The United States and the Nazi Holocaust

PERSPECTIVES ON THE HOLOCAUST

A series of books designed to help students further their understanding of key topics within the field of Holocaust studies.

Published:

Anti-Semitism and the Holocaust, Beth A. Griech-Polelle

The Holocaust in Eastern Europe, Waitman Wade Beorn

Holocaust Representations in History, Daniel H. Magilow and Lisa Silverman

Postwar Germany and the Holocaust, Caroline Sharples

Forthcoming:

Sites of Holocaust Memory, Janet Ward

The United States and the Nazi Holocaust

Race, refuge, and remembrance

BARRY TRACHTENBERG

BLOOMSBURY ACADEMIC
LONDON • NEW YORK • OXFORD • NEW DELHI • SYDNEY

BLOOMSBURY ACADEMIC
Bloomsbury Publishing Plc
50 Bedford Square, London, WC1B 3DP, UK

BLOOMSBURY, BLOOMSBURY ACADEMIC and the
Diana logo are trademarks of Bloomsbury Publishing Plc

First published in Great Britain 2018
Reprinted 2018, 2019

Series design by Jesse Holborn
Cover image: Jewish Protest In New York City, 1933. (© Bettmann/ Getty Images)

A catalogue record for this book is available from the British Library.

Library of Congress Cataloging-in-Publication Data
Names: Trachtenberg, Barry, author.
Title: The United States and the Nazi Holocaust : race, refuge, and remembrance / Barry Trachtenberg.
Description: New York : Bloomsbury Academic, [2018] |
Includes bibliographical references and index.
Identifi ers: LCCN 2017042050 (print) | LCCN 2017043330 (ebook) |
ISBN 9781472567215 (PDF eBook) | ISBN 9781472567208 (EPUB eBook) |
ISBN 9781472567185 (pbk. : alk. paper)
Subjects: LCSH: Holocaust, Jewish (1939–1945)–Foreign public opinion, American. | Holocaust, Jewish (1939-1945)–Historiography. | United States–Foreign relations–1933–1945. | Jews–United States–Attitudes. | United States–Ethinic relations.
Classifi cation: LCC D804.45.U55 (ebook) | LCC D804.45.U55 T73 2018 (print) |
DDC 940.53/18072073–dc23
LC record available at https://lccn.loc.gov/2017042050

ISBN: HB: 978-1-4725-6719-2
PB: 978-1-4725-6718-5
ePDF: 978-1-4725-6721-5
eBook: 978-1-4725-6720-8

Series: Perspectives on the Holocaust

Typeset by Newgen KnowledgeWorks Pvt. Ltd., Chennai, India
Printed and bound in Great Britain

To find out more about our authors and books visit
www.bloomsbury.com and sign up for our newsletters.

For Albert J. Winn, 1947–2014

and

Gary Steller, 1946–2017

Contents

Figures

Acknowledgments

I am grateful to Rhodri Mogford at Bloomsbury for soliciting this book and to Beatriz Lopez and Kalyani Shankar for seeing it through the publication process. My interest in the relationship of the United States and the Nazi Holocaust began a quarter century ago while a master's student at the University of Vermont, and I remain indebted to Professors Doris L. Bergen, Mark A. Stoler, and David Scrase for their guidance and encouragement as I first engaged with these questions. I am also thankful to Jack Sutters of the American Friends Service Committee archives and Wendy Chmielewski of the Swarthmore College Peace Collection for their suggestions and assistance.

While at the University at Albany, I benefitted from conversations about this project with several friends, colleagues, and graduate students, including Malka Evan, Nolan Altman, Fardin Sanai, Lawrence Lichtenstein, Arthur Brenner, Carl Bon Tempo, Kori Graves, Monica Kim, Paul Stasi, Mitch Aso, Meredith Weiss, Bret Benjamin, Vesna Kuiken, Stacy Veeder, Eric Morgenson, Laura Auketayeva, and Kyle Stanton.

In 2014, I was invited to be the Balmuth Visiting Lecturer in the History Department at Skidmore College by Tillman Nechtman and to teach an advanced undergraduate course on the United States and the Holocaust. My thanks to Professor Nechtman for that opportunity and to the students in the course, especially Dorothea Trufelman and Sophie A. Don, for their engagement and willingness to explore this topic. Also in 2014, I presented portions of early chapters to participants in the Holocaust Educational Foundation of Northwestern University's Summer Institute on the Holocaust and Jewish Civilization, who provided many helpful suggestions, especially regarding racial violence in early-twentieth-century American history. Roger Brooks also encouraged me to consider what is at stake in the historical debates related to this topic and the reasons for its continued contentiousness.

Brad S. Hill, Eugene Sheppard, Lisa Leff, Adam Strom, Paul Mathewson, Jonathan Wiesen, Rachel Deblinger, and Melissa Jane Taylor generously shared with me many invaluable sources and suggestions on various parts of this work. Bill Swersey of HIAS kindly facilitated the permissions to reprint photographs from *New Neighbors*. Tim Chambers of Anchor Editions assisted me with the Dorothea Lange photograph.

At Wake Forest University, where I now hold the Michael H. and Deborah K. Rubin Presidential Chair of Jewish History, I regularly benefit from discussions on Jewish history and the Holocaust with many colleagues, including Dean Franco, Annalise Glauz-Todrank, Penny Sinanoglou, Mir Yarfitz, Lisa Blee, Ben Coates, Susan Rupp, and Michael Hughes. I am grateful to Debbie and Mike Rubin for their deep intellectual curiosity and support for Jewish Studies, to Dean of the College Michele Gillespie for providing me with the time to complete this manuscript, and to Kaeley McMahan of the Z. Smith Reynolds Library for tracking down many hard-to-find sources.

I am particularly grateful to Rebecca L. Erbelding of the United States Holocaust Memorial Museum for sharing her incomparable expertise at many stages of this project. Allison Brown of Henry Street Editing improved the manuscript tremendously and kept me on deadline. Both Daniel Greene of Northwestern University and Anna Hájková of the University of Warwick read the manuscript in its entirety, made many important suggestions, and saved me from several embarrassing errors. Any remaining errors, of course, are my sole responsibility.

Jennifer Greiman remains my dearest companion, intellectual sounding board, and best friend. Our child, Harley Simone, is the light of our lives.

Over the years, I have had many conversations with Albert J. Winn and Gary Steller about the ethical demands placed on us by the Holocaust and its study. I dedicate this book to their memory.

Introduction

It would not be entirely inappropriate to tell the history of the Nazi Holocaust with only a passing reference to the United States. In many respects, the United States was marginal to this cataclysmic event that had Europe at its center. The genocide against European Jews, Roma, people whom the Nazis perceived as disabled, and others took place far from American soil, and far from most Americans' view. There were no Nazi death camps or mass atrocities committed in the United States, nor was the country the scene of combat during World War II. As Auschwitz survivor Ruth Kluger reminds us in her memoir *Still Alive: A Holocaust Girlhood Remembered*, "Americans have no idea what it is like to be bombed."[1] By the time US leaders had learned of the mass slaughter of Jews, their capacity to intervene, should they have wanted to, was severely limited by the circumstances of the war itself. Sadly, even if the United States had fulfilled the wishes of those who later criticized it for inaction—if it had more vigorously protested Hitler's rise to power, changed immigration laws and policies that prevented hundreds of thousands of Jews from finding sanctuary, and taken military action to curb the murder of civilians—there is no reason to presume that there would not have still been a Holocaust and millions of victims to mourn.

Nevertheless, there remain very important historical questions to be considered about the United States and the Holocaust. Given its geographical distance from the fighting, resources, and size, the United States had the capacity to shelter a much greater number of refugees from Nazism than it ended up providing. It was home to large numbers of people—Jews and non-Jews alike—who publicly declared their willingness to provide for refugees and to ensure that they would not become a public burden. Furthermore, after the war's end (and until just recently), the United States was home to the world's largest postwar Jewish community, which shouldered much of the responsibility for coming to terms with Nazism's assault on Judaism and the Jewish people. In addition, the Holocaust has come to occupy a central place in American society, with Holocaust memorials and museums found in cities and towns across the country, Holocaust education in school curricula from grade schools to the university level, and a seemingly endless stream of Holocaust-related films, books, and other cultural and academic works.

Popular perception of the relationship of the United States and the Holocaust tends to fall into one of two realms: either US troops were great liberators who freed concentration camp victims at the end of the war, or the country was so unwilling to intervene in the murder of European Jews that it was nearly complicit with the genocide. The first of these understandings holds up President Roosevelt and the US military as fearless enemies of fascism and foes of tyranny. The second asserts the opposing view, depicting the United States as itself so deeply antisemitic that it deliberately ignored all evidence of the mass murder of Jews and emphatically refused to intervene to stop it.[2] Both positions cast the United States as having had a unique role to play—a view based on assumptions about the country's unrivaled power and its ability to influence events in Europe, about its history as a nation founded and shaped by immigrants, and about its status as a beacon of liberty and democracy. In each of these viewpoints, however, the gap between the assumptions of American exceptionalism and the actual limits of American influence is quite vast. In fact, as with most other countries not directly involved with the Holocaust, the United States' actions were motivated primarily by its own perceived self-interest rather than humanitarian concerns or overt antisemitism. Decisions about whether to boycott Germany after the Nazi Party's rise to power in 1933, to change the country's immigration laws as the crisis worsened over the course of the 1930s, or to engage in military action to stop the murder of European Jews were made only after assessing their impact on the country's domestic and international goals.

Advocates for the rescue of European Jews—both within government and outside of it—fought to steer the United States toward a more altruistic stance, but American sympathy toward oppressed peoples was severely diminished by what seemed to be more pressing concerns about the country's economy, the security of its borders, and, most importantly, its changing racial makeup. While it is certainly reasonable to wish that the full extent of German Jewry's plight had been understood at the time and that such an understanding would have promoted greater action on their behalf, the reality was that the United States in the 1930s and early 1940s was no more immune from racist, isolationist, and nativist attitudes than most of the other countries that were unwilling to give sanctuary to large numbers of Jewish refugees or otherwise intervene to save Jewish lives.

The United States—meaning the government, its inhabitants, and its institutions—was neither a *perpetrator* of the Holocaust nor a *victim* of it. Rather, as this book shows, from the rise of the Nazi Party to power in January

1933 until the present day, it has inhabited several roles that exist apart from these two positions. Not only was the United States a *bystander* to the Holocaust, but it also acted as Germany's *adversary* during the war, and its military efforts contributed to Nazism's downfall. But it was also at times an *enabler* of the Nazi regime's persecution of its victims: US leaders decided not to amend laws that effectively prevented more refugees from finding sanctuary in the country and chose to maintain economic and diplomatic ties with Nazi Germany until the United States' entry into the war. Conversely, the United States was also an occasional *rescuer* of imperiled Jews in its various attempts to find a solution to the refugee crisis before entering the war and by its role in liberating concentration camps at the war's end. In the war's aftermath, it became an *inheritor* of the legacy of the Holocaust as it provided a home to many survivors and became the site of Holocaust memorials, monuments, and museums. At the same time, the United States was also a *beneficiary* of Nazi expertise, as many German scientists were provided sanctuary after the war's end in order to fight the Cold War against the Soviet Union.

It is perhaps because of the ambiguity of America's role in the Holocaust and the unprecedented scope of killing that occurred in Europe that historical accounts of this subject have often reached wildly contrasting conclusions, with scholars oftentimes adopting either wholly condemnatory opinions of the United States' response or entirely laudatory ones. Academic debates have occasionally made their way into public view, and some have escalated into attacks that go far beyond the sort of criticism that typically appears in book reviews, academic conferences, or other settings where historians dispute one another's findings.[3]

Scholarship on the United States and the Holocaust first appeared in the late 1960s, soon after the first comprehensive studies of the Holocaust were published. With few exceptions, books that have most strongly influenced popular perception of the United States are those that have severely criticized President Franklin Roosevelt and the officials working within his administration, as well as American Jewish leaders, insisting that they utterly failed to meet their moral obligation toward European Jews. These authors conclude that the United States was too permissive of the Nazi regime throughout the 1930s, too antisemitic to offer sanctuary to German Jews, and too indifferent to attempt to rescue Europe's Jews, in spite of what they assert was the widely available information at the time that Germany was seeking to exterminate them completely.[4] Their challengers, who have tended to be less successful in influencing popular opinion, insist that the United States acted morally and justly in this period, and took all reasonable steps to help Jews and stop the genocide.[5] Other historians, focusing on the postwar era, have argued that the United States has abused its position as one of the main inheritors of the Holocaust's legacy, for example, by overemphasizing its place within American society, or by manipulating the memory of the Holocaust for political or monetary gain.[6]

The journalist Lawrence Zuckerman has argued that the subtext for scholars' often severe criticism of President Roosevelt—which stands starkly at odds with the support given to him by the large majority of Jews during his administration—is concern over protecting US support for the State of Israel.[7] In an article entitled "FDR's Jewish Problem," Zuckerman asserts that by creating a historical narrative that blames Roosevelt (and the American Jews who supported him) for *not* coming to the aid of threatened Jews then, these scholars can more effectively make the case for the United States to give uncritical support today for Israel as a Jewish homeland that will ostensibly protect Jews from any possible future threats. If "betrayal happened before," the logic goes, "it can happen again."[8] Zuckerman chides this scholarship for holding the United States to a standard different from that which is typically applied to other rescuers:

> If Roosevelt's scholarly critics acknowledge this achievement [that the president can be given credit for saving hundreds of thousands of threatened Jews], they do so only grudgingly, and they argue he could have and should have done more. But so-called righteous gentiles—non-Jews who risked their lives to save Jews during the Holocaust, such as Oskar Schindler, whose famous "list" contained the names of 1,098 people—are not normally criticized for how many more Jews they could have saved. Instead, they are celebrated for those they did save in the face of the cruel and relentless determination of the Nazism to murder Jews. The question is why FDR's list is now more often noted for the names it left out than for those it included.[9]

By categorizing the large body of scholarship on the United States and the Holocaust in this way, I do not mean to imply that it has not contributed to our understanding, nor that President Roosevelt and his administration acted in what were the best interests of European Jews. Rather, I suggest that the tendency of much of this literature to adopt absolutist depictions—either in full opposition or defense of the United States'—often obscures what is in fact a more complicated history. To adopt the term of the literary scholar Michael André Bernstein, much of the literature on the United States and the Holocaust has often engaged in "backshadowing." Bernstein defines "backshadowing" as "a kind of retroactive foreshadowing in which the shared knowledge of the outcome of a series of events by narrator and listener is used to judge the participants in those events as though they too should have known what was to come."[10] Bernstein was speaking of the propensity among some observers to criticize the actions of Jewish victims of Nazism for not recognizing what should have been—according to these observers—obvious signs of the genocidal intentions of the regime. They view the Holocaust as the inevitable outcome of a series of highly visible and sequential actions and hold Jews responsible for not acknowledging the impending murder and acting sooner to evade it. The Holocaust survivor and writer Primo Levi put it more plainly in an essay written near the end of his life, in which he described the sort of questions that survivors such as himself inevitably receive when relating their stories to audiences: "Why did you not escape? Why did you not resist? Why did you not avoid capture 'beforehand'?"[11] The assumption behind these questions (which are more accusations than inquiries) is that Jews bear at least partial responsibility for their own destruction because of their supposed inaction.

This sort of "what if?" speculation is increasingly common in writing about the Holocaust, argues Gavriel D. Rosenfeld, who has studied the phenomenon of counterfactualism among Holocaust historians and dates its beginnings to the early 1960s.[12] In this vein, much of the literature on the United States and the Holocaust criticizes America for steps that it did not take, arguing explicitly that acting otherwise would have unquestionably produced far more favorable outcomes. The difference between interrogating the actions of European Jews and those of the United States, of course, is that America was not a victim of Nazi crimes and had a range of options available to it in the years 1933–45, when the Nazis were in power. Nevertheless, in spite of the insistence of both the United States' accusers and defenders, we cannot know what would have happened had the country and its leaders chosen to act otherwise. We can only try to understand what were the possibilities available to various influential historical actors at any particular moment and what led them to choose as they did. We can critically examine—and this book offers such an assessment—the steps they took and how their decisions were shaped by historical forces, opportunities, and constraints.

This book, therefore, considers the structural factors that determined the plight of German Jewish refugees seeking to find sanctuary in the United States. In particular, it argues that in order to understand how and why the United States' relationship to the Holocaust has developed in the way that it has we must address the shifting racial status of Jews in America. Since the founding of the United States, its population has been divided into racial categories, with power and privilege bestowed to those classified as white. Yet whiteness has never been a fixed category, except in that it is permanently denied to African Americans. In fact, the history of the United States in the twentieth century was, in many respects, the history of "the color line," as the historian W. E. B. DuBois famously predicted in his foundational 1903 text, *The Souls of Black Folk*.[13] In more recent years, a growing body of literature has demonstrated that over the course of the twentieth century the racial position of Jews was constantly changing (and still is).[14] Contrary to how most

American Jews of European descent are viewed today, in the first half of the twentieth century, Jews were not necessarily accepted as white, but whiteness was something that they could "achieve." Their ambiguous racial status had a profound impact on how they were perceived by non-Jews, how they understood their own position with in American society, and what kind of religious, economic, political, and social choices they made.

Jews' racial status has also shaped how the United States has contended with the Holocaust, from the Nazis' rise to power until the present day. In the decades between the two world wars, this influenced both popular perceptions of refugees as well as the ways that American Jews responded to the worsening situation in Europe. Rather than point to systematic antisemitism as the sole (or even primary) cause for America's mixed record in welcoming Jews fleeing Germany, this books shows that antisemitism was but one component of a much larger system of segregation and racial exclusion that pervaded society. After the war, as Jews of European ancestry came to be perceived as among the ranks of white Americans, the Holocaust took on increasingly greater importance. The establishment of a Holocaust museum on the National Mall in Washington, DC, in the early 1990s, was the most powerful sign that Jews had secured their position within the ranks of "mainstream" America.

Chapter 1, "The United States and Jewish Immigration in the Interwar Period," concerns how the United States responded to Nazism in the years 1933–39, a period that begins with the Nazi takeover of power in Germany and ends with the start of World War II. In order to tell that history, and in particular how the United States responded to hundreds of thousands of desperate Jewish refugees seeking shelter within its borders, this chapter examines the immigration laws that were put into effect in the years following World War I. It addresses the rise of new isolationist and nativist sentiments that gripped much of the country after that war, and shows how the Great Depression that struck in 1929 exacerbated many Americans' suspicions toward foreigners and toward US intervention in events abroad. New anxieties among white Americans regarding the racial makeup of recent immigrants from Eastern and Southern Europe—including approximately two million Jews who had arrived since the last decades of the nineteenth century—brought about radical changes in immigration laws that were designed to preserve white majority rule. This chapter demonstrates that this intense racial questioning provided much of the context that influenced how the United States contended with Hitler's treatment of Germany's Jewish population. Although on the eve of war the president sought to be a world leader in solving the growing refugee crisis, his efforts failed in large measure because of his unwillingness to challenge the entrenched racial hierarchy, which did not deem endangered Jews worthy of special consideration.

Chapter 2, "Rescue during Wartime," discusses how the onset of war gave rise to new suspicions about Jewish refugees, which were part of a growing distrust of foreigners and racial minorities, as well as new concerns over protecting US borders. In the first two years of the war, when the United States was officially neutral, popular sentiment against US involvement prompted a rise in antisemitic rhetoric, as increasingly loud voices encouraged leaders not to go to war in order to serve "Jewish interests." At the same time, American Jewish organizations sought desperately to identify ways to assist the rapidly increasing number of endangered Jews, including pressuring the government to allow more refugees to enter the country. Jewish organizations and news outlets also sought to raise awareness of the growing atrocities against European Jews in order to garner sympathy for their plight, but often to little avail. When the United States entered the war at the end of 1941, hostilities against the country's racial and ethnic minorities increased, in spite of the government's efforts to project a new national unity in the face of common enemies. Although the United States was fighting a foe in Europe that was trying to remake the world order based on notions of "Aryan" racial supremacy, escalating racism at home led to race riots around the country, the entrenchment of racial segregation in the military, and the imprisonment of persons of Japanese ancestry, many of whom were US citizens. This climate of racial unrest hardened the resolve of those within the government who sought to tighten restrictions on Jewish refugees. Only in the last year of the war did the administration take steps to lessen the crisis with the creation of the War Refugee Board, whose officers, working with Jewish organizations, tirelessly sought ways to aid imperiled European Jews.

The end of World War II and the Holocaust did not bring about an end to the difficulties faced by Jewish victims of Nazism. Chapter 3, "Jewish Refugees and Displaced Persons in Postwar America," shows that while US troops were widely celebrated as liberators, the Jewish survivors of Nazism whom they rescued faced daunting challenges while under the care of the Allies, who were entirely unequipped (and often unwilling) to provide for their needs. Advocates for survivors worked tirelessly to improve how the US military treated them and to change immigration laws so as to admit displaced persons (DPs) into the country outside of the existing immigration system. Not only were most DPs prevented from relocating to the United States in order to begin new lives, but those survivors who did faced nearly insurmountable obstacles in the first decade after their arrival. While they encountered an American Jewish community that was willing to assist them in the first months of their transition, the aid they received was often short-lived and came with unrealistic expectations about survivors' ability to adapt to their new environment. As many survivor memoirs and testimonies indicate, their presence was often an unwelcome reminder of Jewish victimization during the recent war and raised concerns as to whether they would interfere with American Jews' rapid integration into the white middle class.

As American Jews were coming to terms with the Holocaust, the country as a whole was beginning to learn about it. Although the name "Holocaust" did not come into wide use for several decades after the end of the war, Americans slowly learned about the systematic attempt to exterminate European Jewry. (Nazi efforts to annihilate Roma and persons perceived to be disabled are still only becoming recognized today.) Chapter 4, "America Confronts the Holocaust, 1945–1960s," traces this growing awareness and shows that it was accomplished in a variety of ways. The first of these were popular accounts written by Jewish victims of Nazism, such as Anne Frank's, whose diary was adapted first for Broadway and then for Hollywood, and not without controversy. During the war, Hollywood studios began to depict the plight of European Jews, and newsreels taught many Americans about Nazi crimes. After the war, American filmmakers were slow to take up the Holocaust as a central theme in their works, but in the late 1950s, films began to portray the plight of Jews and found receptive audiences. The new medium of television also helped to shape Americans' understanding of the Holocaust, as programs brought news of how DPs were transitioning to life in the United States, as well as the trials of prominent Nazis, directly into American homes. Scholarly investigations, first initiated by historians who had experienced Nazi persecution and who were able to draw upon Nazi wartime documents captured by US troops, further added to knowledge about the Holocaust.

By the final decades of the twentieth century, the Holocaust had moved to the center of American life. Chapter 5, "America Embraces the Holocaust, 1970s–the Present," traces this development and shows that the embrace—as reflected in the building of Holocaust monuments, memorials, and museums around the country; a regular stream of books and films; the ongoing criminal prosecutions of suspected Nazis; the creation of school curricula; and the dramatic growth of the scholarly field of Holocaust studies—is linked in part to changes within the Jewish community, which attained new levels of acceptance into the American white mainstream. As Jews secured their position within white society, remembrance of the Holocaust served as a way for them to maintain their communal distinctiveness and to advance Jewish interests. Recognition of the Holocaust has been one way that political leaders regularly show their respect to American Jews, who have become an important political constituency and economic force. The status of American Jewry also led to a period of sustained questioning of America's initial response to Nazism and the Holocaust and the decisions by Jewish leaders during the war, asking whether they had tried hard enough to pressure President Roosevelt to take action. The importance accorded to the Holocaust is also tied, this chapter shows, to the growing accumulation of knowledge internationally about the Holocaust, which has become recognized worldwide as a tragedy with consequences for all of humanity.

1

The United States and Jewish immigration in the interwar period

The 1939 journey of the MS *St. Louis* lasted only a period of a few weeks; yet, for many, it has come to symbolize American indifference to the desperation of German Jews seeking safety from Nazi oppression. According to the standard telling, a ship of German Jewish refugees arrived in the United States after being denied entry into Cuba, its initial destination. Rather than allow the passengers to enter the country and find safety from Nazi persecution, President Franklin Roosevelt cruelly turned the ship away. Out of options, the *St. Louis* returned to Europe and soon thereafter, its passengers, abandoned to their fate, died in the Holocaust. This account, with occasional variations, is frequently evoked as emblematic of how the United States responded to the Nazi Holocaust. Some see in the story of the *St. Louis* evidence of American apathy toward the plight of Hitler's victims. Others have gone so far as to argue that it proves that the United States acquiesced with German plans to exterminate European Jewry. Some see proof of a particular American antisemitism while others point to the *St. Louis* as an ethical lesson in order to advocate on behalf of refugees from subsequent conflicts. As it turns out, the actual history of the *St. Louis* is far more complicated than this account allows. When understood correctly, it is less an example of how the United States responded to the Holocaust than it is an illustration of the extent to which this difficult period is misunderstood and misrepresented.[1]

A more accurate summary of events is that in mid-May 1939, the *St. Louis*, which was part of the Hamburg-American line (known as Hapag), departed Hamburg, Germany. After a stop in Cherbourg, France, the ship headed for Havana, Cuba, with 937 passengers. Most travelers were German Jewish émigrés who held landing permits issued by the Cuban government. Of these, 743 were on a waiting list to receive visas to enter into the United States and had arranged to stay in Cuba until their documents would arrive. For some time, Cuba had served as a temporary refuge for German Jews awaiting their entry into the United States via an immigration quota system that had been in place since 1924. According to the law, the number of persons identified as members of any particular nationality was fixed and—reflecting the racist intentions of the 1924 law—varied according to the perceived "whiteness" of the country's inhabitants, with Western European countries allotted significantly higher quotas than Eastern or Southern European ones.[2] Under the quota for Germany, which President Roosevelt had unilaterally combined with Austria's following its 1938 annexation by Germany, the number of available immigration visas was 27,370. By the time of the *St. Louis*'s departure, the wait for visas under the German quota was many years long and included well over 300,000 names.[3] For Jews desperate to get out of Germany, Cuba served as a convenient place to reside until they were permitted to enter the United States via the quota system.

However, in the days just prior to the ship's departure, tensions in Cuba over the growing number of European Jews escalated and internal feuds within the Cuban government prompted President Federico Laredo Brú to tighten the rules for new arrivals, requiring them to procure additional approvals to land in Cuba. Although Hapag officials were notified of the change, the *St. Louis* left Hamburg on the optimistic assumption that the new rules did not apply to its passengers, since they had already received permission to enter Cuba. Upon landing in Havana two weeks later on May 27, however, the passengers discovered that most of them would not be permitted to enter. Twenty-eight had papers that allowed them to disembark and the rest were confined to the ship.

Even as the ship was en route to Cuba, the American Jewish Joint Distribution Committee (a relief organization popularly known as "the Joint"), working closely with officials from the State Department in Washington, began to advocate on behalf of the passengers, warning the Hapag line that its passengers might not be granted entry into Cuba. Its agent in Havana entered into negotiations with the Cuban government, but they were unable to reach a settlement.[4] The story of the refugees' increasingly desperate plight was picked up in the press and reporters were sympathetic to the passengers. On June 2, the *New York Times* reported that the anxiety of the refugees was palpable:

> Late this afternoon the St. Louis was surrounded by boats filled with relatives and friends of those on board. Police patrolled the liner's docks and forbade any except government officials to approach too closely or to step

> on the floating dock alongside the ship. Huge spotlights attached to the vessel's sides lighted the surrounding waters tonight.
>
> The St. Louis's passengers, many sobbing despairingly, lined the rail and talked with those in the surrounding boats, some of whom remained several hours.

One passenger was quoted as saying, " 'If we are returned to Germany,' he lamented, 'it will mean the concentration camp for most of us.' "[5] Another, a Breslau attorney named Max Loewe, cut his wrists and jumped overboard out of desperation for his wife and children, who were also aboard the ship.

FIGURE 1.1 *Passengers crowd the deck of the MS* St. Louis.

In spite of thousands of telegrams in support of the refugees sent to President Brú by concerned Americans, the ship left the port of Havana on June 2. While the ship sailed in the waters of the Caribbean, advocates for the passengers sought a wide range of alternatives to returning the ship and its passengers to Germany. Plans to post a $500 bond for each passenger (approximately $450,000, or nearly $8 million in today's dollars) or to allow the passengers to disembark into Santo Domingo came to no avail. Others suggested allowing the refugees to enter into the United States either outside of or ahead of their place on the waiting list, but this was deemed untenable both by State Department officials who were opposed to any relaxing of immigration laws (and had no authority to change them even if they wanted to) and by the president's own advisors, who did not want to threaten his Good Neighbor policy of nonintervention in Latin American countries' internal affairs. Popular sentiment in the country was decidedly opposed to any relaxation in immigration laws. Furthermore, permitting such a move would have forced those who had waited for their quota number to come up to wait even longer for their turn to enter the country. Among the more callous proposals was one to encourage the United States to request that the German government not permit refugees to leave unless they were certain of the passengers' destinations.[6] Complicating matters even more was the fact that while the crisis of the *St. Louis* was under way, tense debates were occurring in a Congressional committee over proposed legislation that would have allowed as many as 20,000 German refugee children to enter the United States outside of the normal quota system. As the ship approached the Florida coast, a United States Coast Guard ship and plane monitored its progress. The ship did not, as some later accounts have claimed, fire a "warning shot" across the bow of the *St. Louis*.[7]

None of the proposals to identify homes for the passengers in North, Central, or South America was successful. As the *St. Louis* prepared for the return journey back to Europe, the *Times* dubbed it "the saddest ship afloat today" and, as did most critics, placed responsibility squarely on the Cuban government for its refusal to negotiate a solution to the crisis:

> She is steaming back despite an offer made to Havana yesterday to give a guarantee through the Chase National bank of $500 apiece for every one of her passengers, men, women and children, who might land there.... [President Brú's] cash terms have been met. But the St. Louis still keeps her course for Hamburg. No plague ship ever received a sorrier welcome.[8]

As the *St. Louis* headed toward Hamburg, the Joint found havens for the passengers in Europe. In what was heralded at the time as a successful outcome, refugees disembarked in Great Britain, the Netherlands, Belgium, and France.

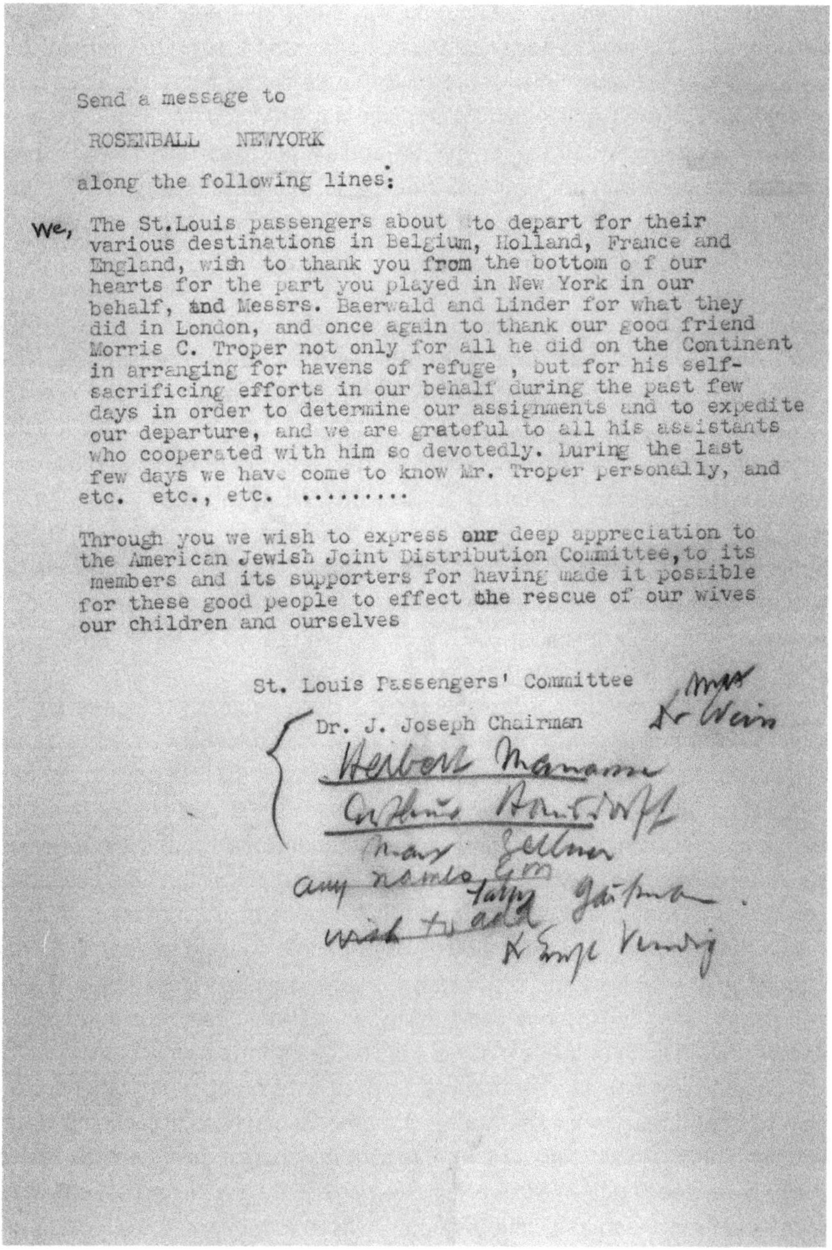

Send a message to

ROSENBALL NEWYORK

along the following lines:

We, The St.Louis passengers about to depart for their various destinations in Belgium, Holland, France and England, wish to thank you from the bottom of our hearts for the part you played in New York in our behalf, and Messrs. Baerwald and Linder for what they did in London, and once again to thank our good friend Morris C. Troper not only for all he did on the Continent in arranging for havens of refuge , but for his self-sacrificing efforts in our behalf during the past few days in order to determine our assignments and to expedite our departure, and we are grateful to all his assistants who cooperated with him so devotedly. During the last few days we have come to know Mr. Troper personally, and etc. etc., etc. ....

Through you we wish to express our deep appreciation to the American Jewish Joint Distribution Committee, to its members and its supporters for having made it possible for these good people to effect the rescue of our wives our children and ourselves

St. Louis Passengers' Committee

Dr. J. Joseph Chairman

any names wish to add

FIGURE 1.2 *Typewritten English translation of a message sent by the members of the MS* St. Louis *Passenger Committee to the Joint Distribution Committee in New York, thanking them for their efforts to finding places of refuge for the Jews on board the MS* St. Louis.

Although many anticipated that another war was on the near horizon, the passengers were relieved to have avoided being forced to return to Germany and awaited the time when they could finally settle in the United States. Three months later, Germany invaded Poland and started World War II in Europe. In May 1940, eleven months after the *St. Louis* crisis was resolved, Germany invaded Western Europe. While 532 of the former passengers found themselves in Nazi-occupied Europe, 254 of them perished during the war and Holocaust.

In spite of the attention paid to the *St. Louis*, it was not the only ship affected by the change in Cuban laws. The *Orinoco*, which set sail from Cuxhaven, Germany, for Cuba with 200 German Jewish passengers, was recalled once it was clear that they would not be permitted to disembark in Havana.[9] The French liner *Flandres*, with 104 refugees aboard, was denied entry into Mexico after being prohibited from docking in Havana a few days after the *St. Louis* and returned to France.[10] A British vessel, the *Orduña*, with 120 Jewish passengers aboard, arrived in Cuba the same day as the *St. Louis*, and 72 of them, who did not have appropriate landing permits, were not allowed to disembark. Some were successful in finding sanctuary in South America. After a complicated and harrowing journey, 55 of these passengers were able to enter the United States in 1940.[11]

The plight of the *St. Louis* highlights the desperation of refugees so anxious to escape Germany in mid-1939 on what was widely believed to be the eve of war. As a story of German Jews seeking to get to Cuba prior to entering the United States who eventually find sanctuary in France, the Netherlands, Belgium, and Britain, it reveals the truly international aspect of the refugee crisis. It demonstrates how the post–World War I preoccupation with passports, visas, and border controls restricted the freedom of movement and determined the fate of hundreds of thousands of people seeking to escape Europe during the prewar Nazi era. It shows the extent to which isolationist concerns and racist views in America easily trumped humanitarian considerations. It shows that, in spite of these many obstacles, the efforts of officials within the US government and representatives from private relief organizations were able to bring about what seemed at the time to be a positive ending to the matter. It also reveals how structural racism in America governed the fate of many Jews seeking to escaping Nazi Germany. In its desire to preserve white racial supremacy and to isolate the country from foreigners, the US Congress had passed legislation in the 1920s that exacerbated the refugee crisis in the 1930s and provided Hitler with evidence to claim that the world had turned its back on German Jews.

Subsequent events in the summer of 1939, culminating with the beginning of World War II in Europe on September 1 quickly overshadowed the memory of the *St. Louis*. It was not until the late 1960s and early 1970s that historians writing on the response of the United States to the Holocaust began to recast it as either an example of American indifference to or (in extreme cases) collusion with Nazi goals to exterminate European Jewry. In time, the *St. Louis* began to serve as a metonym for how the United States responded to the larger refugee crisis. The plight of the *St. Louis* is featured prominently in the permanent exhibition of the United States Holocaust Memorial Museum (USHMM). It has been the subject of countless news articles, several monographs, a feature film, and, more recently, political protests in the first days of the Trump presidency. While President Roosevelt and government officials could have likely extended themselves further on behalf of these refugees, they acted entirely in accordance with the prevailing sentiment in the United States and with the governments of most other countries in the Americas. The plight of the *St. Louis*, therefore, is less accurately viewed as a specifically *American* failure and more correctly seen as a global one in which the United States played its own part.

What is curious about the common portrayal of the *St. Louis* is that the fate of its passengers was exceptional for its time. The United States stands out in the period just prior to the onset of war, more correctly, because its immigration policies, as racist and restrictive as they were, had actually granted the passengers the right to enter the country, once their quota number was up. The fate of the passengers aboard the *St. Louis* was at odds with that of most refugees who had secured the right to enter the United States. In fact, from mid-March 1938 through October 1941 (corresponding to the period from Germany's annexation of Austria until Germany forbade Jewish emigration), 1,288 ships carrying refugees successfully docked in the United States, with 110,960 self-identified "Hebrews" aboard. Of those, 68,984 self-identified as Jews born in Germany.[12] The United States in this period permitted more German Jews to enter than did any other country. The *St. Louis* was not "turned back" because its passengers were Jews, as popular wisdom holds, but because of something even worse: its passengers were forced to act within a monstrous system that prioritized secure borders and racial hierarchies over basic humanitarian concerns.

Just as the plight of the *St. Louis* is widely misunderstood, the common understanding of the United States and the entire refugee crisis—which argues that the country refused to open its doors to Jews fleeing Nazi persecution—also requires significant revision. Scholarly and popular critics of the United States tend to focus their attention on several key areas of influence. The first of these are the beliefs and actions of President Roosevelt and his administration. His opponents argue that he was either wholly indifferent to the worsening crisis, or worse, in possession of such antisemitic views that he was virtually an accomplice to the murder of European Jewry. For evidence, they point to occasional antisemitic statements by Roosevelt himself and to the fact that he tolerated the presence of antisemites in the State Department who actively sought to curtail immigration. They highlight his reluctance to challenge a Congress that was decidedly anti-immigrant and his refusal to take unilateral actions on behalf of imperiled refugees. Another factor to which critics have pointed are infamous antisemites, such as the industrialist Henry Ford and the popular radio priest Charles Coughlin, who committed vast time and resources to shape American popular opinion about Jews and created a climate that was hostile to expanded immigration.[13] Furthermore, many condemn the efforts of American Jewish leaders for failing to pressure the Roosevelt administration to shift government policy regarding refugees, when in fact there was no formal policy concerning refugees at all. They portray Jewish leaders as being too concerned with protecting their social standing and their limited political access to risk coming to European Jewry's defense.[14]

This chapter offers a reassessment of the United States and the plight of German Jews in the 1930s, before the start of the widely expected World War II and the as-yet-unimaginable Nazi Holocaust. Rather than present the refugee crisis strictly as a product of the personalities and prejudices of individual historical actors, such as the president, notorious antisemites, or prominent Jewish leaders, it pays greater attention to the decidedly more significant underlying structural factors that determined the plight of German Jewish refugees seeking to find sanctuary in the United States. It demonstrates how American beliefs in isolationism and nativism combined with white racial anxieties after World War I to set the stage for the subsequent crisis. It argues that the uncertain racial status of American Jewry in the interwar years influenced both popular perceptions of refugees as well as the ways that American Jews responded to the worsening situation abroad. Rather than point to systematic antisemitism as the sole (or even primary) cause for America's mixed stance toward Jews fleeing Germany, it shows that antisemitism was one component of a much larger system of segregation and exclusion that pervaded nearly every aspect of society.

Isolationism and white racial anxiety after World War I

For German Jews hoping to find sanctuary in the United States, the refugee crisis that emerged with the rise of Nazism could likely not have come at a worse time. The United States' role as a global power was unrivaled after World War I, yet most Americans after the war believed that their country had extended itself too far in coming to the aid of its European allies and that it paid too heavy a price for its involvement in world affairs. The immediate postwar years saw a growing belief, particularly among many white Americans, that the United States was weak politically, morally, and racially and that the country needed to recover its previous strength and homogeneity. As cosmopolitan values became dominant over agrarian ones, increasing numbers of people who felt displaced by the political, economic, social, and cultural changes under way in the 1920s pointed to foreigners and racial minorities as the source of the disruption.

After World War I, many Americans wanted to focus on domestic issues and did not believe that the United States had achieved any material or moral benefit due to its involvement abroad. As historian Christopher McKnight Nicholas has shown, encounters with nonwhites abroad during the war led many to fear that American imperial ambitions would bring increased numbers of "lesser" peoples into the country itself.[15] Advocates of a policy known as "isolationism" argued for avoiding both colonialist enterprises and the "entangling alliances" against which Thomas Jefferson had famously warned. Isolationism gained strength over the course of the 1920s. It was also an economic and cultural movement that preached nationalism, nativism and anti-immigrant sentiments and professed hostility toward urbanization, racial and religious minorities, and industrialization. It found expression in "patriotic" organizations, restrictionist labor union policies, agitation against civil rights advocates, and new immigration policies. After the war, President Warren G. Harding, who was elected in 1920 and who died after just two years in office, had promised Americans that his presidency would mark a "return to normalcy" and a renewed focus on domestic affairs. Although the United States' imperial reach into Latin America in fact expanded in the 1920s under President Calvin Coolidge, the country remained apart from the League of Nations and most other postwar international organizations. In signing the 1928 Kellogg–Briand Pact, the country pledged never again to resort to war to resolve international disputes. Even President Roosevelt, who was not an isolationist, signed the 1935 Neutrality Act, which invoked an embargo upon "the export of arms, ammunition, and implements of war to belligerent countries."

Isolationism was most prominently reflected in growing resentment against immigrants. From the early 1880s until the mid-1920s, approximately twenty-five million migrants entered the United States, largely from Southern and Eastern Europe and with significant numbers from Latin America and Asia. These new arrivals—coming in unprecedentedly large numbers, often with little financial resources, and at a moment when the United States was rapidly industrializing—did not assimilate as quickly as had previous waves of European migrants. They retained their ethnic and linguistic differences longer than many previous immigrant groups, settled in cities, and filled the ranks of the newly forming working classes. While large numbers quickly found employment in areas of industrial growth including factories, mines, meatpacking districts, and sweatshops, many Americans viewed them as racial, economic, political, and religious threats to the existing order. Among the immigrants were over two million Jews who arrived chiefly from the Russian empire to escape political turmoil, poverty, and antisemitism. Many faced hostility and occasional violence. Even in the eyes of their sympathizers, immigrants were expected to Americanize quickly by adopting English, dressing in contemporary fashions, and assuming a more relaxed stance toward Jewish law and ritual obligations.

The widespread anxiety over these immigrants received legitimacy from the scientific field known as eugenics.[16] Articulated as a public good, eugenics was concerned with the cultivation of desired hereditary traits among humans by promoting reproduction among those considered to have healthy genes and by preventing it among those who were deemed to be inferior. In the name of "racial improvement," the eugenics movement hosted "better baby" and "fitter family" competitions and promoted the use of contraceptives to prevent the birth of "unfit" children. In the last years of the nineteenth century, states began to enact legislation that prohibited those with hereditary illnesses from marrying in the name of combating mental illness, criminality, and disease. Soon, states turned to the practice of forced sterilization. At its core, eugenics was a means by which those of white Northern European ancestry sought to preserve their racial dominance. Most often, poor people and members of racial minority populations were targeted out of a belief that their "inferior" status was a consequence not of inadequate social, environmental, or material conditions but of biological ones that could not be otherwise remedied. Some eugenicists in the United States went so far as to advocate for "euthanasia"—a polite term for medical killing—as a way to eradicate unwanted hereditary traits. Historian Stefan Kühl has shown that eugenics was an international movement, as practitioners in the United States worked closely with counterparts abroad, in particular with those in Germany during the Weimar era and the prewar years of the Nazi regime. American eugenicists gave "nearly unanimous support," he shows, for Nazi legislation such as the 1933 Law for the Prevention of Hereditarily Diseased Offspring, which resulted in the forced sterilization of over 400,000 Germans.[17] While most American eugenicists began to distance themselves from their German counterparts after the passing of the 1935 Nuremberg Laws that prohibited sexual relations between "Aryans" and Jews, a few even continued their support for the murder of people perceived to have disabilities under the Nazi T-4 program that began in the first days of World War II.[18]

Along with eugenicists' efforts to eradicate all forms of disability, they also legitimized preexisting policies of racial segregation and discrimination and shaped US immigration policy. The great numbers of migrants from Eastern and Southern Europe of the late nineteenth and early twentieth centuries led many to clamor for restrictions that would "restore" the national and racial percentages that had existed prior to their arrival. Sharing these concerns, Congress passed the Emergency Quota Act in May 1921, which limited the number of new immigrants to just 3 percent of the number of residents from that same country who had been in the United States in 1910, according to the US Census. This restricted total immigration to approximately 350,000 residents per year.[19] President Wilson refused to sign the bill but it was passed by Congress a second time in a special session and signed by President Harding in May 1921. In 1922, Congress renewed it for an additional two years. Historian John Higham has noted that this new policy created a series of very public immigration emergencies, as steamship companies raced one another to land on American shores and deposit their passengers ahead of their rivals, in order to gain entry under the new quotas. Those ships and their unfortunate passengers who "lost" (by arriving after the quotas were met) were forcibly returned to Europe.[20]

Such restrictions were still insufficient to many race experts, who clamored for even tighter controls. In September of 1921, the Second International Eugenics Conference at the American Museum of Natural History met to consider the immigration issue. Those gathered unanimously supported tighter immigration controls, believing that the "melting pot" theory was flawed, since there was no guarantee that racial "impurities" would be eliminated with the mixing of races. As the *New York Times* reported, "The theory held by some eminent anthropologists that all races have an equal capacity for development and that all race questions, even the negro question, is to be solved in the long run by race mixture, was vigorously combatted." Eugenicists proposed even tougher immigration laws to "maintain our historical republican institutions through barring the entrance of those who are unfit to share the duties and responsibilities of our well-founded government."[21]

On account of the broad support for more stringent controls, in 1924 Congress passed the Johnson–Reed Act, which limited the annual number of immigrants who could be admitted from any country further to just 2 percent of the number of people from that country who were already living in the United States in 1890, twenty years earlier than the benchmarks set by the 1921 legislation. The quota for all of Russia was limited to 2,248 persons. From Poland it was 5,982 and from Romania it was just 603.[22] By contrast, the quota for Germany was 51,277 and for Great Britain (including Northern Ireland), it was 34,007. In 1929, Congress adjusted these quotas further, so that Germany's allotment was reduced to 25,957 and Great Britain's was increased to 65,721.[23] To avoid ships rushing to the border, hopeful migrants now had to apply at US consulates abroad in order to secure a visa for entry. Under the law, in any single month the number of visas issued from a country was not permitted to exceed 10 percent of that country's annual quota. The law was aimed at further restricting Southern and Eastern Europeans as well as prohibiting entirely the immigration of East Asians and Asian Indians. The act did not put into place any limits on nationals from Latin American countries. Congressional opposition was minimal and public support was widespread. The racist intent of this legislation is well exemplified by Senator Ellison DuRant Smith of South Carolina, who stated:

> Thank God we have in America perhaps the largest percentage of any country in the world of the pure, unadulterated Anglo-Saxon stock; certainly the greatest of any nation in the Nordic breed. It is for the preservation of that splendid stock that has characterized us that I would make this not an asylum for the oppressed of all countries, but a country to assimilate and perfect that splendid type of manhood that has made America the foremost Nation in her progress and in her power, and yet the youngest of all the nations. I myself believe that the preservation of her institutions depends upon us now taking counsel with our condition and our experience during the last World War.[24]

The legislation was broadly popular and validated the concerns of isolationists, nativists, and eugenicists. It also enacted a system that made it much more difficult for Jews of any nationality to find sanctuary in the United States following the Nazi takeover of Germany in 1933. More immediately, Jewish immigration into the United States was radically curbed since most Jews who sought to enter the United States in the 1920s did so from those parts of Europe that after 1924 faced the most restrictive quotas. Prior to this legislation, recent Jewish immigration (from all countries) had at times totaled well over 125,000 (such as in 1892, and from 1905 to 1908). In 1921, it was more than 119,000. In each year following the 1924 legislation, by contrast, the number of all Jewish immigrants entering the United States from any country never reached 20,000 until 1939.[25]

When the Great Depression struck the United States in 1929, hostilities toward immigrants increased dramatically and restrictionists argued that the country's borders should be closed entirely to all new arrivals.[26] Responding to these demands, in September 1930, under President Hoover's direction, the State Department enacted the "LPC Proviso," which put into effect strict new standards that denied visas to immigrants who were considered Likely to become a Public Charge. Those not in possession of sufficient financial resources or a guaranteed job in the United States were required to procure affidavits from family or friends who agreed to provide for their well-being. As the historians Richard Breitman and Allan Lichtman point out, "The new restrictions cut immigration from European countries on average to about

10 percent of quota levels."[27] Keeping the number of visas to the lowest possible levels became a value highly promoted among State Department officials working in embassies, consulates, and legations.[28] A consequence of the Depression and the new immigration changes was that in 1931, there was more emigration from the United States than there was immigration into it. It is important to note that many of those who left the United States in the 1930s did not do so voluntarily. Rather, as many as one million Mexican nationals and US citizens of Mexican ancestry were forcibly (and most often illegally) deported in a policy that continued through the Roosevelt administration until the late 1930s.[29] In some of the most brutal instances, police in Los Angeles cordoned off entire neighborhoods and rounded up Mexicans and Mexican Americans with little regard for their citizenship, immigration status, or longevity in the country. In the name of "repatriation" (which was a euphemism for expulsion), authorities denied them their due process rights and summarily deported them to Mexico. In many instances, families found themselves separated on either side of the border or cast into a country with which they had only historic ties, with little personal connections or knowledge of the Spanish language.

American Jews in the land of color lines

The mass influx of new immigrants arriving in America from Southern and Eastern Europe in the late nineteenth and early twentieth centuries unsettled what were generally accepted racial categories. David R. Roediger has argued that most of these new immigrants—Slavs, Greeks, Hungarians, Jews, and Italians among them—fell "in between" the preexisting color divisions that separated white and black and created a new "messiness" in the racial order that was sorted out over the first half of the twentieth century.[30] Although these migrants and their descendants were ultimately accepted into white society, he has shown that, "early in the twentieth century, it was by no means clear that immigrants from Eastern and Southern Europe would escape the condemnations of white supremacists."[31] In response to this uncertainty, most Jews came to accept that in order to achieve peace and prosperity, they, like other European migrants, needed to assimilate into the white middle class and they sought economic, housing, and educational opportunities to assist them in this process. Additionally, as historian Eric L. Goldstein has shown, "identification with whiteness, Jews came to find, not only gave them greater chances for advancement but also allowed them to experience what it was like *not* to be the focus of national hostility and resentment."[32] Oftentimes, Jews publicly and strenuously objected to the country's policies of racial oppression and exclusion against African Americans, yet many also sought to mimic white behaviors by seeking access to exclusively white institutions, deliberately hiring African American women as domestic servants, and in some cases, moving into restrictive white residential communities.

North America had long been a final destination for Jewish immigrants, dating back to the first Jews who arrived in the 1650s. By the period in between the two world wars, Jews numbered approximately 3.5 percent of the total US population. They included speakers of English, Russian, German, Yiddish, French, and Polish. Some belonged to Reform, Orthodox, or Conservative religious denominations and many belonged to none at all. Politically speaking, most leaned toward liberal and even some leftist causes, yet they could be found among the ranks of Republicans, Democrats, Socialists, and the nonpartisan. Newly arriving Jews from Eastern Europe tended to vote Democrat (or Socialist) and were primarily members of the working class. Most wished to partake in the promise of a democratic society that would allow them the religious freedom, physical safety, and economic opportunity that they had often sorely lacked.[33]

While Jews were working to become a part of white middle class society, there were forces gathering to keep them out. To some observers, Jews, as a dispersed people with no state of their own and of indeterminate racial composition, seemed to be the most visible group profiting from the changes under way in the first decades of the twentieth century. This was part of a growing antisemitic trend in Europe that had begun in the last decade of the nineteenth century and which escalated in the interwar years. In the United States, the industrialist Henry Ford, for instance, spent much of the 1920s agitating against what he perceived to be the pernicious influence of Jews in American society.[34] Convinced of a Jewish conspiracy, Ford was responsible for funding the publication and distribution of 500,000 copies of the notorious antisemitic *Protocols of the Elders of Zion*, a text that purportedly revealed plans for Jewish world domination. For much of the decade, he used the weekly *Dearborn Independent* to promote antisemitic pieces that were published in his name. In an essay published in May 1921, for example, he spoke directly to the uncertain racial status of Jews within American society:

> The only absolute antidote to the Jewish influence is to call college students back to a pride of race. We often speak of the Fathers as if they were the few who happened to affix their signatures to a great document which marked a new era of liberty. The Fathers of our nation were the men of the Anglo-Saxon-Celtic race. The men who came from Europe with civilization in their blood and in their destiny. The men who crossed the Atlantic and set up civilization on a bleak and rock-bound coast; the men who drove north to Alaska and west to California; the men who opened up the tropics and subdued the arctics; the men who mastered the African veldt; the men who

> peopled Australia and seized the gates of the world at Suez, Gibraltar and Panama; men who have given form to every government and a livelihood to every people and an ideal to every century. They got neither their God nor their religion from Judah, nor yet their speech nor their creative genius—they are the Ruling People. Chosen throughout the centuries to Master the world, by building it ever better and better, and not by breaking it down.
>
> Into the camp of this race, among the sons of the rulers, comes a people that has no civilization to point to, no aspiring religion, no universal speech, no great achievement in any realm but the realm of "get," cast out of every land that gave them hospitality, and these people endeavor to tell the Sons of the Saxons what is needed to make the world what it ought to be.[35]

Ford was by no means alone in his diatribes against Jews. Antisemitism appeared overtly, such as in campaigns for "Christ Democracy" by the American fascist group known as the Silver Shirts, and in more subtle forms, such as with calls to preserve the white majorities at elite colleges by restricting the number of Jewish students.[36] One of the most notorious antisemites was the "Radio Priest" Charles Coughlin, who laced his popular radio broadcasts throughout the 1930s with speeches against Jewish bankers, Bolsheviks, and New Dealers. Although antisemitism never became the basis of a political movement, such as was occurring in Europe, antisemitic tensions grew over the course of the 1930s and raised anxiety among many American Jews about their status.

Of equal concern to many Jews was what Goldstein has identified as a persistent public questioning in the interwar period on the so-called Jewish Question which—in its American incarnation—openly pondered whether Jews and Judaism were truly compatible with white, Christian, American society.[37] These were not purely "scientific" or hypothetical debates, but, considering the systematic persecution and segregation faced by African Americans, at stake were Jews' legal right to marry and vote for whom they chose, the right to live, work, and be educated where they desired, and their overall social standing. It was common for debates on Jews' racial status to appear in the press. Such discussions considered whether Jews are "white" like other Europeans or are closer to Middle Eastern, Asian, or African peoples. Did they perhaps comprise a distinct "Hebrew" race? Goldstein points to, for example, a 1926 debate in *The Forum* on "The Problem of Anti-Semitism."[38] *Forum* editors invited the eugenicist and racial anthropologist Lothrop Stoddard, for whom race was a "concrete fact," to consider whether Jews comprised a distinct racial group. In seeking to "discover what blood or bloods flow in his [meaning Jews'] veins" he declared that their "exclusiveness and group-separatism" was a biological trait.[39] Debates of this sort were not limited to the 1920s, but were a constant presence in the 1930s as well. Even as late as the summer of 1941, at the time when Germany broke its pact and invaded the Soviet Union and began the mass slaughter of Jews, the *Atlantic Monthly* published a multipart essay, "The Jewish Problem in America," by social critic Alfred Jay Nock. This misguided essay sought to relieve rising antisemitism, but concluded that Jews' were an "Oriental" people living in an "Occidental" society.[40]

In this context of racial interrogation, widespread opposition to liberalizing the newly restrictive anti-immigration legislation, and economic uncertainty, most American Jews during the first years of the Nazi regime were concerned as much, if not more so, for their own status than for German Jews abroad. Jews in the United States tended to be highly aware of the situation affecting the German Jewish community, but they did not always assume that they were living in a country that would be tolerant of Jewish political activism. Liberty, equality before the law, and religious freedom were not taken for granted by most Jews, but were rights that had to be protected and safeguarded. Considering that there began a refugee crisis in Germany at the very moment when the racial position of Jews in America was historically at its most unstable, it is unsurprising that the United States was unwilling to open its doors to a larger number of Jews, that many American Jews were uneasy about testing the limits of their political authority, and, as we will see, that so many American Jews looked uncritically to Roosevelt as their protector.

America responds to Nazism

Hitler's rise to power in January 1933 drew a swift rebuke from American Jewish leaders who feared for the safety of German Jewry. Jews in Germany were a tiny minority, just 523,000 of a population of 67 million, 400,000 of whom were citizens. Public statements and organized activity by American Jewish groups against the new government in Germany were nearly instantaneous. While the Jewish community in Germany itself adopted a much more restrained approach out of fear of Nazi reprisals, groups such as the American Jewish Congress (AJ Congress) quickly took an aggressive stance toward the Nazi regime. Hitler's rise to power provided an opportunity for the up-and-coming AJ Congress to assert itself as a significant force within the Jewish community. Within days of the takeover of power, it denounced the Nazi government for its extreme antisemitism and expressed its hope that the German people would recognize the danger that it posed. In its statement, the organization declared:

> It has been widely recognized that the appointment of Adolf Hitler, head of the National Socialist Party, to the chancellorship of the Reich, creates a grave situation for the Jews of Germany. This party, of which Hitler is the

> titular head, has been teaching that the difficulties of the Reich subsequent to the great war, are due to the Jews and has been preaching hatred and violence toward Jewish life and Jewish culture.
>
> Everybody knows the sort of psychopathic emotion which underlies doctrines of this kind, and everybody recognizes the real grounds in the international situation to which this emotion is due. But the great German people are noteworthy among Europeans for their firmness of character, natural justice and intelligence. It is in these qualities of the German masses, and in the sober common sense of the parties at present collaborating with Hitler, and particularly in the leadership of President Hindenburg, that we place our faith in this grave hour.[41]

It may be difficult to understand given subsequent events and the length of time that Hitler ultimately led Germany, but in the days and weeks following his initial appointment, it was unclear to everyone just how long this government would last and the extent of the threat that he posed to German Jewry.[42] Ruling coalitions in Germany had risen and fallen with great frequency since the end of World War I. It was quite reasonable at the time to anticipate that Hitler's reign would end as quickly as it had begun. With new Reichstag (Parliament) elections called on March 5, 1933, many expected that Hitler's time in office would be mercifully brief. However, when the Reichstag building was set on fire on the evening of February 27, Hitler asked President Hindenburg to invoke Article 48 of the Weimar Constitution and initiate a formal state of emergency. Hitler successfully manipulated this event to claim that Communists were plotting to attack German society. Civil liberties and constitutional protections of freedom of assembly, speech, the press, and communications were immediately suspended. A severe crackdown on political opponents cemented Nazi rule. In the elections that occurred just six days later, the Nazi Party won almost 44 percent of the vote, a gain of ninety-two seats. Weeks later, Hitler proposed the infamous Enabling Act, which was passed by a two-thirds majority and allowed him effectively to rule by decree. A government that many expected to last only a short time quickly defied all of its rivals' expectations and left his opponents at home and abroad unsure of how best to respond. Attacks on Jews in Germany, especially those who had emigrated from Eastern Europe or were prominent politically or culturally, began almost instantly and many fled to neighboring states such as Poland, France, and the Netherlands. In the first five months that the Nazis were in power, over 18,000 Jews left Germany, a number that would more than double by the end of that year.[43]

In the weeks and months after Hitler's rise, Jewish individuals, groups, and communities around the United States spontaneously looked to (then President-elect) Roosevelt for assistance and voiced their opposition to Nazism in the press. The Jewish community in Perth Amboy, NJ, for example, passed a resolution requesting Roosevelt to promote "a better understanding between the German government and the Jewish people there."[44] Jewish periodicals in the weeks and months following January 30, 1933, are filled with articles, letters to the editors, and opinion pieces reflecting the general anxiety and concern for the plight of German Jewry. The *Jewish Morning Journal* called Hitler one of the great tragedies to have befallen the Jewish people in their history and considered Hindenburg's decision to appoint him to power a "public slap in the face for the Jews of Germany and the rest of the world."[45] The Jewish Telegraphic Agency, based in New York since 1922, ran dozens of stories on the rise of Hitler to power and the threat posed to the German Jewish community in first weeks of the new regime. Its dispatches, which were reprinted in Jewish newspapers throughout the United States, told in great detail of the first threats posed by the Nazi government. It published reports filled with stories of street violence, the April 1 boycott of Jewish businesses, the expulsion of Jewish university faculty, and the harassment of Jews trying to cross the German–Austrian border. It published articles highlighting the determination of the organized Jewish community to maintain its resolve and adopt a "wait and see" attitude.[46] The Yiddish language daily *Forward*, which had a readership of 275,000 and was the largest newspaper for Jewish readers in the country, published the news from Germany on its front page throughout 1933. With headlines such as "Hitler-Government Revokes All Freedoms in Germany by Introducing State of Emergency" (March 1) and "Slaughter of German Jewry Is Possible Every Minute" (March 3), the socialist-oriented *Forward* kept its readers informed of the latest developments in the early days of the Nazi regime. As Gennady Estraikh has shown, one of its Berlin correspondents, the renowned Jewish demographer Jacob Lestschinsky, was arrested less than two weeks after the Reichstag fire and was released only when the US State Department interfered. Another of its correspondents, the Menshevik leader Raphael Abramovitch, fled the country after being tipped off about his imminent arrest.[47]

Franklin Roosevelt assumed the presidency on March 4, just one day before the election that cemented the Nazi hold on power in Germany. Very quickly, the AJ Congress, led by Rabbi Stephen Wise, sought to mobilize support for strong action from the administration against the Nazi regime. Acting on its own initiative and contrary to the wishes of the more established Jewish leadership, such as the American Jewish Committee (AJ Committee), the State Department, and Jewish organizations in Germany itself, the AJ Congress called for a boycott of German goods and organized a mass rally on March 27 at Madison Square Garden. The demonstration featured speeches by former New York State Governor Alfred E. Smith, Fiorello H. LaGuardia (who would be elected mayor of New York City later that year), President of the American

FIGURE 1.3 *An estimated 100,000 people gather in front of Madison Square Garden in Manhattan to participate in a mass march to the Battery to protest the Nazi persecution of German Jews, May 10, 1933.*

Federation of Labor William Green, Rabbi Wise, the editor of the *Forward* Abraham Cahan, and many others. With 20,000 participants reportedly in attendance, and as many as a million (most of whom were assumed by the press to be Jews) participating in simultaneous rallies, fasts, and meetings around the country, speaker after speaker condemned the Hitler regime and encouraged Germany's citizens to repudiate him. Governors of many states across the country sent in telegrams of support, as did members of Congress. The rally and calls for boycott were part of a worldwide phenomenon among Jewish communities, as similar actions were held in Brazil, Argentina, Greece, Egypt, and Palestine. In his speech, Governor Smith appealed to the German people to denounce the regime in the name of "human love and brotherhood":

> Well, all I can say about this is that where there is a good deal of smoke there must be fire. And the only thing to do with it, not only in our interest alone but in the interest of the future of the German people, is to drag it out into the open sunlight and give it the same treatment that we gave the Ku Klux Klan. And it don't make any difference to me whether it is a brown shirt or a night shirt.[48]

Many speakers at the rally made clear distinctions between the Nazi government and the German people (condemning the former and declaring their solidarity with the latter), and paid particular attention to the anti-Jewish ideology of Nazism. As the AFL's Green stated:

> We will not remain passive and unconcerned when the relatives, families and brethren of the Jewish members of our great economic organization are being persecuted and oppressed. We will come to their defense because the bonds of brotherhood which bind us so closely in a great economic organization make their great human problems a part of our own.[49]

The Budapest-born Rabbi Wise, whose speech was reprinted in its entirety in the *New York Times* the following day, insisted upon German Jewry's right to be counted among the ranks of the German people and not as antithetical to it:

> How could we, of the household of Israel, fail to cherish and honor the German people, and of the great peoples of earth, a people that has made monumental, indeed eternal, contributions to human well-being in domains of religion, literature and the arts. How could we fail to cherish and to revere the people of Goethe and Schiller, Immanuel Kant and Hegel, Beethoven and Wagner, Heine and Einstein?[50]

He also acknowledged that while the Jewish community in Germany had opposed the rally, he criticized their cautious approach as allowing Nazism to flourish, stating that: "We have no quarrel with our Jewish brothers in Germany and their leaders, but their policy of uncomplaining assent and of super-cautious silence has borne evil fruit."

Founded in 1918 with the goal of presenting a unified Jewish presence and asserting Jewish national ambitions at the 1919 Paris Peace Conference, the AJ Congress was much more disposed than other American Jewish organizations to take a public approach in its activism.[51] Zionist in its orientation, the AJ Congress attracted a wider following than did groups such as the AJ Committee, which the AJ Congress often regarded as elitist and outmoded. The AJ Congress sought to organize Jewish power at the ballot box and promoted a vision of American Jewry as a distinct ethnic group within the ranks of white society. Under the leadership of Wise, the AJ Congress regularly sought to raise awareness of the danger of Hitler's Germany and to press the Roosevelt administration to act on behalf of threatened Jews.[52] Throughout the 1930s, Wise often served as the most visible representative of American Jewry. Politically liberal, he was a founder of the National Association for the Advancement of Colored People in 1909 and of the American Civil Liberties

Union in 1920. He was a strong supporter of unions and, with the exception of Roosevelt's first political campaign (he backed the Socialist candidate Norman Thomas), most Democratic candidates to the presidency. Throughout the 1930s, Wise charted a course that sought to emphasize American Jewry's support for Roosevelt, while encouraging him to intervene more strenuously on behalf of German Jews. However, given the rather modest political and economic clout that American Jews possessed in the 1930s, Wise's ability to influence the Roosevelt administration was limited. He also faced pressure by the more staid AJ Committee to adopt a cautious approach to his advocacy and from the left by the working-class Jewish Labor Committee (which formed in 1934 and joined with non-Jewish groups in a boycott of German goods) to assume a more aggressive one.[53]

The United States in the 1930s saw a steady stream of demonstrations and publications against Nazism. A year after the first mass rally was held in Madison Square Garden, the AJ Congress convened a mock trial of Nazism before a crowd of 20,000 in which Hitlerism was judged to be an offense against civilization.[54] Twenty "witnesses" appeared, including Alfred E. Smith and (now) Mayor LaGuardia, who gave evidence against the tyrannical regime. The prominent attorney Samuel Seabury made the case that the injuries facing Jews in Germany were of consequence to all people, not Jews alone and concluded that "persecution of one is an injury to all."[55] In addition, many pamphlets and books denounced the regime, such as the 1933 *Brown Book of the Hitler Terror* that was published by the Communist-backed World Committee for the Victims of German Fascism and widely distributed in both English and Yiddish.[56] Another work, *Nazism: An Assault on Civilization* (1934), featured a preface by the German-born senator from New York Robert F. Wagner and contributions by the journalist Dorothy Thompson, the President of the New York City Board of Alderman Bernard S. Deutsch, the German Jewish novelist Ludwig Lewisohn, and Rabbi Wise, among others.[57] This work spelled out in detail the arrest and mass incarceration of pacifists, leftists, and unionists as well as the loss of freedoms and civil rights for all Germans. Essay after essay describes the regime as thuggish, violent, and criminal.

In addition to the AJ Congress, AJ Committee, and the Jewish Labor Committee, other organizations such the National Coordinating Committee for Aid to Refugees and Emigrants (founded by the American Joint Distribution Committee), the Hebrew Immigrant Aid Society, the American Friends Service Committee, the Women's International League for Peace and Freedom, and the German Jewish Children's Aid were either formed to address the refugee situation or dramatically expanded their existing mission to confront it. These groups sought to facilitate the immigration of German Jewish refugees by identifying financial sponsors and assisting with their resettlement and retraining in the hope of demonstrating to US immigration authorities that the refugees would not become a public charge.

Some private initiatives, such as one by Alvin Johnson to bring refugee academicians to the United States, led to the establishment of the University in Exile at the New School for Social Research in New York City. While this program was successful in bringing a total of 180 scholars to the United States between 1933 and 1945, it also marked the beginning of a disturbing phenomenon during the refugee crisis that extended through the war years: on several occasions, refugees with status, important connections, and wealth were often granted exceptions to the general rule that kept the vast number of "ordinary" refugees out of the United States. Access for such "elites" reinforced existing notions that not all lives were considered equal. As historian Karen J. Greenberg has noted, "Opportunism clearly overshadowed humanitarianism in the rescue of scholars. Repeatedly, the universities and colleges agreed to take a refugee scholar only if he was a leader in his field ... Once quality was in question, anti-Semitism and xenophobia reared their heads in implicit and explicit forms."[58]

American journalists working as foreign correspondents in Germany also sought to raise the alarm about the treatment of Jews and sent back dire reports of the repression occurring in the new regime. As Michaela Hoenicke Moore shows, reporters such as Dorothy Thompson and William Shirer were unified in their antipathy toward Nazism, although they differed in terms of identifying the cause for its electoral success and popular support.[59] They were forced to walk a fine line between reporting their findings accurately to their audience and not provoking the government to expel them (as was Thompson in 1934). Most insisted on making clear distinctions between the German people and their government but varied at times in their opinion on the extent to which the persecution faced by German Jews was specific to them or part of a much larger campaign against those considered enemies of the state. Journalists based in the United States, by contrast, often took a comparatively softer line toward Germany and displayed more skepticism toward reports of abuses against Jews. Especially in the first years of Hitler's regime, many newspapers and magazines around the United States used Nazism to critique Roosevelt's New Deal proposals, to tout its effectiveness as a bulwark against Bolshevism, or as an opportunity to raise isolationist fears of US involvement in European affairs. Journalists writing for the African American press often viewed Nazi treatment of Jews in light of the struggle for racial equality in the United States and decried the "hypocrisy" of white Americans protesting racial discrimination in Germany while not waging a similar battle at home.[60] As Hoenicke Moore concludes, "Even as public opinion polls showed that ever-increasing numbers of Americans were appalled by Third Reich repression and alarmed by the rising tide of totalitarianism in Europe, the debate on their country's role and responsibility only became more conflicted."[61]

US policy and the Jewish refugee crisis

More than any other figure, President Roosevelt's response to the threat of Nazism has faced the greatest scrutiny. His critics accuse him of refusing to come to Jews' rescue because of his supposedly deeply held antisemitic beliefs and point to the more than 190,000 unused spaces in the combined quotas from Germany and Austria during the period of the Nazi regime.[62] His most ardent defenders view him as Jews' greatest advocate and argue that his many attempts to assist refugees were constrained by legal obstacles and popular opinion.[63]

In spite of critics who argue that Roosevelt either was overtly hostile to European Jews or that he did all that was possible in the existing circumstances, the historians Richard Breitman and Allan J. Lichtman have persuasively argued that Roosevelt's legacy is not so easily characterized as entirely opposed to or in favor of Jewish refugees. In *FDR and the Jews*, they show that Roosevelt's position shifted over the course of his presidency. The first of his many stances coincided with his initial term, from 1933 until the 1936 campaign. During this time, which coincided with the period of increasing discrimination and persecution of Jews in Germany (but long before mass killing began), Roosevelt was focused almost entirely on passing and implementing his New Deal legislation to end the Depression and was little concerned with the fate of German Jews. Only with the 1936 election did he begin to take steps to relax immigration restrictions that barred the way for hopeful Jewish refugees. In his second term, which saw the situation for German Jews grow especially dire, his policies led the United States to provide refuge to over 100,000 Jews. He also gave his support for a Jewish state in Palestine and encouraged the British government to allow for more Jewish colonization. In the late 1930s, Roosevelt became particularly active in trying to find solutions to the worsening crisis. Since he did not put his own domestic agenda at risk, his efforts were not particularly effective, however.[64] Once the war began, however, a third position emerged in which he prioritized security concerns and feared that his foreign policy would suffer if he advocated further on behalf of imperiled Jews. Roosevelt's final position emerged at the end of 1943. He established the War Refugee Board which sought to aid refugees and again pressed the case for a Jewish state in British-controlled Palestine. In this final phase, Roosevelt came to realize that the Nazis' campaign against Jews was distinct from their general war aims. In assessing Roosevelt's legacy, Breitman and Lichtman portray Roosevelt's response to the refugee crisis not easily depicted as having been either wholly positive or negative:

> FDR was neither a hero of the Jews nor a bystander to the Nazis' persecution and annihilation of Jews. No simple or monolithic characterization of this complex president fits the historical record. FDR could not fully meet all competing priorities as he led the nation through its worst economic depression and most challenging foreign war. He had to make difficult and painful trade-offs, and he adapted over time to shifting circumstances. His compromises might seem flawed in the light of what later generations have learned about the depth and significance of the Holocaust, a term that first came into widespread use many years after FDR's death. Still, Roosevelt reacted more decisively to Nazi crimes against Jews than did any other world leader of his time.[65]

Much of Roosevelt's early attitudes toward the refugee situation was driven by political concerns. Given his start in New York State, he learned early in his political career of the importance of ethnic voting blocks. Although he held antisemitic views that were all too typical of his social and racial status, they did not prevent him from forming close relationships with Jewish advisors (such as Felix Frankfurter), hiring Jews to serve in his administration, or enthusiastically courting Jewish voters. Overall Jewish support for his presidency was extraordinarily high (between 70 and 80 percent) and was based more on his economic policies than any other issue, since Jews were among those often financially ruined in the first years of the Depression.[66]

Immigration reform on behalf of German Jews was a vexed question from the outset of his presidency. There was little support anywhere for repealing the 1924 immigration law. Rather, the issue was the tightly enforced LPC proviso, which was the primary obstacle that prevented most refugees from entering into the United States within the quota system. Soon after Roosevelt took office, Labor Secretary Frances Perkins and Felix Frankfurter urged him to sign a presidential order lifting the Hoover-era mandate but members of the State Department, which was staffed by a number of anti-immigrant and antisemitic figures, used the argument that the United States should not interfere in the internal affairs of a foreign country—even Nazi Germany—and successfully blocked the plan. This set up a series of "immigration wars" between Labor and State within the first Roosevelt administration.[67] Whereas Labor was motivated to act out of humanitarian concerns, State's overriding priority was to maintain the strict controls that had been in place for the previous decade. Organized labor, whose voting strength was far superior to that of Jewish voters, likewise resisted any efforts to lower obstacles for immigration out of fear of exacerbating the unemployment crisis. During the course of Roosevelt's first term in office, the Labor Department crafted various proposals for assisting German Jewish refugees gain entrance into the United States—such as a bonding initiative by which money would be posted to ensure that an immigrant would not require public assistance—but none of them gained sufficient traction. Such attempts were not helped by the fact that many of Roosevelt's opponents sought to characterize him as overly beholden to Jewish interests and antisemitic agitation—especially in the Midwest—grew stronger during his term. In all, Breitman and Lichtman conclude, by the end of fiscal year 1936, approximately 60,000 "potential German immigrants, most of the Jewish, may have failed to find refuge in the United States because the Roosevelt administration continued policies that denied them visas despite available quota slots."[68] This claim must be understood, however, in light of the fact that during the first years of the Nazi regime, most German Jews did not seek to leave the country. They expected, in the words of historian Saul Friedländer, "to weather the storm," and hoped that the situation would soon stabilize. Following the emigration of more than 37,000 Jews (many of whom were not citizens) in 1933, the annual number of Jews emigrating in the years 1934–37 (to any country) was never more than 25,000. This was in spite of Nazi policies that encouraged Jewish emigration (while extracting as much of their wealth as possible). German officials even cooperated for a time with Zionist organizations to relocate German Jews in Palestine. Under the Haavara (Hebrew: Transfer) Agreement, as many as 60,000 emigrated to British-controlled Palestine between 1933 and 1939, when the arrangement was finally halted by German officials.[69]

In the years that coincided with Roosevelt's second term in office, the situation for Jews within Germany worsened dramatically. In 1936, when Germany held the Summer Olympics in Berlin (which the United States and other Western countries declined to boycott), the pace of anti-Jewish activity temporarily eased. Although Germany acted aggressively in other realms, such as with the remilitarization of the Rhineland in March, measures against Jews escalated only gradually that year. The Aryanization (state-supported theft) of Jewish businesses continued, and state decrees continued to exclude Jews from aspects of public life.

In 1937, Germany assumed a much more aggressive posture, both internationally (such as with the aerial assault of Basque city of Guernica, Spain, in April and its growing interference in Austria) and domestically, with the increased seizure of Jewish-owned businesses. That year, 23,000 Jews left Germany, bringing the total to between 129,000 and 140,000 émigrés, approximately 25 percent of the January 1933 Jewish population. In response to the worsening situation, the State Department began to loosen the tight LPC prohibitions on immigrants, allowing for more discretion by consular officials. In doing so, the United States outpaced Palestine in providing refuge to the largest number of German Jewish emigrants, 11,520 or 38 percent of the total (filling 42.1 percent of available visas under the quota).

In 1938, Germany provoked several crises that had dramatic effects on the refugee situation and prompted changes in US policy. The first of these was the annexation of Austria, known as the *Anschluss*. Fulfilling a long-held dream of German pan-nationalists, and following stepped-up pressure by Austrian Nazis and German authorities, on March 12, the Wehrmacht crossed the German–Austrian border. In what has become known sarcastically as the "Blumenkrieg" (war of flowers), soldiers encountered no resistance and were instead welcomed by cheering crowds. Later that day, Hitler entered the country and greeted supporters. He again returned to Austria on April 2 and spoke before a crowd of 200,000. The incorporation of Austria into Germany—a violation of the Treaty of Versailles that garnered no significant reprisals by either the countries of Europe or the United States—brought an additional 185,000 Jews (almost all of whom lived in Vienna) under German rule. The consequences of this were particularly brutal. Thousands of Jews were arrested without cause, many of whom were sent to the Dachau concentration camp. By April, authorities began to construct the Mauthausen camp, which became operational in August (and in which 14,000 Jews and over 80,000 non-Jews would perish by the end of World War II). Within a few months, the legislation to which German Jews had five years to become accustomed was enacted and immediately enforced. In response to the violence, theft, arrest, and loss of rights, many Austrian Jews scrambled to leave the country as quickly as possible. In the last seven months of 1938, over 11,500 Austrian Jews emigrated.[70]

After the *Anschluss*, the refugee situation grew to a full-blown crisis and Jews in Germany began to fear for their lives. More than 1,000 persons a day came to the Hilfsverein der Deutschen Juden (Relief Organization of German Jews) in Berlin looking for guidance. Jews trying to escape Germany in 1938 were more desperate, had few financial resources, and little to offer the countries that would host them. In response, many of the states that had once been willing to accept Jewish migrants, such as South Africa or many Latin American countries, became concerned with the cost of absorbing the financial and social costs related to their immigration, and strictly limited immigration or curtailed it altogether. In April 1938, *Foreign Affairs* published as the lead story an essay by the journalist Dorothy Thompson entitled "Refugees: A World Problem," which began by outlining the collapsing situation in Europe:

> As I write this article the news from Europe is distressing in the extreme. Hitler is in Vienna. Central Europe is in turmoil, as every small state of the Danubian Basin feels the increasing pressure of Nazidom. Great Britain, and, following her leadership, France, are considering whether—and if so

FIGURE 1.4 *Journalist Dorothy Thompson and New York City Mayor Fiorello H. LaGuardia, October 1, 1940.*

> how—to protect Czechoslovakia, and whether—and if so how—to save even a modified League of Nations. The Soviet system seems in a state of serious disintegration. The war in Spain continues, to what final denouement we cannot yet foresee. But one thing is certain: these chaotic situations cannot fail to add to a problem which is already a world headache—the problem of dispossessed racial and political minorities.[71]

As Thompson discussed, the refugee problem was increasing beyond Germany's borders and the instability was provoking a much larger crisis. She described how the rise of antisemitism in Germany led to spikes throughout central and east central Europe: in Czechoslovakia, Rumania, Hungary, and Yugoslavia, "if any more countries fall under Nazi domination, or come under Nazi influence, a further growth of anti-Semitism will hardly be avoided." Thompson estimated that in the spring of 1938, there were four million refugees in the world, with Jews suffering the worst of the atrocities due to their "race" and the fact that they tend to be "political liberals." She noted with alarm that the rise of mass migration was provoking the rise of radical forms of nationalism in response, and creating a "Jewish question" in countries where it had not existed previously—such as in the United States. Arguing that "until now the problem has been largely regarded as one of international charity. It must now be regarded as a problem of international politics," she advocated for the creation of a new world body to deal with the problem on a mass scale. She realized that any international proposal to resettle Jewish refugees might prompt other antisemitic countries to begin expelling their Jewish residents, but, Thompson argued, the situation was so grave that none of the available solutions was ideal. "The best that can be hoped," she wrote, "is that if this is done the fate of the persecuted can be softened by compromise."[72] Thompson saw, correctly as it turned out, that the problem faced by Jews was not one for Jews alone to solve, but rather one that posed challenges for the entire Western world, and therefore, the burden of finding a solution should fall on the West as a whole:

> Jews and Christians alike are forced to contemplate the fact that when, with one sweeping gesture, the Nazi leader of Germany outlawed the relatively small Jewish population of his country he declared a war in which the Jews of the whole world became potential victims of aggression. Both Jews and Christians must face the fact that the stand he took is unacceptable to those who profess western principles of democratic law and order. Both Jews and Christians therefore must collaborate to prevent the problem which Hitler created from gathering force as it rolls along.[73]

The escalating crisis prompted Roosevelt to take up renewed interest in immigration reform. In spite of opposition from members of Congress, he unilaterally combined the quotas for Austria and Germany, which now stood at 27,370, and allowed Austrian Jews to avail themselves of the unused portion of the German quota. As the historian Melissa Jane Taylor has shown, American foreign offices were initially taken off-guard by changes in administrative lines of authority within the State Department that had occurred as a result of the annexation of Austria. This allowed for significant variation in how individual offices responded to the dramatic rise in visa requests. The way in which individual consular officials interacted with applicants was often decisive as to whether or not a visa would be granted. The officials stationed in Vienna stand out for having factored in humanitarian considerations (while staying within the law) into their decisions while other consulates in Europe adhered more strictly to the State Department's historic practice of keeping the number of visas allotted to a minimum.[74] As a result of Roosevelt's decision to combine the quotas and the willingness of these consular officials to challenge the State Department's mindset, the quota for Germany was filled for the first time in fiscal year 1939.

Nine days after the *Anschluss*, Roosevelt began to organize the creation of an international conference to establish an organization to handle refugee affairs. He and his advisors realized that, even in spite of the worsening situation in Europe, opening up the borders of the United States would be wholly unpopular in Congress and with the American people. Rather than use the authority of his office to influence the public and risk further his own standing (which had been severely damaged in his failed attempt to add seats to the Supreme Court), Roosevelt instead reached out to over thirty countries, primarily from Latin America and Europe, to come together in the hope of finding an international solution.

Held over July 6–14, the conference in Évian, France, has been widely disparaged by critics for the near absolute unwillingness of its participants to offer immediate refuge to imperiled German Jews. With little to offer the gathered countries, the United States did not sufficiently lay the groundwork for a successful outcome. The invitation to the conference made no specific reference to the Jewish crisis. The United States sent as its representative Myron Charles Taylor, an industrialist without diplomatic experience. No Jewish organizations (from any country) were formally invited to send delegates and their representatives only had an advisory role. Many administration officials were concerned that any action that was seen to be explicitly on behalf of "Jewish interests" would raise the specter of further antisemitism and prompt other countries to follow Germany's lead and force their own Jewish

FIGURE 1.5 *English representative Lord Winterton delivering a speech at the Evian Conference, July 12, 1938.*

residents to emigrate. Complicating matters further was that both the British and French representatives, in talks prior to the conference, insisted that the proposed new body, the Intergovernmental Committee on Refugees, be subordinate to the League of Nations, a position that the United States refused to accept. Several countries, including France and Latin American nations, were reluctant to upset their diplomatic relations with Germany.[75]

With over 200 people in attendance, the conference was viewed by many with cautious optimism. Journalist Anne O'Hare McCormick considered it a "Test of Civilization." Writing on July 4, just days before the gathering, McCormick drew a parallel between the founders of the United States and their desire to be divorced from the problems of Europe and the isolationists of her own time who wished similarly to avoid involvement in overseas affairs. However, she argued, "this relative independence increases our responsibility." She viewed the conference as a moral challenge to the United States, to see whether it was capable of living up to its newly inhabited role as a world power, and presciently raised the question of the self-reckoning the United States would endure should it fail to meet its responsibility: "How deeply do we believe in our Declaration of the elementary rights of man? Whatever other nations do, can America live with itself if it lets Germany get away with this policy of extermination, allows the fanaticism of one man to triumph over reason, refuses to take up this gage of battle against barbarism?"[76]

The New York Times likened the conference to a game of poker with all sides waiting for one of the major players to make an opening bid.[77] On July 6, the opening day of the conference, Stephen Wise, now leader of the World Jewish Congress (an organization founded in Geneva in 1936 to represent the interests of global Jewry), sent a memorandum to the delegates at the conference, imploring them to place the Jewish crisis at the forefront of their agenda and reminding them that they were likely the only hope for Jews trapped within Nazi Germany and that they must stand up for the "fundamental principles of justice and humanity." He wrote, "At a time when policies of brutal force and oppression of political, racial and religious minorities disgrace our century, the initiative of President Roosevelt has been a ray of hope; may it permit us to save a part at least of the victims and give them new opportunities."[78] Wise went on to remind the delegates that should they not identify a solution to the present crisis; it was likely to expand far beyond Germany into the countries of Eastern Europe, where far greater numbers of Jews were also threatened with persecution and involuntary emigration:

> Following the nefarious example set by Germany, several European states have, for some time, been enacting legal and administrative measures

> designed to evict [the] Jewish population from employment and professions, to deprive Jews of their nationality and to force them to emigrate. In so doing, these states are violating their constitutions which guarantee to Jews equality of rights, and disregard the rights pledged to Jewish minorities by the peace treaties [following World War I].[79]

Although the United States convened the conference and made the refugee crisis a matter for international concern, its refusal to alter its own immigration laws provided sufficient cover for the gathered countries to decline to open its borders further. Without leadership from the United States, Britain, or France, there was little impetus for countries such as Canada, Nicaragua, Brazil, or the Netherlands to extend themselves. Of all the assembled countries, only the Dominican Republic extended an offer, promising refuge to an unimaginably large number of 100,000. In reality, the Dominican Republic's overture was designed to deflect criticism off of its leader, Rafael Trujillo, who a year earlier oversaw the ethnic cleansing of 12,000 Haitian immigrants. Approximately 3,000 Jewish refugees survived as a result of Trujillo's largess.[80] The rest of the countries only agreed to organize the Intergovernmental Committee, which was given no authority and achieved little practical results. In his July 20 report to the Secretary of State Cordell Hull, Taylor remained optimistic about the outcome of the conference, but viewed the countries of Latin America (and not the United States, which made no offer to admit more refugees) as the weak point that might threaten continued efforts to find places of sanctuary.[81]

As predicted, in the months immediately following the Évian conference, the refugee situation grew worse. The German seizure of the Sudetenland, the German-speaking region of Czechoslovakia, in September, prompted more Jews to take flight. Although the United States continued to allow the immigration quota for Germany to be filled, other possible sites of sanctuary in the Americas began to refuse Jewish refugees, with the exception of Bolivia. By fall, all Jews in Germany and Austria were required to have their passport stamped with the red letter "J," thus marking them as Jewish refugees to the world.

Events within Germany grew more dire when, in the last days of October, Germany expelled approximately 12,000 Polish Jews who were still residing in the country.[82] Many of them were at risk of losing their right of residence within Poland, following a law passed by the Polish parliament at the end of March which allowed the government to strip citizenship from any Pole who had lived continuously for more than five years outside of the country. By this time, an estimated 50,000 Polish Jews still resided within the (now enlarged) borders of Germany. The Polish order was scheduled to go into effect on October 30 out of fear that Germany might expel these residents back into

Poland, where antisemitism was also on the rise. Instead, passing the act prompted Germany to round up Polish Jews (as well as approximately 3,000 Czech Jews), summarily arrest them, and force them across the border in the days just before the October 30 deadline. Most refugees were forbidden to take anything with them other than a few German marks. Polish authorities refused to accept the expellees, and for days, they languished at the border until Jewish organizations were able to negotiate with the Polish government for their return.

In Paris, a seventeen-year-old Polish Jew by the name of Herschel Grynszpan learned that his family was among those Jews forcibly repatriated. Grynszpan was living illegally in Paris at the time, having been rendered stateless by the March legislation in Poland. His family, who had resided in the German city of Hanover since before World War I, was arrested on October 27. According to his father Sendel's testimony at Adolf Eichmann's 1961 trial in Jerusalem, "Then they took us in police trucks, in prisoners' lorries, about twenty men in each truck, and they took us to the railway station. The streets were full of people shouting: '*Juden raus* to Palestine!' "[83] After being marched to the railway station, they were brought to the Polish border and forced to march over a mile into Poland and ended up in a refugee camp outside of the town of Zbaszyn.

Having received word of his family's treatment and unable to provide them assistance, on November 7, Herschel went to the German embassy and asked to see an official. He met Ernst vom Rath, a member of the SA and a career diplomat, whom he shot. Vom Rath died of his injuries two days later—a date that coincided with the fifteenth anniversary of the 1923 Beer Hall Putsch, the first Nazi attempt to overthrow the German government. In response, Nazi authorities in Germany organized what has become known as *Kristallnacht* over the night of November 9–10. At the instigation of Minister of Propaganda Joseph Goebbels, Jewish communities, shops, homes, and religious organizations were attacked across Germany. Although the violence appeared to be a spontaneous action by the general public, it was in fact conducted almost entirely by members of the SA and Hitler Youth. By the time the violence had ceased, nearly 100 Jews had been murdered and hundreds more wounded, 267 synagogues were destroyed, and more than 7,500 Jewish-owned businesses were in ruins. The Gestapo and Schutzstaffel (SS) arrested more than 26,000 Jewish men and detained them in concentration camps, and many died as a result of their ill-treatment. German Jews themselves were held responsible for the damage and the community was fined one billion Reichsmarks (approximately 400 million dollars). The government put into effect dozens of new anti-Jewish laws, including the acceleration of the "Aryanization" of Jewish property and the increased removal of Jews from the public realm.[84]

Following *Kristallnacht*, it was clear to most Jews in Germany that there was no future for them within the country and that flight was likely the only way to survive. As the historian Herbert A. Strauss discusses, prior to 1938, German Jewish emigration had been an orderly matter. When Jews left, they tended to do so via legal means, were able to pay their own way, and most often brought a significant number of their possessions with them. They tended to have a clear destination and prospects for supporting themselves in their new homes. Following the crises of 1938, emigration became a "Hobbesian" affair with German Jews trying to flee by whatever means possible and to wherever possible. Emigration organizations chartered ships for passengers without visas or even clear destinations in the hopes of finding a place of refuge.[85] The response of the various countries to where German Jews hoped to find sanctuary was mixed. Countries around Germany began enacting tighter regulations, for fear of being overwhelmed by refugees. By contrast, in what became known as the *Kindertransport*, Great Britain admitted 10,000 children on an emergency basis between 1938 and 1940.

In 1938, humanitarian organizations in the United States desperately sought to find ways to alleviate the refugee crisis. Among the most active non-Jewish organizations was the American Friends Service Committee, which began assisting Jews soon after Hitler's rise to power. The AFSC's leader Clarence E. Pickett had traveled to Germany in 1934 as a result of hearing many "grim and bitter stories" about the persecution of that country's Jews.[86] Upon arriving at the Quaker center in Berlin, Pickett witnessed hundreds of Jews seeking to get out of Germany. As he later recounted in his memoirs, he realized his good fortune for the first time: "We had taken our privileges of American citizenship pretty much for granted all our lives, and had assumed they came without money and without price, but here we began to understand what a precious possession was ours, highly coveted by a growing number of uncertain citizens of Germany."[87] During his 1934 Berlin trip Pickett met with Dr. Leo Baeck, the president of the Reichsvertretung der Deutschen Juden (a Jewish umbrella organization formed in 1933), who conveyed to him the extent of the isolation and confusion felt by German Jews. "He pointed out that Jews were in Germany before the time of Christ, that they loved Germany, and wanted to stay."[88]

In December 1938, Pickett returned to Germany for a third and what would be his final visit. The AFSC's refugee workload had increased tremendously, to the point of it being the organization's primary focus of concern, and Pickett believed he needed to witness first-hand the changes that had taken place in the four years since his last visit. He was shocked by the enormity of suffering and persecution and the near-universal desire of Germany's Jews to escape. As he later described, he felt his greatest sense of obligation as a US citizen and as a Christian when one Jewish man beseeched him, "Don't put food and hunger first. For the love of God, get us out!"[89] During this visit, Pickett and his fellow Quaker leader Rufus M. Jones met with Gestapo leaders and requested to investigate the suffering of German Jews and undertake relief efforts within the country. They reminded the officials that the AFSC had been responsible for feeding more than a million German children during the blockade of Germany at the end of World War I and of its many programs that continued to support needy Germans. They were provided with assurances that they would be able to continue with their relief work in the country.[90]

As a result of Pickett's visits to Germany, the increasingly dire reports from Berlin, and *Kristallnacht*, the AFSC began to develop programs to get refugees out of Germany and safely into the United States.[91] For the next two years, until the start of World War II in Europe, the AFSC founded resettlement communities and hostels for displaced German Jews, such as the Scattergood school in Iowa and Quaker Hill in Richmond, Indiana. Knowing little English, having few connections, and with little hope of finding jobs on their own, refugees received training in the hope that they would go on to live full, productive lives in the United States.[92] The AFSC also arranged various seminar schools, such as the one at Vermont's Goddard College, to assist refugees to become better accustomed to the new country.[93]

Hoping to follow the model of the *Kindertransport*, refugee advocates also promoted a similar plan in the belief that public sympathy in the United States was such that it might be possible to allow for the entry of more refugees. In early 1939, a group calling itself the Non-Sectarian Committee for German Refugee Children (which was headed by Pickett) organized to pass a bill that would allow the admission of 20,000 German children, outside the quota system, over the course of 1939 and 1940.[94] The bill did not specifically favor Jewish children, for fear of provoking an antisemitic backlash against the legislation. Introduced by Senator Robert F. Wagner (D-NY) and Representative Edith Nourse Rogers (R-MA) in February 1939, the bill was the first challenge to existing immigration law. The authors of the bill fashioned it to be as nonthreatening as possible. As part of the legislation, private agencies would provide for the needs of all the children, at no cost to the government. Support formed quickly and decisively. In order to combat the charge that these children, although years away from working, would take away jobs from US workers, unions such as the Brotherhood of Railroad Trainmen, the International Ladies' Garment Workers' Union, the AFL, and the CIO were recruited to support the bill.[95] As most resistance was expected from the Southern Congressional delegation, prominent Southerners such as Monte Lemann, former president of the Louisiana Bar Association, and Frank Preston, general secretary of the Children's Home Society of Virginia, gave their support.[96] Dozens of child welfare organizations approved the arrangement.[97] The list of proponents included such prominent names as Eleanor Roosevelt, Herbert Hoover, Henry Fonda, John Steinbeck, and Helen Hayes.[98] By April 1939, over 5,000 (mostly Quaker) families had offered to take the children into their homes. One letter from Grand Rapids, Michigan, to the AFSC stated:

> All right-thinking people, I believe, should support this bill. We also have a personal interest, in that we should like to care for one of the children so admitted, with a view to adopting the child, if possible, but in any event to give it the love and the care from which it has been deprived by the cruelty of men or circumstances.[99]

Opposition, however, quickly mounted from Southern Senators and organizations such as the American Legion, the Daughters of the American Revolution, Junior Order United American Mechanics, the Patriotic Order Sons of America, and the American Coalition of Patriotic Americans.[100] The most effective argument against the bill spoke of the need "at home" for the type of charity being offered to foreigners. Although most of the opponents had never before spoken with such passion concerning poverty in the United States, they argued that it was objectionable to provide for another country's children while thousands of US children were living without proper care and services. These arguments proved effective despite the fact that child welfare agencies nearly unanimously endorsed the bill.

Using tactics such as calls for repeated hearings and "amend[ing] the bill to death," the opponents of the Wagner–Rogers bill were finally able to kill the proposed legislation, thus preventing the admittance of 20,000 children into the country.[101] The AFSC leader Clarence Pickett recalled the testimony of Rabbi Wise, who, at the final hearing, read the Forty-Sixth Psalm:

> When in that great resonant voice of his he had finished quoting the Psalm, first in Hebrew and then in English, there was hardly a dry eye among the visitors at the hearing. Then, in his most eloquent voice, he pleaded for the admission of these children.
>
> The facts and the logic, the eloquence and the fervor, seemed to me all on the side of the bill, but those of us who supported it plugged away in vain. The bill never came out of committee.[102]

The Roosevelt administration had given only lukewarm support to the proposal, which was being debated amid the crisis facing the passengers aboard the MS *St. Louis*. The State Department was actively opposed to it.[103] This would be the only wide-scale effort to change immigration policy; refugee organizations had to combat not only popular opinion but also resistance from agencies within the government.

***

On January 30, 1939, the sixth anniversary of the Nazi takeover of power, Hitler spoke at length on the Jewish Question before the Reichstag and called attention to the fact that most countries of the world were unwilling to welcome large numbers of Jews. He revealed his belief that most countries of the world likewise shared his antisemitic beliefs and mocked:

> If the rest of the world cries out with a hypocritical mien against this barbaric expulsion from Germany of such an irreplaceable and culturally eminently valuable element, we can only be astonished at the conclusions they draw from this situation. For how thankful they must be that we are releasing these precious apostles of culture, and placing them at the disposal of the rest of the world. In accordance with their own declarations they cannot find a single reason to excuse themselves for refusing to receive this most valuable race in their own countries. Nor can I see a reason why the members of this race should be imposed upon the German nation, while in the States, which are so enthusiastic about these "splendid people," their settlement should suddenly be refused with every imaginable excuse. I think that the sooner this problem is solved the better; for Europe cannot settle down until the Jewish question is cleared up. It may very well be possible that sooner or later an agreement on this problem may be reached in Europe, even between those nations which otherwise do not so easily come together.
>
> The world has sufficient space for settlements, but we must once and for all get rid of the opinion that the Jewish race was only created by God for the purpose of being in a certain percentage a parasite living on the body and the productive work of other nations. The Jewish race will have to adapt itself to sound constructive activity as other nations do, or sooner or later it will succumb to a crisis of an inconceivable magnitude.

***

By late spring, the threat of war loomed ever larger. In 1939, 78,000 Jews fled Germany (27,000 of them to Poland). Jews throughout Europe, fearing war, began looking for sites of refuges abroad and found that their options were rapidly diminishing. In the United States, the quotas for Germany were filled, while those for neighboring countries were not. The British White Paper of 1939 severely limited Jewish immigration to Palestine because of the seemingly intractable conflict between Jewish settlers and the indigenous

Palestinian population. Most Latin American countries closed their doors. With the onset of war in late summer 1939, options for European Jewry—and the United States' ability and willingness to assist them—would narrow even further. As Chapter 2 will demonstrate, the stance of the United States toward the escalating refugee crisis as well as the Holocaust grew more complicated as concerns for rescue often took a backseat first to the goal of avoiding becoming entangled in the war and then for winning it at all costs.

2

Rescue during wartime

In late July 1943, President Roosevelt received a visitor from Poland who had witnessed firsthand what up until then had been mostly rumors. Jan Karski—a courier for the Polish government-in-exile based in London—sat before the president and described the death and destruction that he had seen in Poland. As a member of the Polish underground, Karski had been smuggled into the Warsaw Ghetto in mid-1942. He also secretly visited what then he believed to have been the Belzec death camp (now thought to have been a sorting camp nearby). While in the ghetto, he met with Jewish leaders, who charged him with the task of conveying a message to Allied governments. In an interview many years later, Karski stated that the message was:

> The Jewish situation is unprecedented, it has never happened before. Hitler cannot be allowed to continue extermination. Consequently, every day counts. Thousands of Jews are being murdered. The Allied Governments cannot treat this war only from a purely military strategic standpoint; they will win the war if they take such an attitude, but what good will it do to us? Hitler will lose the war against humanity, but he will win his war against the Jews. The Allied Governments cannot take such a stand. We contributed to humanity, we gave scientists, for thousands of years. We originated great religions, we are humans.[1]

Prior to his trip to the United States, Karski had brought this appeal to British officials in London, his first stop after he escaped Poland. Although in summer 1941 British officials had learned of Germany's mass killings of Jews in the Soviet Union after they acquired an encoding machine that allowed them to understand secret German radio messages,[2] they doubted the veracity of Karski's report from Poland. They also insisted that by having already taken in large numbers of refugees, they had fulfilled any responsibility they had toward Jewish victims of Nazism.

When Karski arrived in the United States in July 1943, he met with Polish officials and American Jewish leaders, who eventually arranged for him to speak in secret with the president. After a lengthy discussion of Poland's fate, including the Nazi occupation and the presence of Soviet communists serving in the Polish underground, he moved to the Nazi slaughter of Jews and spoke of the death camps that by then had become fully operational. He later recalled saying: "Mr. President, before having left Poland I was charged with this mission by the most important Jewish leaders. They organized for me two visits in the ghetto. I saw an extermination camp, the name is Belzec ... Mr. President, the situation is horrible. The point is that without outside help the Jews will perish in Poland. The end of them."[3] According to the report that Karski wrote immediately after the meeting, he also conveyed to Roosevelt that Nazi intentions toward Polish Jews were qualitatively different from their intention toward ethnic Poles:

> The Germans want to ruin the Polish state; they want to rule over a Polish people deprived of its elites ... With regard to the Jews, they want to devastate the biological substance of the Jewish nation ... If the Germans don't change their method of dealing with the Jewish population, if there is no effort at Allied intervention ... the Jewish people of Poland ... will cease to exist.[4]

The Polish ambassador, who was also present at the more-than-hour-long meeting, was convinced that the meeting was a success and reported this back to his superiors in London, who were pleased. Karski had achieved his primary mission, which was to convey to the president the dire circumstances of Poland. The news regarding the plight of Polish Jewry did not seem to stir Roosevelt. The president ended the meeting with a few vague promises of support, promising Karski that "the Allied nations are going to win this war! ... Your country will be alive again, more prosperous than before ... The United States will not abandon your country."[5]

Following his July 1943 meeting with Karski, the president sent word that he would like Karski to discuss his report with several key administration figures, including the secretary of war and the secretary of state, as well as major Jewish leaders. As Karski later told the filmmaker Claude Lanzmann, Roosevelt also asked him to meet with Supreme Court Justice Felix Frankfurter.[6] In his interview with Lanzmann, Karski relayed what he had seen in the Warsaw Ghetto and at (what then he presumed to be) Belzec and also what he had been told by Jewish leaders in Poland. According to Karski's retelling, the conversation went as follows (this includes Karski's comments to Lanzmann):

FF: Young man, do you know that I am a Jew?

JK: Yes, Sir. Mr. Ambassador [a reference to the Polish Ambassador Jan Ciechanowsky] told me about this.

FF: Well, tell me about the Jews. We have here many reports. What happens to the Jews in your country?

JK: [To Lanzmann] I become a machine again ... I told him: The Jewish leaders, the ghetto, Belzec; those fifteen, twenty minutes passed and then stop. Justice Frankfurter sits, looks at me still at this moment. Then tells me the following:

FF: Young man, as I mentioned I have been informed about your activities. I was told that you came out of hell, and I was told that you are going back to hell ... I am no longer young. I am a judge of men; men like me, men like you must be totally honest. I am telling you I do not believe you!

At this point, Karski describes to Lanzmann that Ambassador Ciechanowsky, who was also present at the meeting with Frankfurter, interrupted and vouched for Karski's reliability. To which Frankfurter responded:

FF: Mr. Ambassador, I did not say that he is lying. I said that I don't believe him. These are different things. My mind, my heart, they are made in such a way that I cannot accept it. No! No! ... I am a judge of men. I know humanity, I know man! Impossible!

In describing this conversation to Lanzmann, Karski stated: "I think he believed me, of course; I have no doubt he did his best, whatever he could have done. He took it for granted I was going back to Poland. Probably, he wanted to show me that the world is unprepared, this is an unprecedented problem, a horrible problem."[7] This inability to believe, in spite of reliable eyewitness testimony, was commonplace in the United States not only among government officials, but among the general population as well.

Although Karski did not discuss with Roosevelt the details of what he saw in the ghetto and in the (presumed) extermination camp, this encounter is one that scholars often view as representing a missed opportunity by the US government both to come terms with the immensity of killing and to attempt to rescue European Jewry.[8] Since Roosevelt did not leave any notes of his own regarding the meeting, we cannot know how he perceived Karski's news. His seeming disinterest in the situation facing Polish Jewry may be because the previous week he had met with the American Jewish leader Stephen Wise, who had relayed much of the same information. By contrast, Karski's news regarding Poland was intriguing and new.

To Karski and the leaders of the Jewish underground seeking to stop the extermination under way, as well as to many observers since, the US president was their greatest hope. As Karski himself later related, he believed at the time that the man with whom he met was not only the president of the United States but a "world leader" who could single-handedly intervene and change the course of history for the better.[9] He, like so many others, believed that by getting the right information to the right people, the mass slaughter could be brought to an end.

Even if Roosevelt had wanted to intervene, it is unclear what options were available to him. His authority was limited by laws governing the government's ability to offer refuge to European Jews, by the limits imposed by the course of the war, and by US public opinion, which was neither fully informed about nor particularly sympathetic to the plight of European Jews. As this chapter will demonstrate, during the war years, as the situation for European Jews worsened, the possibilities for the United States to effect change increasingly narrowed. The debate on rescuing and providing refuge to European Jewry was shaped by new concerns for state security during wartime, the increasingly hostile racial climate that existed throughout the country, a continuing ambivalence about the place of Jews within America, and, once information about the plight of Jews was widely (if not accurately) known, a lack of consensus on what would be the most effective response.

The eruption of war and the closing of US borders

In the summer of 1939, the threat of war prompted many to flee for safer realms. The evacuation of Paris began, and French citizens who had been residing in Germany hurriedly fled the country. Many Dutch citizens living in Germany quickly returned to their country in spite of the Netherlands' official declaration of neutrality. With nearly 60,000 US citizens residing in Europe and thousands more present as visitors, embassies began advising those with "no compelling reason to continue their sojourn" to return to the United States immediately. *The New York Times* reported that as early as mid-August, many US citizens cut their stays in order to "get out while the going was good."[10] In the days before war broke out, the State Department helped stranded Americans book passage on ships headed west across the Atlantic. Among them was Lucy Schildkret (who would become the Holocaust historian Lucy Dawidowicz), a Jewish American working at the Yiddish Scientific Institute (known as YIVO) in Vilna, Poland. In her memoir of this harrowing period, she describes taking a train in late August from Warsaw into Nazi Germany itself in order to make her way to a ship in Copenhagen. In Berlin just days ahead of the invasion of Poland, she witnessed the exhilaration among soldiers and the public alike for the coming battle:

> I was in the heart of enemy territory, witnessing a pageant of Nazi war frenzy. The taxi driver had to inch his cab through the traffic. We were afloat in a sea of soldiers, waves of Nazi flags, and the trappings of war. The air

> was heavy with jubilation: cheers, shouts, rousing songs. The German will to fight and to conquer Poland deafened the air.[11]

On September 1, Germany invaded Poland from the west. In accordance with a secret pact that Hitler had signed with Stalin, the Soviet Union invaded Poland from the east three weeks later. Within six weeks, the partition of the country was complete. Nazi forces executed many members of the Polish political and intellectual elite, and murdered thousands of disabled patients in hospitals.[12] Approximately 2 million Jews trapped in the regions under German control were immediately subjected to harassment and terror. They faced the theft of their property, segregation from public life, confinement in ghettos, forced labor, mass deportations, and, eventually, wholesale murder. Jews under the control of the USSR, who numbered 1.3 million, while safe from Nazi persecution and state antisemitism, were forced to contend with often brutal Sovietization campaigns that included forced population transfers, the nationalization of their private property, and the dismantling of their religious institutions.

In Germany, the situation for those seeking to emigrate grew desperate once the war began. There remained more than 250,000 Jews within Germany and annexed Austria. Wartime measures imposed against Jews went into effect and included curfews, new laws segregating Jews from parts of urban areas, the confiscation of property, and food rations that were more severe than those permitted to the "Aryan" population. Jews quickly began to experience what historian Marion Kaplan has aptly called a "social death" in Germany.[13] Over the next two years, an additional 87,000 Jews managed to emigrate, joining the more than 500,000 threatened Jews who had previously left Germany and Austria for sanctuary in British-controlled Palestine, the United States, Great Britain, and a number of Latin American countries, as well as Japanese-occupied Shanghai. Not all who fled had found refuge, however. As many as 200,000 of those who had left Germany still had not found a permanent place to settle.[14]

In February of 1940, Germany began the compulsory deportation of Jews in the General Government, forcing 160,000 Jews into the newly established Lodz Ghetto. By late October, any Jews residing within the General Government were prohibited from emigrating. Saul Friedländer notes that a comment made at the time by Nazi leader Reinhard Heydrich foreshadows the genocide to come. Heydrich realized that Germany's policy of permitting Jewish emigration might eventually backfire in their war against Jews. He was concerned that those who had managed to resettle in the United States might eventually strengthen the Jewish communities there and thus prevent the fulfillment of the Nazi dream of a world without Jews:

> The migration of the Eastern Jews means a continuous spiritual regeneration of world Jewry, as these Eastern Jews, due to their orthodox

religious attitudes, represent a large part of the rabbis, Talmudic teachers, etc., who are much in demand, particularly in Jewish organizations active in the United States. For these American-Jewish organizations, each orthodox Jew also represents an additional element in their constant effort to effect both a spiritual rejuvenation and further cohesion of American Jewry. American Jewry also aims, with the particular help of those Jews newly arrived from Eastern Europe, to create a new basis from which to pursue its struggle, especially against Germany, with ever greater energy.[15]

Britain and France had pledged to come to Poland's defense and declared war against Germany, but after Poland was conquered, fighting in Europe largely ceased until the spring of 1940. During this interim period, known as the "Phoney War," many of those in Western Europe who had fled returned home. Despite the apparent cessation of hostilities, the outbreak of war dampened the US government's support for imperiled refugees considerably as concerns over state security and espionage overshadowed humanitarian considerations. Roosevelt quickly extinguished any hope that he would undertake any of the many emergency measures that groups working for rescue and resettlement had been requesting. A bill introduced in Congress to temporarily resettle European Jews in Alaskan territories that had gained limited support in late August and into the early months of the war never advanced to a vote, nor did it receive support from the president.[16]

Not only did the US government reject most emergency steps on behalf of refugees in the first days of the war but it also quickly reversed its recent shift toward a relatively relaxed enforcement of immigration law. With the start of war, opponents of immigration raised the specter of spies infiltrating the country as a justification to prohibit any new refugees. They proposed measures to fingerprint all immigrants, cut existing quotas even further, and identify potential saboteurs from among applicants. Making matters even more difficult for hopeful refugees, in June 1940, Roosevelt moved the Immigration and Naturalization Service from under the Labor Department to the much more security-conscious State Department, which limited the definition of who was to be admitted to the United States to those in "the American interest."[17]

The fall of France and rescue during wartime

The "Phoney War" came to an abrupt end in spring 1940 with the German invasion of Western Europe. In April, Germany attacked Denmark and Norway to better allow them to block British naval forces and to secure shipments of iron-ore. In mid-May, it overran the Netherlands, Belgium, Luxembourg, and France. On June 14, Nazi forces entered Paris without firing a shot, as its leaders had declared it an "open city" in order to avoid its destruction. The government fled in advance of the military, and four-fifths of its population of just under three million was evacuated.[18] The French capital, which had been home to tens of thousands of refugees (the majority of them Jews) from Nazi Germany since Hitler's takeover of power in 1933, stood largely empty.[19]

The number of Europeans seeking refuge expanded dramatically as these former havens fell under Nazi control. By some estimates, the total number of people fleeing German forces was as high as eight million.[20] Most fled south ahead of the Germany military. A small number managed to travel by train, but others went in automobiles, bicycles, horses, carts, and on foot. As the author Irène Némirovsky (who had emigrated to France from Russia in 1918 and who was murdered at Auschwitz in 1942) wrote in an unfinished novel documenting the Paris exodus, the stream of refugees was seemingly endless:

> Silently, with no lights on, cars kept coming, one after the other, full to bursting with baggage and furniture, prams and birdcages, packing cases and baskets of clothes, each with a mattress tied firmly to the roof. They looked like mountains of fragile scaffolding and they seemed to move without the aid of a motor, propelled by their own weight down the sloping streets to the town square. Cars filled all the roads into the square. People were jammed together like fish caught in a net, and one good tug on that net would have picked them all up and thrown them down on to some terrifying river bank. There was no crying or shouting; even the children were quiet. Everything seemed calm. From time to time a face would appear over a lowered window and stare up at the sky for a while, wondering. A low, muffled murmur rose up from the crowd, the sound of painful breathing, sighs and conversations held in hushed voices, as if people were afraid of being overheard by an enemy lying in wait.[21]

On June 22, France agreed to an armistice that effectively divided the country into two. The northern and coastal regions fell under direct German occupation, while the south—which became known as Vichy France—was placed under French military rule, although in practice the Vichy government served as a proxy for Germany until France was fully occupied in November 1942. By the end of June 1940, most of Western and central Europe was in the hands of Germany and its allies. Following the armistice, those remaining in the occupied area were able to return to their homes quickly. Many of those on the Vichy side, however, were stranded for months before being permitted to return. A German decree enacted on September 27 prohibited Jews on one side of the demarcation line from crossing to the other side, which prompted a lucrative trade in human smuggling. Those Jews who remained in Paris faced the theft of their property, segregation, isolation, and extreme circumstances that for some included round-ups, imprisonment in internment camps, and deportation to killing centers in Eastern Europe.

Jews, like Némirovsky, who were born abroad could not safely return to Paris as they were now at great risk of arrest. This vulnerable group included those who were legally designated *Israelité* (Jews possessing French citizenship) and even more so those designated *Juifs étrangers* (Jewish immigrants). In addition, members of the political left—including significant numbers of socialists and communists—as well as artists and intellectuals who were hostile to Nazi rule were in grave danger. Those who made it to Vichy France but who were stateless or without French citizenship found their situation to be desperate. Anxious to avoid imprisonment in one of several concentration camps in the southern zone, most tried to find a way to leave the country, while some hid and others, including famous anti-Nazi German intellectuals Walter Benjamin, Carl Einstein, and Walter Hasenclever, committed suicide.

As opportunities to flee from ports in Nazi-occupied Northern Europe narrowed, the city of Marseille became an increasingly important destination. For some refugees fleeing the continent, Marseille became a way station while for others it was a terminus point. As France's second largest city and only functioning port in the unoccupied part of the country, Marseille quickly became a destination for tens of thousands hoping to get out of Europe and to safety. One refugee was the German novelist Netty Reiling, who wrote and was known by her pseudonym, Anna Seghers. Born in 1900 into an upper-class Jewish family in Mainz, Seghers joined the Communist Party in 1928. She wrote a number of short stories and novels critical of the Nazi regime that gained widespread attention. Shortly after the Nazi seizure of power in 1933, she fled Germany for Paris, where she continued to write works attacking the regime. Following the invasion of Paris, she fled southward and spent nearly a year in Marseille. From there, with help from a network established by the American journalist Varian Fry and the Emergency Rescue Committee, she managed to escape to Mexico in March 1941.[22]

Her novel *Transit*, published in 1944, was based upon her time in Marseille. In it, she describes how the already dire situation of refugees was made nearly impossible by myriad legal and financial obstacles. Not only did refugees have to secure increasingly rare passage aboard a ship, but they had to acquire an exit visa from the Vichy government, an entry visa for a country of refuge, and transit visas for any countries through they might travel in order to get to safety. Securing such visas, each of which contained an expiration date, often required applicants to obtain affidavits testifying to their financial well-being and physical fitness, procure official consular stamps, produce contracts showing future employment, and present up-to-date identification papers. It was often the case that by the time a person managed to obtain the final document, the first had expired and the applicant would be forced to undergo the hunt for sponsors, papers, and passage aboard a ship all over again. Making matters worse, being caught without proper documents made one subject to arrest, at which point one would be either confined to a concentration camp or handed over to the Gestapo. As Seghers writes:

> A tireless pack of officials was on the move night and day, like dogcatchers, intent on fishing suspicious people out of the crowds as they passed through, so as to put them into city jails from which they'd be dragged off to a concentration camp if they didn't have the money to pay the ransom or to hire a crafty lawyer who would later split the outsize reward for freeing the prisoner with the dogcatcher himself. As a result, everyone, especially the foreigners, guarded their passports and identification papers as if they were their very salvation. I was amazed to see the authorities, in the midst of this chaos, inventing ever more intricate drawn-out procedures for sorting, classifying, registering, and stamping these people over whose emotions they had lost all power. It was like trying to register every Vandal, Goth, Hun, and Langobard during the "Barbarian Invasion."[23]

As the war progressed and the number of refugees in Europe grew larger and their situation more desperate, the possibility that they might find safe harbor narrowed sharply. Not only were there fewer ships leaving Europe and an increasingly shrinking number of safe ports, few refugees had sufficient means, fame, clout, or marketable skills to make them desirable immigrants in the estimation of those countries that had once been at least marginally receptive to people desperate to flee Nazism. Borders that had at one time been open closed quickly once war broke out. Options to find sanctuary in Britain, Palestine, and Latin America were no longer available. As was the case before the war, the United States acted in a similar manner to most other countries. Although it did not formally enter the war until Japan's December 1941 bombing of Pearl Harbor, the imperative to protect the country from possible attack and foreign spies soon overrode humanitarian considerations.

With most governments unwilling to come to refugees' aid, the burden fell to private initiatives. One notable example of such initiatives is the work of Varian Fry, an American journalist in France who, along with a small group of volunteers, was responsible in 1940 and 1941 for assisting approximately 2,000 refugees—many of whom were prominent artists, intellectuals, scholars, and political leaders and their families—reach safety outside of Europe. Fry himself had witnessed firsthand Nazi cruelty toward Jews while working as a journalist in Berlin in the mid-1930s. In the summer of 1940, he moved from New York to Marseille in order to spend what he initially thought would

FIGURE 2.1 *Varian Fry.*

be a month assisting refugees, but he remained in the country for over a year before he was finally expelled because of his aid efforts.

Fry worked on behalf of the Emergency Rescue Committee (ERC), which was established after the fall of Paris to facilitate the rescue of prominent figures who were being especially targeted because of their political or religious beliefs, anti-Nazi activism, or artistry. The ERC received support from writers, artists, and intellectuals associated with the political left, such as the journalist Dorothy Thompson, Alvin Johnson of the New School for Social Research, and the novelists Upton Sinclair and Thomas Mann. Much of the ERC's finances came from the art collector Peggy Guggenheim and heiress Mary Jayne Gold, who worked with Fry and the ERC in Marseille.[24] First Lady Eleanor Roosevelt gave her support to many of the ERC's initial efforts.

Many of those the ERC helped to leave France were former citizens or residents of Germany who had fled the country in 1933, while others were French citizens, or originally from Eastern Europe. As Fry wrote in his memoirs, the refugees in his care were desperate to avoid capture, fearing "that every ring of the doorbell, every step on the stair, every knock on the door might be the police come to get them and deliver them to the Gestapo."[25] There was good reason for this panic, as many of those assisted by Fry and his associates, such as the philosopher Hannah Arendt and novelist Lion Feuchtwanger, had spent time in French concentration camps.

For many refugees unable to secure the necessary paperwork, the ERC utilized escape routes from southern France through Spain to Portugal. Working under the auspices of a legal French aid group known as the Centre Américain de Secours (American Relief Center), the ERC often provided refugees with either genuine or, if necessary, false passports, entry and exit visas, affidavits, and stamps for departure. [26] Fry and others frequently accompanied refugees as they eluded border guards and made their way across the Pyrenees. From Lisbon, refugees could often secure passage on ships to the United States.[27]

Meanwhile, ERC members in the United States desperately tried to convince the State Department to make special exceptions to the quota system by stressing the immediacy of the threat posed to those they were trying to help. The ERC's work and the possibility of the exceptions themselves were made possible by the Emergency Visitor's Visa Program, which had been proposed by James G. McDonald and the President's Advisory Committee on Political Refugees.[28] The program required visa applicants to demonstrate that they posed no threat to national security, and refugees sought to secure letters from prominent Americans to testify on their behalf. For example, a July 1 letter from *Nation* editor and ERC member Freda Kirchwey to labor leader David Dubinsky provides a list of endangered political refugees including the philosopher Julien Benda and the authors André Gide, Francois Mauriac, André Malraux, and Antoine de Saint-Exupéry, and insists, "It contains no Communists. The fact is vouched for by Dr. Thomas Mann ... We were not able to include many addresses because no-one knows where these people are at present."[29]

As Fry's rescue work grew more successful, Vichy authorities redoubled their efforts to put an end to it. Fry and his associates endured arrests, police harassment, and surveillance. Increasingly, Fry came under pressure from the US State Department to curb his activities, as it did not wish to antagonize further its diplomatic relations with Vichy France nor did it want to bring more refugees into the country. When in late August 1941 Fry was again arrested, this time with an expired visa, he was directed to leave the country. By the time of his return to New York, his group had been responsible for assisting many luminaries of European arts, culture, and politics, including the painters Marc Chagall and Marcel Duchamp, the writers Franz Werfel and Victor Serge, and the political activists Otto Klepper and Friedrich Stampfer.

Being a well-known figure with a clear record of persecution was, while helpful, hardly a guarantee that one could secure a place in the United States, however, as the case of Stefan Zweig makes clear. In the first decades of the twentieth century, Zweig, who had been born in Austria to Jewish parents, was one of the most widely read authors in the world. His literary output comprised novels, biographies, librettos, and journalism. As a strong internationalist sympathetic to the plight of his fellow Jews, he was both a friend and critic of Theodor Herzl, the founder of the modern Zionist movement. Zweig's works were among the first to be burned as decadent literature following the Nazi takeover of Germany in 1933, and in 1934, he left Austria for safety in London, and was able to acquire British citizenship. Richard Strauss, for whom Zweig had written the libretto for *Die schweigsame Frau* (The Silent Woman), famously refused to remove Zweig's name from the piece at a 1935 performance, in direct defiance of Nazi demands. The opera was soon banned in response. Following Germany's 1940 invasion of Western Europe, Zweig and his wife Lotte Altmann fled again and managed to secure a temporary visa to come to the United States. For a short period, they lived in New Haven, Connecticut, as guests of Yale University and then in a home in upstate New York, where Zweig began writing his memoir, *Die Welt von Gestern* (*The World of Yesterday*). With their temporary visas expiring in the summer of 1940, Stefan and Lotte moved again. They managed to find refuge in Petrópolis, a mountain town near Rio de Janeiro, Brazil, where they were safe, but isolated and in increasing despair. In February 1942, the day after Stefan completed his memoir, the Zweigs took their own lives.[30]

National security and the US racial order

The US response to the refugee crisis during the war years is often depicted as the consequence of the actions of a small number of influential figures, such as the Assistant Secretary of State Breckinridge Long, who is widely known for his intense hostility to refugees, and Rabbi Stephen Wise, who is frequently portrayed as too timid to wield the clout he possessed. President Roosevelt is often described in turns as having been too weak to stand up to antisemites both within the government and by Republican opponents, too politically fearful of being identified with Jewish causes, or simply too antisemitic to come to the aid of endangered Jews.[31] As discussed in the previous chapter, while it is necessary to consider the actions of influential figures to understand this historical period, it is also insufficient. Long, Wise, and Roosevelt, among others, unquestionably played important roles in shaping the way in which the United States responded to the European refugee crisis, and their actions are discussed later in this chapter. However, too exclusive a focus on the motives of certain individuals can prevent us from realizing the extent to which deeply held views of ethnicity and race in the United States influenced the actions of nearly everyone who was involved and shaped the larger context within which they worked. Although ideologies of biological racism were central to Nazi plans to build a pure Aryan empire, the United States and its policies toward refugees were also deeply influenced by racist ideologies as well.

The response in the United States to the plight of Jewish refugees from the Holocaust is best understood as occurring at a time when there existed widespread fear of aliens, foreigners, and any population group who was widely presumed to be unassimilable into white society. The antisemitism that was influential in shaping the US response to the refugee crisis occurred within a much larger and more complicated racial context that included, but was not exclusive to Jews. Although, as we will see, in comparison to other ethnic groups such as Asian Americas, Latinos, and African Americans, American Jews held significantly more power to respond to ethnic hatred than most other groups, at the time, Jewish refugees were widely considered to be one of many unwanted racial minorities looking to enter the United States against the wishes of the majority of the population. To most Americans, the plight of Jews in Europe might have been unfortunate, and even deeply pitiable, but it was insufficient to force any changes in US border laws.

As discussed in Chapter 1, US immigration law at the time was predicated upon the principle of maintaining a strong majority of people of white, Northern European ancestry. Support for these policies was so widespread among politicians and the public that very few figures or organizations considered challenging them. In the war years, concerns for maintaining white supremacy grew into a full-scale panic that brought about the forced imprisonment of thousands of US citizens and residents on account of their race, racial attacks and riots in some parts of the country, and the continued racial segregation of the armed forces.

Soon after the outbreak of war, stories of spies and foreign agents filled newspapers and radio broadcasts, and espionage was a popular topic of Hollywood films, novels, and comic books. Congressman Martin Dies, a Democratic opponent of the New Deal and chairman of the recently convened Special Committee to Investigate Un-American Activities, began to monitor the activities of German American groups suspected of ties to pro-Nazi activism, as well as of left-leaning groups with suspected links to communism. While speaking in November 1939, Dies estimated that in Detroit alone "some 3,500 persons . . . hold membership in organizations controlled by foreign governments." Such persons, he said, "of necessity do the bidding of their governments in matters of sabotage and espionage."[32] Roosevelt added 150 new agents to the ranks of the FBI and tasked them with rooting out traitors. In the spring of 1940, he approved the use of warrantless wiretaps on those suspected of subversive activity.

In June, the State Department revised the criteria for entry to the United States. Immigrants not only had to demonstrate a legitimate reason for leaving Europe, but also a compelling reason to enter the United States specifically. Embassies and consulates received instructions to employ the strictest standards when processing visa requests and to use their authority to severely limit the number of successful applicants. Although some with close ties to the administration, such as Eleanor Roosevelt and James G. McDonald, attempted to convince the president of the need to aid those seeking to flee Europe, their concerns were quickly trumped by new demands for state security.[33]

In many historical accounts of this period, Breckinridge Long is depicted as the administration figure most responsible for keeping US borders closed to imperiled refugees seeking safe haven.[34] Although Long has been characterized as the architect of US refugee policy, he is more accurately understood, as Breitman and Lichtman have shown, as the most effective instrument of the Roosevelt administration's intended policies toward immigration in the early war years.[35] A close and personal friend of Roosevelt, a Democratic Party operative, and ambassador to Italy from 1933 to 1936, in spring 1940 Long became assistant secretary of state, a position which entailed oversight of the Visa Division. Notoriously nativist, xenophobic, and fearful of spies, Long used his post to hinder any efforts to humanize policy toward imperiled refugees and took many actions that resulted in European Jews being denied visas that might have saved their lives. Long viewed himself as the figure most responsible for holding the administration's line against any attempts to liberalize immigration policy. He successfully blocked the issuance of visas for many refugees who had been recommended for emergency consideration by the President's Advisory Committee on Political Refugees (PACPR), a body established in 1938 by Roosevelt following the Evian Conference and headed by McDonald. In spite of agreements hashed out between the PACPR, the State Department, and the Justice Department to allow the PACPR greater latitude in selecting which applicants would receive visas, Long advised the consular officials tasked with approving visas to adhere to the tightest possible interpretation of the rules. Arcane procedures and inscrutable policies thwarted thousands of refugees, who were left stranded in ports such as Marseille and Lisbon as a consequence of Long's efforts to protect the United States from possible foreign agents. Once the United States entered the war, Long redoubled his efforts to withstand the increasing pressure from American Jewish leaders desperate to help Jews trapped in Europe.

As Roosevelt and the State Department were severely restricting the number of refugees primarily out of concerns for state security, many others were fostering a climate of hostility toward Jews and immigrants in their efforts to prevent the United States from entering the war, and, in particular, going to war against Germany. Keeping up a steady drumbeat of isolationist rhetoric laced with antisemitic canards, figures such as Charles Coughlin, North Dakota senator Gerald P. Nye, demagogue and opportunist Gerald L. K. Smith, and Montana senator Burton K. Wheeler blamed Jewish businessmen and film studio heads for encouraging the United States to go war. On January 29, 1939 (a day before Hitler's famous speech in which he threatened "the annihilation of the Jewish race in Europe"), Coughlin insisted during his weekly radio speech that the United States must not go to war against Germany on behalf of "Jewish interests." He declared that most Americans "are opposed to any policy designed to create a world war for the sake of revenging the ill treatment meted out to any Jew or group of Jews resident in Germany or elsewhere, as long as these Jews or groups of Jews are not American citizens or nationals."[36]

Among the most famous figures to employ antisemitic rhetoric as a means of preventing the United States from entering the war was the aviator Charles A. Lindbergh. Lindbergh's 1927 solo flight across the Atlantic in the *Spirit of St. Louis* had made him one of the most widely admired Americans in the 1920s and 1930s, and the kidnapping and murder of his son generated universal sympathy for him and his wife, Anne Morrow. In the mid-1930s, while living in England to find privacy after his family's tragedy, Lindbergh made several visits to Germany, including one to attend the 1936 Berlin Olympics. He repeatedly expressed his admiration for Hitler and famously dined with Nazi leader Hermann Göring, who awarded him with the Commander Cross of the Order of the German Eagle for his Atlantic flight. (Henry Ford had received the same honor six months earlier.)[37]

Upon his return to the United States in 1939, Lindbergh became an increasingly vocal opponent of war with Germany, not out of a desire for peace, but so that the United States and Europe could maintain a united front against what he saw as a greater peril: the racial threat posed by non-Europeans whom he imagined were poised to strike.[38] As he wrote in an article for *Reader's Digest* in November 1939:

> We, the heirs of European culture, are on the verge of a disastrous war, a war within our own family of nations, a war which will reduce the strength and destroy the treasures of the White race, a war which may even lead to the end of our civilization. And while we stand poised for battle, Oriental guns are turning westward. Asia presses towards us on the Russian border, all foreign races stir restlessly. It is time to turn from our quarrels and to build our White ramparts again … Our civilization depends on a united strength among ourselves; on strength too great for foreign armies to challenge; on a Western Wall of race and arms which can hold back either a Genghis Khan or the infiltration of inferior blood; on an English fleet, a German air force, a French army, an American nation, standing together as guardians of our common heritage, sharing strength, dividing influence.[39]

In late 1940, Lindbergh became active with the America First Committee, an organization founded in September 1940 by isolationists initially affiliated with both the political right and left but who were united in their desire to keep the United States out of war. Very quickly, Lindbergh became one of its chief spokespersons and most sought-after representatives. In a speech made in Des Moines, Iowa, on September 11, 1941, Lindbergh explicitly blamed Jews as one of the key constituents, alongside the British and the Roosevelt administrations, pressing the United States to enter the war:

> Instead of agitating for war, the Jewish groups in this country should be opposing it in every possible way for they will be among the first to feel its consequences. Tolerance is a virtue that depends upon peace and strength. History shows that it cannot survive war and devastations. A few far-sighted Jewish people realize this and stand opposed to intervention. But the majority still do not. Their greatest danger to this country lies in their large ownership and influence in our motion pictures, our press, our radio and our government.[40]

Although hailed by its audience at the time, in the days and weeks following, Lindbergh's speech was widely perceived as having crossed a line into

FIGURE 2.2 *Charles A. Lindbergh (right) standing beside Sen. Burton K. Wheeler.*

"Jew-baiting" and provocation. As historian Lynne Olson has shown, nearly every major newspaper—even many that similarly opposed intervention—denounced the speech, and many compared him to Nazi leaders.[41] Outrage was so great that the backlash against it shook the America First Committee to the core and caused many to leave the group, especially those on the political left who had joined out of a commitment to pacifism. Henceforth, the isolationist position was, in the eyes of its detractors, closely associated with outright antisemitism.

The quotes by Lindbergh demonstrate that attacks on foreigners and immigrants—those carriers of "inferior blood" who threatened America's borders—often went hand in hand with attempts to deny the right of ethnic and racial minorities to be included in the definition of what it is to be an American—"*their* large ownership and influence in *our* motion pictures, *our* press, *our* radio and *our* government." Both were efforts to defend the belief that America was a country for the "White race" that was under assault from attacks from both external and internal threats.

In truth, however, as difficult as the situation was for American Jews, whose overall socioeconomic position improved during the war years, the periodic antisemitism that they faced in the United States was significantly less than the systematic racism that other minority groups regularly encountered. During the war years, even prior to America's entry in it, other minorities endured forced imprisonment, increased segregation, and mass violence. Such an intensive enforcement of racial divisions was in stark contrast to repeated government calls for Americans to put their differences aside and fight for the greater good. Responding to pressure from civil rights leaders A. Philip Randolph and Walter White, who had threatened to hold a mass rally in Washington, DC, on July 1, 1941, Roosevelt issued Executive Order 8802, which prohibited defense industries and the federal government from discriminating based upon "race, creed, color, or national origin." The order opened up employment opportunities for African Americans and for many was a hopeful step toward ending racial segregation. As historian Robert L. Fleegler has noted, Roosevelt took an active interest in "promoting the message of tolerance and national unity."[42] In this vein, the Office of War Information produced a series of posters highlighting the need for racial harmony in the workplace. One poster, for example, portrayed a harmonious multiracial team of workers—last names Du Bois, Hrdlicka, Schmidt, Kelly, Williams, Santini, Lazarri, Cohen, and Nienciewiscz—putting the finish touches on a tank; the poster's text declared the workers were "Americans All" and quoted Roosevelt's executive order. The late 1930s and early 1940s also saw the idea of the United States as a Judeo-Christian nation gain widespread traction as a progressive alternative to the notion, which pro-fascist forces insisted on, that it was exclusively Christian.[43]

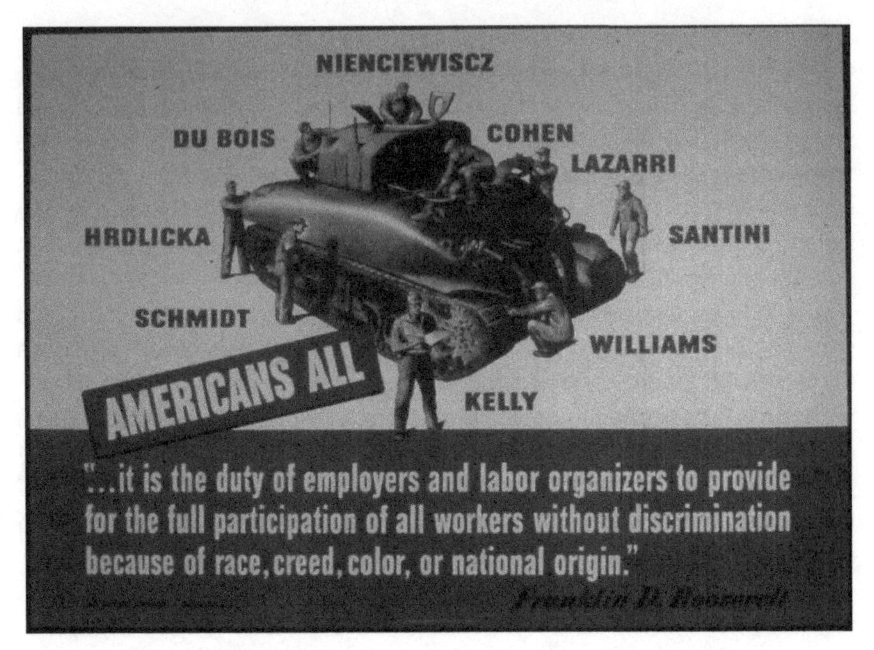

NIENCIEWISCZ
DU BOIS
COHEN
LAZARRI
HRDLICKA
SANTINI
SCHMIDT
WILLIAMS
AMERICANS ALL
KELLY
"...it is the duty of employers and labor organizers to provide for the full participation of all workers without discrimination because of race, creed, color, or national origin."

FIGURE 2.3 *"Americans All."*

As well-intentioned as these steps to reduce racial and economic injustice were, they were far more symbolic than substantive. The United States remained deeply polarized along racial lines as many white Americans sought to preserve their supremacy, often in the name of state security, through legislation, coercion, and outright violence. The most shameful example of this occurred following Japan's bombing of the US naval base at Pearl Harbor and the subsequent entry of the United States into the war. On February 19, 1942, Roosevelt issued what would become his most infamous decree. Executive Order 9066 authorized the secretary of war to designate certain areas of the United States as military zones "from which any or all persons may be excluded, and with respect to which, the right of any person to enter, remain in, or leave shall be subject to whatever restrictions the Secretary of War or the appropriate Military Commander may impose in his discretion."[44] The order paved the way for the forcible deportation and incarceration from the West Coast of tens of thousands of persons of Japanese ancestry, nearly two-thirds of whom were US citizens.[45] Those who were born in Japan and had not earned US citizenship were classified as "enemy aliens" (as were non-citizen Germans and Italians residing in the United States). No such systematic was taken against Americans of German ancestry, although Germany had many highly vocal sympathizers in the United States during the 1930s and first two years of the 1940s.[46] EO 9066 was the most extreme expression of a wave of racism against persons of Japanese ethnicity that emerged following the December 7, 1941, attack. Suspicions of espionage and fear of a fifth column that was preparing a full-scale attack on the United States spread rapidly throughout the country, and the situation was especially tense in California, Oregon, and Arizona, where anti-Asian attitudes had been a fixture since the middle of the previous century. Despite the lack of any credible evidence demonstrating that this community represented a particular threat to the United States, throughout the spring of 1942, Japanese Americans were expelled from their residences. In what was a form of organized theft akin to German efforts to "Aryanize" Jewish property before the war, Japanese Americans were forced to sell their homes, businesses, and other property at cut-rate prices, and they were incarcerated in hastily built concentration camps in the US interior. Many prominent Americans publicly opposed the imprisonment of Japanese Americans, but the large majority of citizens supported the measures in the name of state security. Racist caricatures were common in newspapers and journals (with even the left-leaning cartoonist Theodor Seuss Geisel—"Dr. Seuss"—joining in), and signs telling Japanese persons to "keep moving" were posted in many places along the West Coast.[47]

Deportations to the camps were at times brutal affairs, with prisoners confined to temporary "Civilian Assembly Centers," which in many instances were barely refurbished stables at horse tracks, before being moved to more permanent facilities. As one prisoner recounted, "Suddenly, you realized that human beings were being put behind fences just like on the farm where we had horses and pigs in corrals."[48] Most often, deportees were allowed to bring only what they could carry. They were imprisoned in poorly made barracks, where they suffered from a lack of clean water, inadequate health care, and meager rations. Few accommodations were made for the schooling of the 30,000 children. In all, approximately 110,000 persons were imprisoned, a number that represents over 85 percent of all Japanese Americans present in the country at the time. Only in late 1944 did a pair of rulings by the Supreme Court lay the groundwork for the release of inmates. The court declared that while the deportations were legal under the law, the incarceration of US citizens on the basis of their ethnicity was not. In the first half of 1945, most prisoners were released and given a token sum and a bus ticket. It was only decades later that the United States formally recognized its responsibility and paid modest restitution to former prisoners.

In spite of Roosevelt's 1941 Executive Order forbidding discrimination in the government, the 125,000 African American soldiers who served in the war overseas in the US military faced severe racism in the armed forces. As historian Henry Louis Gates Jr. has noted, "The military was as segregated as the Deep South."[49] Placed into segregated units, many, such as the famous Tuskegee Airmen, served with distinction. Most African American soldiers

FIGURE 2.4 *A young man arrived at 2020 Van Ness Avenue, the meeting place of the first contingent to be moved from San Francisco to the Santa Anita assembly center in Arcadia, California.*

and sailors, however, were assigned to menial labor and were not permitted to handle weapons except in cases of extreme shortages of white combat troops. White officers regularly assigned those African American soldiers who remained in the United States dangerous work. At the Port Chicago Naval Magazine in Concord, California, for example, 320 sailors, a majority of whom were African American, died on July 1944 while loading munitions onto a ship bound for the Pacific theater of war. The sailors given this specialized assignment were not trained and were pushed by their superiors to work as quickly as possible and through the night, making an already dangerous job even more treacherous. When the explosion occurred, the fireball was visible for miles. All of those on duty at the pier died instantly. Nearly 400 others nearby were injured. The following month at the nearby Mare Island Naval Shipyard, African American sailors were once again ordered to load munitions in a similarly dangerous manner and they refused out of concern for their safety. In the end, over 200 men were tried and convicted for disobeying orders, and fifty were convicted of mutiny. Each of the fifty received a sentence of fifteen years of hard labor and a dishonorable discharge. After the war, most gained their release, in large part as a result of the efforts of NAACP attorney Thurgood

Marshall. Their plight was widely viewed as an example of the discrimination faced by African Americans in the military.[50] Only at the war's end were some naval units integrated on a limited basis. An Executive Order by President Harry S. Truman in 1948 finally brought an end to racial segregation in the armed forces.

Racial tension between whites and Mexican Americans also increased during the war years. In the summer of 1943 in Los Angeles, the "Zoot-Suit Riots" pitted white sailors in the US Navy and their supporters against young Mexican American men, who were targeted by the combination of their ethnicity, age, and distinctive dress. These young men wore Zoot suits, high-waisted, baggy suits with wide lapels and shoulders that were popular in the late 1930s and 1940s. The suits were a matter of contention not only because they required a substantial amount of cloth during wartime rationing, but even more so because they were an external sign of assertiveness and pride among ethnic and racial minorities, including African Americans, Latinos, and Italians. As the historian Stuart Cosgrove has claimed, "The zoot-suit was a refusal: a subcultural gesture that refused to concede to the manners of subservience."[51]

After a disturbance in early June 1943, police arrested dozens of "zoot-suiters," and fights between Mexican Americans and white sailors on leave became more frequent. Soon, vigilante groups of servicemen began patrolling sections of East Los Angeles in search of young men to humiliate by stripping them of their attire and then often brutally assaulting them.[52] A small incident between sailors and Mexican Americans soon led to rumors that zoot-suiters had attacked a group of servicemen and their wives and girlfriends. Starting on June 3 and over the next four days, thousands of white sailors stormed Latino neighborhoods to hunt for young men in revenge. Police often gave their support, and the local white-owned press showered overwhelming praise for the sailors' actions. Sailors searched bowling alleys, cinemas, and street cars looking to attack Latino young men, sometimes targeting African Americans and Filipinos as well. One petty officer defended the violence by saying, "We're out to do what the police have failed to do—we're going to clean up this situation to the satisfaction of ourselves and the public."[53] After ten days of what was the largest racial disturbance in the city to date, ninety-four civilians and eighteen servicemen suffered injuries. Other cities, too, were not immune from organized racial assaults that year. In Detroit, for example, in the same month as the riots in Los Angeles, white mobs attacked African American communities, backing down only once federal troops intervened. The vast majority of those killed and wounded were African American.[54] That same summer, race riots also occurred in Harlem, New York City, and Beaumont, Texas.

Within this climate of racial violence, the status of Jewish Americans remained unsettled, although their situation was much less treacherous than that of other minorities. During the war, Jewish Americans were not forcibly confined like most Japanese Americans, nor were they placed into segregated military units as were African American troops, nor were they the victims of mob violence like many Latino Americans. Over half a million Jews (of an estimated overall population of just under 4.7 million) served in the military. Throughout the twelve years of his administration, Roosevelt set a tone of inclusiveness and promoted a national vision that welcomed the participation of Jewish Americans, especially if they downplayed their ethnic and religious differences.[55] Nevertheless, some Americans still regarded Jews as possible spies for the Nazis, even though Nazi assaults on German Jewry were highly publicized. To others, they were suspect because of their alleged ties to Bolshevism. As a result, American Jews' loyalty to the United States was repeatedly called into question. The perceived fragility of their recent social and economic "progress" in joining white America had a chilling effect on some of those Jewish leaders who wished to convince Roosevelt to loosen immigration policies and to intervene militarily on behalf of imperiled Jews in Europe. Given the racial violence that did exist, many American Jews were concerned that pressing their case too hard might prompt a backlash that would threaten their status at home and weaken further their ability to help Jews abroad.

US responses to reports from Europe

Historians have discussed at length the question of what was known in the United States about the Holocaust as it was unfolding in Europe.[56] Officials in the United States and Great Britain learned of the Nazi plans to murder Jews in Nazi-occupied countries in the summer of 1942. Many of the very European Jews who were being targeted for destruction only learned of their fate upon arriving at killing centers.[57] In addition, it was only much later that information about other groups who had also been targeted for extermination, such as people perceived to have been disabled, Roma, and Jehovah's Witnesses, became known and incorporated into a general understanding of the Holocaust.

As the example of Justice Frankfurter demonstrates, the notion that an entire population would be targeted for complete and absolute elimination was beyond many people's comprehension at the time. The term "Holocaust" was not widely used to refer to the Nazi effort to exterminate European Jewry until the late 1970s and early 1980s. As well, the word "genocide" was coined only in 1944 as a result of the scholarship of Raphael Lemkin, a Polish Jewish jurist who arrived in the United States in 1941 and who studied the extermination of Armenians by Ottoman Turks during World War I. During World War II, then, there was neither an agreed-upon terminology nor an understanding of the extent of the Nazi extermination program, largely because information about the mass murder of European Jews did not arrive all at once and when it did, was often understood as crimes of war. Although American Jewish communities tended to comprehend the larger picture sooner than most others, it was only with the deportation of Hungarian Jewry to death camps in spring 1944 that news about the mass slaughter of Jews began to attract sustained attention in the press and by public officials. Prior to that time, few people recognized that Germany was specifically targeting European Jewry outside of its general war aims. As the historian Walter Laqueur has argued, although intelligence officials in both the United States and Great Britain regularly saw reports of mass killings of Jews, few of them pieced it together into a coherent picture of Nazi plans for the complete murder of European Jewry. He writes, "Ignorance was probably a more important factor than antagonism toward Jews."[58] Those few who did possess first- or secondhand knowledge of the genocide sought desperately to get the information to Allied leaders, but they had little success, for their stories were, in the words of the historian Deborah Lipstadt, "beyond belief."[59] Although stories regarding the murder of Jews appeared regularly in reports to the US government, in the general press, and in discussions that took place within the American Jewish community, it would not be until after the war, when scholars assembled the fragments of information, that the public came to understand the full scale of the Nazi program of genocide.[60]

Questions regarding when US leaders learned about the mass killing of Jews imply a more pressing set of concerns: What did those do with the knowledge that they had? Did (or should) the knowledge that Jews were being specially targeted prompt a change in military strategy? Could more have been done to intervene specifically on behalf of Hitler's Jewish victims? Those who criticize President Roosevelt for his response to the refugee crisis also tend to condemn him for not intervening militarily with the goal of saving Holocaust victims. Roosevelt's defenders, by contrast, argue that there were few opportunities to target Nazi killing centers, and that any attempt to do so would have diverted much-needed resources away from the larger military effort to defeat Germany. Similarly, those who accuse Rabbi Wise—and, by extension, most American Jewish leaders—of failing to vigorously press the issue of refugee assistance also criticize him for not pressing Roosevelt harder to save European Jews, while his defenders point both to his limited influence on the president and to the many actions he did take as evidence of his unrelenting activism on behalf of European Jewry.

By the time the United States entered the war in Europe in late 1941, the situation for Jews in Nazi-occupied territories had become catastrophic.

Germany had broken its non-aggression pact with the Soviet Union in late June 1941 and staged what would be the largest military invasion in history. Hitler's goal was to destroy the USSR politically and to end communist rule. Special death squads, known as *Einsatzgruppen*, followed behind military units and shot more than 1.5 million Jews. Political opponents, persons perceived to be disabled, and Roma were likewise summarily killed. By the end of that year, frustrated at its slow military progress against the USSR, Germany began to strengthen its territorial holdings. To complete its "Final Solution" to the Jewish question, it established a system of death camps. By late summer 1941, the pesticide Zyklon-B had already been tested on Russian prisoners of war at the Auschwitz camp and preparations were under way to expand the camp into a massive killing facility. In late September, *Einsatzgruppen* forces murdered more than 33,000 Jews in a ravine at Babi Yar, outside of Kiev. By early December, the Chelmno extermination camp—where Jews were killed in gas vans—became operational.

The year 1942 was even worse. In the first half of the year, the murder of Jews from ghettos in the east and concentration camps in the west began at Auschwitz, Treblinka, Sobibor, Belzec, and Majdanek. Historian Doris L. Bergen has summarized the scale of the killing: "In early 1942 ... 75 percent of the Jews who would be murdered in the Holocaust were still alive. By the Spring of 1943, 75 percent of the approximately 6 million who would be killed were already dead."[61] News of atrocity killings made its way into newspapers and occasional diplomatic documents during the first years of the war and American Jewish leaders tried desperately to raise a state of alarm, but it was unclear what steps could be taken to end the slaughter. In the summer of 1942, the United States did not yet have military forces in Europe, nor did it have diplomatic ties with Germany or any means to respond to the news other than with public statements of reproach and threats of future retribution. At a July rally in Madison Square Garden called by the AJ Congress and other Jewish organizations, 20,000 people gathered. A telegram sent by President Roosevelt for the first time publically acknowledged, however indirectly, the fact that Jews were particular targets of Nazis:

> Americans who love justice and hate oppression will hail the solemn commemoration in Madison Square Garden as an expression of the determination of the Jewish people to make every sacrifice for victory over the Axis powers. Citizens, regardless of religious allegiance, will share in the sorrow of our Jewish fellow citizens over the savagery of the Nazis against their helpless victims. The Nazis will not succeed in exterminating their victims any more than they will succeed in enslaving mankind. The American people not only sympathize with all victims of Nazi crimes but will hold the

> perpetrators of these crimes to strict accountability in a day of reckoning which will surely come.
>
> I express the confident hope that the Atlantic Charter and the just world order to be made possible by the triumph of the United Nations will bring the Jews and oppressed people in all lands the four freedoms which Christian and Jewish teachings have largely inspired.[62]

Among the first significant reports to reach Western leaders of Germany's intention to systematically murder European Jewry came the following month, in the form of a telegram in August 1942 from Gerhart Riegner, secretary of the World Jewish Congress in Geneva. News had reached him that Nazi leaders were considering a plan to murder 3.5 to 4 million Jews in the coming fall. Riegner's telegram warned:

> Received alarming report stating that, in the Fuehrer's Headquarters, a plan has been discussed, and is under consideration, according to which all Jews in countries occupied or controlled by Germany numbering 3½ to 4 millions should, after deportation and concentration in the East, be at one blow exterminated, in order to resolve, once and for all the Jewish question in Europe. Action is reported to be planned for the autumn. Ways of execution are still being discussed including the use of prussic acid. We transmit this information with all the necessary reservation, as exactitude cannot be confirmed by us. Our informant is reported to have close connexions with the highest German authorities, and his reports are generally reliable. Please inform and consult New York.[63]

Riegner's original source, although he did not know it at the time, was the German industrialist Eduard Schulte, who, fearful that the Nazis would bring about Germany's destruction, regularly leaked sensitive information to Swiss and Polish intelligence officers who relayed it on to the British and Americans. Schulte had access to prominent members of the Nazi Party through his business contacts. He passed on the information he had learned about the Nazi extermination program to a representative of the Swiss Jewish community, who gave it to Riegner. In early August, Riegner met with British and US diplomats in Switzerland and asked them to transmit the information to their governments and to Stephen Wise. State Department officials were skeptical of its veracity because of the spectacular nature of the claims and out of a recognition that the United States was largely powerless to intervene should the report be accurate. Rather than forward the telegram immediately to Wise, the State Department withheld it from him for several weeks. Wise received a copy, however, through the efforts of the British MP Samuel Silverman, to whom Riegner had also sent a copy.[64] For Wise, the cable was confirmation of

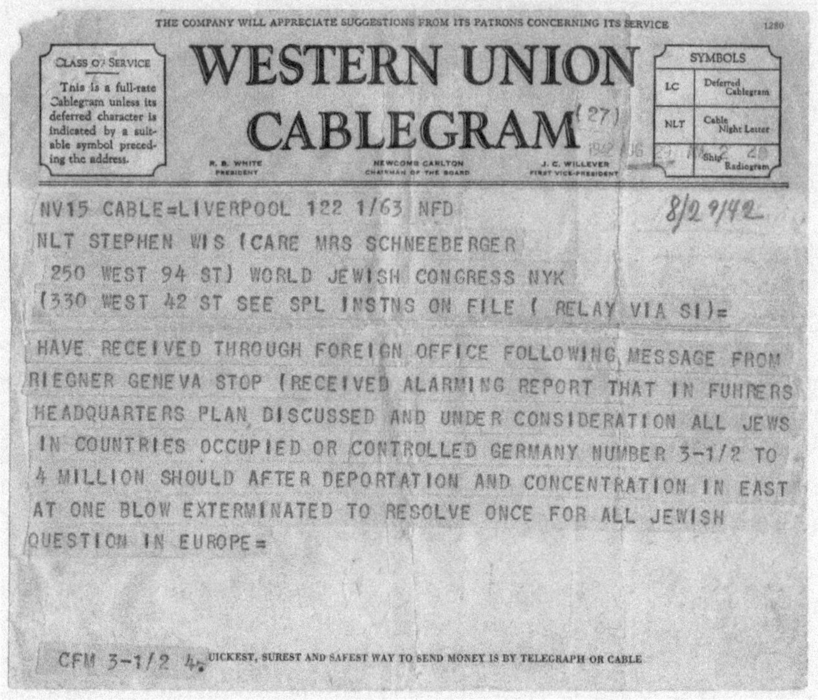

THE COMPANY WILL APPRECIATE SUGGESTIONS FROM ITS PATRONS CONCERNING ITS SERVICE 1280

CLASS OF SERVICE
This is a full-rate Cablegram unless its deferred character is indicated by a suitable symbol preceding the address.

WESTERN UNION
CABLEGRAM

R. B. WHITE PRESIDENT · NEWCOMB CARLTON CHAIRMAN OF THE BOARD · J. C. WILLEVER FIRST VICE-PRESIDENT

SYMBOLS
LC Deferred Cablegram
NLT Cable Night Letter
Ship Radiogram

NV15 CABLE=LIVERPOOL 122 1/63 NFD 8/29/42
NLT STEPHEN WIS (CARE MRS SCHNEEBERGER
250 WEST 94 ST) WORLD JEWISH CONGRESS NYK
(330 WEST 42 ST SEE SPL INSTNS ON FILE (RELAY VIA SI)=

HAVE RECEIVED THROUGH FOREIGN OFFICE FOLLOWING MESSAGE FROM RIEGNER GENEVA STOP (RECEIVED ALARMING REPORT THAT IN FUHRERS HEADQUARTERS PLAN DISCUSSED AND UNDER CONSIDERATION ALL JEWS IN COUNTRIES OCCUPIED OR CONTROLLED GERMANY NUMBER 3-1/2 TO 4 MILLION SHOULD AFTER DEPORTATION AND CONCENTRATION IN EAST AT ONE BLOW EXTERMINATED TO RESOLVE ONCE FOR ALL JEWISH QUESTION IN EUROPE=

CFM 3-1/2 4.

THE QUICKEST, SUREST AND SAFEST WAY TO SEND MONEY IS BY TELEGRAPH OR CABLE

FIGURE 2.5 *Gerhart Riegner telegram (front).*

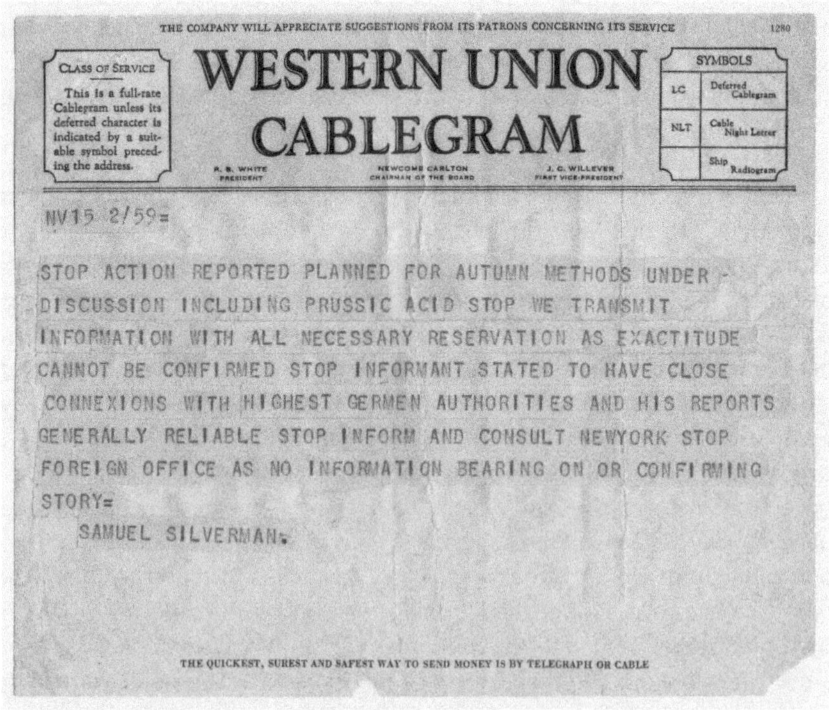

THE COMPANY WILL APPRECIATE SUGGESTIONS FROM ITS PATRONS CONCERNING ITS SERVICE 1280

CLASS OF SERVICE
This is a full-rate Cablegram unless its deferred character is indicated by a suitable symbol preceding the address.

WESTERN UNION
CABLEGRAM

R. B. WHITE PRESIDENT · NEWCOMB CARLTON CHAIRMAN OF THE BOARD · J. C. WILLEVER FIRST VICE-PRESIDENT

SYMBOLS
LC Deferred Cablegram
NLT Cable Night Letter
Ship Radiogram

NV15 2/59=

STOP ACTION REPORTED PLANNED FOR AUTUMN METHODS UNDER DISCUSSION INCLUDING PRUSSIC ACID STOP WE TRANSMIT INFORMATION WITH ALL NECESSARY RESERVATION AS EXACTITUDE CANNOT BE CONFIRMED STOP INFORMANT STATED TO HAVE CLOSE CONNEXIONS WITH HIGHEST GERMEN AUTHORITIES AND HIS REPORTS GENERALLY RELIABLE STOP INFORM AND CONSULT NEWYORK STOP FOREIGN OFFICE AS NO INFORMATION BEARING ON OR CONFIRMING STORY=

SAMUEL SILVERMAN.

THE QUICKEST, SUREST AND SAFEST WAY TO SEND MONEY IS BY TELEGRAPH OR CABLE

FIGURE 2.6 *Gerhart Riegner telegram (back).*

rumors that he had been receiving for months that Nazis were deporting Jews to the east in order to kill them.[65]

Throughout the fall, additional reports arrived in Washington and confirmed Riegner's claims. In early December 1942, Roosevelt met—for the first and only time—with a delegation of Jewish American leaders. Headed by Rabbi Wise, the delegation conveyed the many reports they had received concerning Nazi actions against European Jewry. Just days prior to this meeting, both the *New York Times* and the *Times* of London published dramatic stories on the murder of Polish Jewry, reporting that at least one million Jews had been put to death. Another million were at risk of dying from starvation and disease. With surprising accuracy, the story reported on the selection process that determined which Jews would live and which would die. "Poland is now a mass grave," the *New York Times* declared. "Jews from all Europe are brought to the Warsaw ghetto and separated into two groups: the able-bodied young and the children, old and sick, who are dispatched eastward to meet sure death."[66] Dr. Ignacy Schwarzbart of the Polish National Council was the source for the newspapers; his source in turn was Jan Karski.

Wise and the delegation informed the president that as many as two million Jews had already been killed by the Nazis (we now know that number was closer to four million). They provided accounts of specific atrocities, such as the murder of thousands of Jews in Riga, Latvia, in December 1941 and the death of Jews in camps in Transnistria, where 75,000 Jews were thought to have been killed. The delegation relayed information that most of German and Austrian Jewry have been deported and that the Warsaw Ghetto had less than 10 percent of its former inhabitants. They warned of a Nazi "policy of immediate liquidation of those who cannot work." They asked Roosevelt to make this information known to the larger world, to try to stop the killings, and to request that neutral countries intervene. Had Roosevelt wanted to change US immigration law, however, options for rescue were severely curtailed. There were no Allied troops yet in Europe. There was no way for Jews in the east facing mass extermination to travel across Nazi-occupied Europe to relatively safer ports in Western Europe, few ships to ferry them across the Atlantic, and no military vessels available to chaperone them in the middle of the war. Roosevelt once again promised Wise that he would hold Nazi leaders accountable for their actions and expressed his concern for all victims of Nazi aggression. Wise put a brave face on the meeting and the *New York Times* headline optimistically declared, "President Renews Pledges to Jews."[67]

Two weeks later, in response to a memorandum by the Polish government-in-exile detailing the mass murder of Jews in German-occupied Poland, Britain and the United States issued a joint declaration stating that "the German authorities, not content with denying to persons of Jewish race in all the territories over which their barbarous rule has been extended, the most elementary human rights, are now carrying into effect Hitler's oft-repeated intention to exterminate the Jewish people in Europe." It went on to "condemn in the strongest possible terms this bestial policy of cold-blooded extermination" and declared that "such events can only strengthen the resolve of all freedom-loving peoples to overthrow the barbarous Hitlerite tyranny. They [Britain and the United States] reaffirm their solemn resolution to insure that those responsible for these crimes shall not escape retribution, and to press on with the necessary practical measures to this end."[68]

Rescue advocacy in the United States

Despite the legal constraints on immigration and the generally inhospitable climate for refugee advocacy, and the challenges of conducting wartime refugee assistance work within Europe, there existed a large array of private organizations in the United States that endeavored to assist those threatened by Nazism. These included long-standing Jewish and Christian relief and aid groups, Jewish self-defense organizations, labor groups, and international societies dedicated to peace and freedom. The most effective organization to intercede on refugees' behalf was the American Jewish Joint Distribution Committee. Founded soon after the start of World War I to aid endangered Jews in Eastern Europe and Palestine, the Joint established a vast network to distribute relief and welfare. With the rise of Nazism to power, the Joint sent aid to the German Jewish community—totaling $5 million prior to the start of war in 1939—to support schools, medical facilities, vocational programs, and housing. Its representatives assisted Jews in navigating the often tortuous visa processes, identifying countries that would house them, finding passage on ships, and covering their travel expenses. As the scholar Sara Kadosh notes, prior to the war, the Joint had aided over 100,000 refugees from Nazism.[69] When war erupted, the Joint expanded its efforts to assist Jewish communities by aiding Polish Jewry, even managing to get aid to Jews imprisoned within the Warsaw Ghetto.

After the United States entered the war, the Joint was prohibited by law from operating openly in countries under German occupation, but it worked closely with the Treasury (which tended to be friendly toward their activities) and State (which tended to be more hostile) Departments to obtain licenses to transfer funds to neutral countries, which allowed them to continue their work. As Kadosh states, while Joint officials in the United States were wary of running afoul of the law, its representatives in Europe often skirted it in order to assist Jews in peril. Following the German invasion of France, the Joint moved its offices to Portugal and worked with the small local Jewish community there to assist refugees who had arrived from Spain. The Joint leased ships to bring Jews from Lisbon to safety in the Americas and in at least one instance gave money to a Jewish underground resistance movement in France. Its representative in Switzerland managed to send funds to endangered Jews throughout occupied Europe and to support many Jews who remained in hiding. The Joint also provided economic support to the Jewish refugees in Shanghai and sent care packages to prisoners in concentration camps. In addition, it led the effort to negotiate with Nazi leaders to ransom Jewish lives for war materiel. Over the course of the war, the Joint spent more than $50 million in relief and rescue efforts, money that had been donated primarily by the American Jewish community.

Jewish self-defense organizations, too, played a prominent role in pressuring the US government to intercede on behalf of European Jewry. The historians Breitman and Lichtman have noted that "Jewish organizations engaged in lonely and frustrating efforts to expose Nazi crimes against Jews."[70] Throughout the war years, groups such as the AJ Committee, the AJ Congress, the Jewish Labor Committee, and the Bergsonites (a circle of activists around the Revisionist Zionist leader Hillel Kook) worked to, variously, raise awareness of the catastrophe facing European Jewry, send funds abroad and provide assistance to those Jews who managed to find safety, persuade the Roosevelt administration to relax immigration regulations, and make the case for military intervention.

Some historians have sharply criticized these groups for the different strategies that they pursued, their regular infighting over tactics, and their overall lack of coordination, claiming that Jewish political clout was weakened in the absences of a unified strategy.[71] With nearly five million Jews living in the United States during World War II, there was a wide range of views on what would be the most effective way for Jews to respond to the crisis. It is not clear that a unified approach would have been any more effective at changing government policy. Some Jewish leaders and groups, following tried and true methods, favored a strategy of quiet intervention in the hopes of influencing Roosevelt without provoking a backlash from vocal and influential antisemites. Others favored bolder efforts. Groups such as the AJ Congress and the Jewish Labor Committee staged rallies and large gatherings, while others still, like the Bergsonites, held grand pageants and demonstration, and took out hundreds of newspaper advertisements in an attempt to shame the administration into action.

During the war years, Jewish groups on both the political left and right periodically denounced Wise for his relationship to Roosevelt. Some charged him with being too close to Roosevelt and serving as the president's "court Jew" (a term of derision used to describe those who seek to protect at all costs their access to prominent leaders and their social position). Wise was condemned for his seeming hesitancy to pressure Roosevelt to take stronger action and for publicly defending the president's decision not to intervene more strenuously on behalf of European Jewry. In an inverse of the criticism he received in 1933 for calling for a boycott of German goods against the wishes of the government and other Jewish organizations, he was attacked for his spring 1941 decision to respect the government's economic boycott of Germany and other Axis powers by agreeing to halt all shipments of aid to Jews in ghettos.[72] Attempts by advocates to pressure Roosevelt on the issue of rescue tended to irritate the president. Historians Breitman and Lichtman question whether more strenuous activity by the AJ Congress might have brought about an end to any communication with the White House about the situation facing European Jewry.[73]

If any group could be charged with disrupting the Jewish consensus on how best to advocate on behalf of European Jewry, it was the circle that formed around the Lithuanian-born Hillel Kook, or Peter Bergson, as he came to be known. A leader of the right-wing Revisionist Zionist movement, which called for the creation of a Jewish state in Palestine without concessions to the indigenous Palestinian Arab population, Bergson had come to the United States with Vladimir (Ze'ev) Jabotinsky, Revisionism's founder, in 1940 to raise funds for Jewish military units and build support for the movement. Bergson regularly drew the ire of the established Jewish community for his decision to work outside of the mechanisms established by the more mainstream AJ Committee and AJ Congress. His web of organizations, such as the Emergency Committee to Save the Jewish People of Europe and the Committee for a Jewish Army of Stateless and Palestinian Jews, quickly became notorious for methods that included direct appeals to the public through shocking newspaper advertisements, public demonstrations, extreme litigiousness, and the recruitment of celebrity endorsers. As a group of ultranationalists determined to create a homeland for the Jews in Palestine, Bergsonites had little interest in working within the American context or building a movement of consensus that would strengthen Jewish-American ties. At the same time, as the scholar Judith Baumel has shown, Bergson was far more effective in harnessing the power of the media than were other Jewish leaders.[74] Bergson's followers were among those who pressured the Roosevelt administration to establish the War Refugee Board, which played a significant role in rescue efforts during the last year of the war. Most of the money the Bergson groups raised went to its propaganda efforts and not the material assistance of European Jews, however. Critics denounced the Bergson group for promoting a Jewish form of fascism and committing financial misdeeds.

Many non-Jewish groups also sought to spread awareness of the fate of European Jews. The Information Service of the Federal Council of the Churches of Christ in America dedicated its April 24, 1943, edition of weekly report to the topic "The Mass Murder of Jews in Europe," which was a review of "documentary evidence concerning the systematic repression and progressive elimination of the Jews in Nazi-controlled Europe."[75] This four-page report argued that "the quantity of the evidence is so enormous, the sources are so varied and their correspondence in substance and import so close even in detail as to compel belief." The report noted that tens of thousands of Jews in Germany, Austria, and Czechoslovakia had disappeared, that Poland had become a "Slaughter House," and following the German invasion of the Soviet Union, hundreds of thousands of Jews were being shot, gassed, and electrocuted.

Although their efforts are mentioned only in passing in histories of the United States and the Holocaust, the Women's International League for Peace and Freedom (WILPF) played a significant role in the overall refugee effort. Formed during World War I, the WILPF dedicated itself to "universal disarmament, the abolition of violence," and the "ultimate goal [of] the establishment of an international economic order founded on meeting the needs of all people and not on profit and privilege."[76] By working to protect the rights of political prisoners, protesting the deportation of suspected communists, and countering the spread of US imperialism, the US chapter of the WILPF, founded under the direction of Nobel Peace Prize–winner Jane Addams, had grown by 1940 to 13,000 members with over 100 branches.[77] Throughout the war, the WILPF's refugee committee, led by scholar and pacifist (and future Nobel Peace Prize recipient) Emily Greene Balch, tirelessly struggled alongside other organizations to save Europe's Jews, using its contacts with prominent individuals, lobbying to influence US immigration law, securing affidavits for refugees, and raising public awareness about the plight of Hitler's victims. WILPF members in Europe were often persecuted by the Nazi regime for being part of an international organization, and its refugee committee in the United States worked to get its members—many of whom were Jews—out of Europe and to provide for the well-being of refugees once they arrived.

Mercedes Randall, the national education chairman for the WILPF's US chapter, made a significant contribution to the rescue movement with the publication in March 1944 of a pamphlet, "Voice of Thy Brother's Blood: An Eleventh-Hour Appeal to All Americans," as part of the WILPF's campaign to change Roosevelt's policy toward Jewish refugees.[78] Historian David S. Wyman has cited Randall's essay as the "only comprehensive discussion of the European Jewish disaster issued by an American Christian [non-Jewish] source during the Holocaust."[79] With an introduction by Harry Emerson Fosdick—the "most celebrated preacher in America"—and an epilogue by Emily Greene Balch, "Voice of Thy Brother's Blood" documented the situation in Europe and the various attempts by American Jewish organizations to aid European Jewry.[80] Randall indicated that over three million Jews had already perished and that millions more were soon to die. She discussed the possible options for the remaining Jews: existing immigration laws could be changed to allow more Jews into the United States, temporary asylum could be given, financial help could be provided to neutral countries who were already sheltering refugees, or Palestine could be opened up to Jewish immigration.[81] Recognizing that the United States had done little to help Europe's Jews, Randall ended her essay with the following charge:

> The heart of the problem is whether *we*, as active citizens in a democracy, care enough, and care deeply enough, to bring our wishes home to our legislators. Governments are not willing to undertake action unless there is a large and influential body of public opinion behind them. Neither do they act in defiance of public wishes. The responsibility of whether or not the War Refugee Board [discussed below] succeeds in its mission rests squarely upon us. The guilt will be ours, if through our indifference, our fears and our prejudices we become accessories to the greatest crime in recorded history—the mass crucifixion of a people.[82]

With the financial support of various Jewish organizations and other contributors, 50,000 copies of "Voice of Thy Brother's Blood" were initially printed, and one was sent to every member of Congress, each daily newspaper (1,780 in total), and 150 radio commentators. Following a second printing, 25,000 were sent to the addresses on the Federal Council of Churches' mailing list of ministers and community leaders.[83] The response to Randall's pamphlet was overwhelmingly enthusiastic. The WILPF received droves of letters of support from organizations and institutions such as Barnard College, the *Nation*, the Jewish Joint Distribution Committee, the American Jewish Conference, and the Farmers' Union of America. There was an April 20 editorial in the *New York Herald Tribune*, sermons across the country from sympathetic preachers, and countless other positive responses, including ones from John Foster Dulles and Norman Thomas.[84]

The American Friends Service Committee (AFSC) was another non-Jewish organization that worked relentlessly to aid Jews once war broke out. As early as 1938 it took responsibility for printing and distributing a booklet that the AJ Congress developed and which outlined the case for supporting Jewish refugees. The AJ Congress was concerned that had they printed it, the booklet would not have been as effective.[85] As an outgrowth of its work helping refugees file claims and applications, during the years 1939–43, the AFSC provided shelter to refugees in various hostels across the United States and in pre-entry transit points, such as Cuba, and also provided material aid and training so they could begin their new lives in their new country.[86] The AFSC hostels had a dual purpose. It was no secret that one purpose was to get the recent immigrants out of New York City, where the vast majority had settled and services for them were overwhelmed.[87] Outside of the city, refugees would have greater opportunities to develop new job skills, and learn English, history, and social studies. Yet for the AFSC, larger issues were at stake. The advocates used the hostels as evidence to counter the arguments of those who sought to halt the influx of immigrants from Europe. Opponents often charged that the newcomers were unable to adapt fully to society and that they lacked the knowledge, dedication, and even the social skills required of true citizens. If the AFSC could train refugees to succeed and assimilate into American society, then yet another anti-immigration argument could be defeated. The activists hoped the low-cost hostel model could be developed on a much larger scale, at little expense to the government.[88] The advocates argued that the refugees were not a burden but an asset not to be overlooked. As the journalist and refugee activist with the World Jewish Congress Kurt R. Grossmann wrote in the *Nation*, who better to have on one's side in a time of war than the "implacable foes of fascism?"[89]

US policy, intervention, and the War Refugee Board

On the eve of Passover, April 19, 1943, as the Jewish Combat Organization (Zydowska Organizacja Bojowa or ZOB) of the Warsaw Ghetto began what would be a nearly month-long uprising against Nazi troops seeking to deport the remaining inhabitants of the ghetto (approximately 42,000), diplomats from the United States and Britain gathered in Bermuda in response to critiques over their inaction concerning the ever-growing number of wartime refugees. For months, groups such as the AJ Congress and the Emergency Committee to Save the Jewish People had been holding mass demonstrations around the country to prompt Roosevelt to take more aggressive action on behalf of European Jews. Sympathetic members of Congress and Parliament as well as prominent clergy in both countries called upon their leaders to act. At a March 1 rally led by Rabbi Wise, which featured the Zionist leader Chaim Weizmann, New York City Mayor Fiorello La Guardia, and New York Senator Robert Wagner, an eleven-point resolution was passed that called for negotiating with Germany for the release of Jews held in Nazi-occupied territories, establishing safe havens in neutral or Allied countries, reforming US immigration law in light of the crisis produced by the war, opening up British-controlled Palestine to Jewish immigration, providing food to starving victims, and declaring the intention of the Allied powers to prosecute the guilty parties.

Advocates for the condemned Jews had high expectations for the twelve-day Bermuda conference. It quickly became clear, however, that the meeting was organized in such a way as to preclude any meaningful outcome. Each side sent only a small handful of delegates. No Jewish organizations were invited to participate, and the deliberations were kept from public view. The US delegation, whose members had been personally chosen by Breckinridge Long, were opposed to any relaxation of immigration policies.[90] Neither Britain nor the United States was willing to modify its immigration policies (including, in the case of Britain, the policies of its colonial possessions), and neither wished to divert any resources from the war effort.

The conference produced no new solutions to the crisis and was widely characterized as a charade. Following the gathering, the Emergency Committee to Save the Jewish People took out a large advertisement in the *New York Times* that declared, "To 5,000,000 Jews in the Nazi Death-Trap, Bermuda Was a Cruel Mockery."[91] Upon learning of the failure of the Bermuda conference and the crushing defeat of the Warsaw Ghetto fighters, the Polish Jewish leader Szmul Zygielbojm committed suicide in London. In the note that he left behind, directed to the president and prime minister of Poland, he declared:

> The responsibility for the crime of the murder of the whole Jewish nationality in Poland rests first of all on those who are carrying it out, but indirectly it falls also upon the whole of humanity, on the peoples of the Allied nations and on their governments, who up to this day have not taken any real steps to halt this crime. By looking on passively upon this murder of defenseless millions tortured children, women and men they have become partners to the responsibility.
>
> . . . By my death, I wish to give expression to my most profound protest against the inaction in which the world watches and permits the destruction of the Jewish people.[92]

Zygielbojm's suicide was covered widely in the *New York Times*, which reprinted his suicide note in full.

As reports of the mass murder of Jews mounted over the summer and fall of 1943, the AJ Congress, the Emergency Committee to Save the Jewish People, and other advocacy groups stepped up their efforts to persuade Roosevelt to intervene on behalf of refugees. Although its efforts angered Rabbi Wise and more mainstream Jewish leaders due to their stridency, the Emergency Committee sponsored advertisements in newspapers across the country and held rallies, pageants, and demonstrations to raise attention and criticize the president, and recruited celebrities and notables to their cause. These efforts were not in vain. In November, while Roosevelt was out of the country for a month beginning in mid-November to attend the Tehran Conference with Churchill and Stalin, legislators in both the House and Senate introduced resolutions that recommended the president establish an agency devoted to refugee rescue. Additionally, the State Department was facing mounting criticism from members of Congress and the Treasury Department for its handling of refugee affairs.[93] On the day after Thanksgiving, Long testified before the House Foreign Affairs Committee in order to defend his department's actions. He claimed that the State Department was doing all that was possible to assist refugees and claimed that any new organization would only complicate ongoing rescue efforts. During his testimony, he falsely claimed that the United States permitted 580,000 refugees into the country since Hitler's ascension to power and implied that these were primarily Jews. The actual number was closer to 190,000, and the United States had in fact only permitted 18.3 percent of the allowable immigration quotas to be filled between the years 1934 and 1943.[94] Days later, during a meeting between Treasury and State Department officials, Treasury Secretary Henry Morgenthau Jr. called Long aside and directly accused him of obstructionism and antisemitism. When his testimony became public soon after, Long faced severe criticism and calls for his dismissal. (Within a year he was demoted and he retired from the State Department entirely.)

Finally, after the British Foreign Office declared unequivocally that it was unwilling to provide for any more Jewish refugees and following strong lobbying by Treasury officials frustrated with the State Department, on January 22, 1944, Roosevelt signed Executive Order 9417.[95] It declared that "it is the policy of this Government to take all measures within its power to rescue the victims of enemy oppression who are in imminent danger of death and otherwise to afford such victims all possible relief and assistance consistent with the successful prosecution of the war," and to carry out this commitment it formally established the War Refugee Board (WRB). This marked a significant shift in the president's approach to the refugee issue. The WRB was formally placed under the responsibility of the heads of the State, Treasury, and War Departments, although it was located within the Treasury building and led and staffed primarily by Treasury officials.

The creation of the WRB was met with widespread enthusiasm. It received one million dollars from the president's emergency fund and nearly a million and a half dollars in private donations.[96] Over the next twenty months (sixteen of them during wartime) the WRB, the only nonmilitary US governmental agency dedicated to the relief and assistance of the victims of Nazi aggression, managed an impressive lists of accomplishments. Headed by Treasury official John Pehle, the WRB quickly cleared many of the administrative hurdles that had been put into place by the State Department and that had prevented the transfer of funds abroad. It facilitated relationships with various rescue and relief organizations, such as the Intergovernmental Committee on Refugees, the United Nations Relief and Rehabilitation Administration, the Red Cross, the American Joint Distribution Committee, and the AJ Congress. It appointed representatives in various European states who would relay accurate information about the plight of refugees there and who could provide direct aid when possible. For example, Pehle appointed Ira A. Hirschmann, who was involved in major philanthropic enterprises in New York, to be the WRB's representative in Ankara, Turkey. Hirschmann was able to help smooth obstacles and clear the red tape that had prevented refugees traveling through Turkey to reach sanctuary in British-controlled Palestine. He also assisted the Joint lease ships that would transport refugees from Romania and the Balkans. The WRB placed other representatives in North Africa, Sweden, Switzerland, Portugal, and England. Most famously, it supported the activities of the Swedish diplomat Raoul Wallenberg, who provided protective passports and shelter to tens of thousands of threatened Hungarian Jews. The WRB also drafted Roosevelt's March 24, 1944, warning to Germany that those responsible for the murder of Jews would be punished at the war's end and that it was the responsibility of all German citizens to help Jews escape Nazi violence.[97]

In the summer of that year, the WRB seriously considered the proposal that the United States should intervene militarily to stop deportations to Auschwitz and passed on recommendations to the military. It also contended with the various proposals to pay ransom (in the form of war materiel and soft goods) to Nazi and Hungarian leaders for the lives of imperiled Jews. The proposals were rejected by the United States and Britain on both ideological and practical grounds. In November, the WRB pressed the United States to bomb the gas chambers at Auschwitz (other groups, such as the Orthodox Vaad ha-Hatzala, had previously made similar calls), but the request never went beyond the assistant secretary of war, who deemed it unfeasible and a diversion from Allied war aims, and the issue was likely never brought before Roosevelt.[98]

Whether the United States could have intervened militarily to save Jewish lives, in particular by bombing the gas chambers at Auschwitz or the railway lines leading to it from Hungary, is a heated question that has engaged historians and commentators for several decades, but one that was not widely discussed at the time.[99] Compared with the question of providing sanctuary to threatened Jews, there is significantly less activity to report. Unlike the refugee issue, the possibility of humanitarian military intervention was not considered intensively during the war itself and became a subject of debate only many years afterward. Few advocacy groups pressed the case for armed intervention and none pressed it with the vigor that they reserved for the possibility of rescue. The reasons for this are rather straightforward. For most of the war, US forces were not in a position to reach targets inside Poland.

Only in the beginning of 1944 could US bombers reach Hungary (which was invaded by Germany in March and began deporting Jews to Auschwitz in May) and the Auschwitz killing center without having to stop to refuel.[100] More importantly, the existence of operations at Auschwitz were largely unknown to most American Jewish leaders until summer 1944. The I. G. Farben industrial complex that was located a few miles from the gas chambers, and which was staffed primarily with slave labor from camp, came under repeated bombing in late August. The only major attack on the death facilities at Auschwitz was one launched by the prisoners themselves when members of the *Sonderkommando* (the prisoner unit forced to dispose of corpses from the gas chambers) in October of that year blew up one of the crematoria with explosives smuggled to them by a number of Jewish women working as part of the camp's underground resistance movement. The rebellion was quickly crushed and over 400 members of the underground and *Sonderkommando* were killed.

With its November 1944 report, "German Extermination Camps—Auschwitz and Birkenau," the WRB was among the first governmental agencies to report in detail on the systematic murder of millions of civilians. The account detailed the living conditions of prisoners, their classification via variously colored triangles, the murderous treatment by SS guards, the layout of the camps, the armament factories, and the murder by gassing and cremation of inmates. It included a "rough ground plan" of the gas chambers and crematoria in Birkenau. That same month, Himmler brought an end to mechanized killing at Auschwitz and the camp was liberated by Soviet forces in late January 1945.

The WRB also pressed the Roosevelt administration to consider providing safe havens for refugees within the United States' own borders, claiming that otherwise it had little leverage to persuade other countries to do so. In summer 1944 President Roosevelt agreed to a plan allowing the resettlement of nearly 1,000 refugees from camps in Allied-occupied parts of southern Italy (many of whom had arrived there by escaping through Yugoslavia). For some time, the WRB had been pressing the president to make a public commitment to helping refugees, and on June 9, he announced that he was designating Fort Ontario, in Oswego, New York, as a site for temporary resettlement. The WRB was tasked with identifying which refugees were most suitable for relocation. In July, a group of 982 refugees, most of whom were Jews and representing fourteen national groups, sailed for New York.[101] By presidential order, they were admitted into the United States outside of the immigration quota system and were expected to return to their homes at the end of the war.

Near the end of the war, the WRB helped provide hundreds of thousands of care packages for the Red Cross to distribute to recently liberated concentration camp prisoners. Although the WRB is commonly cited as having saved as many as 200,000 persons,[102] historian Rebecca L. Erbelding argues convincingly that such a number is most certainly an exaggeration and that, in fact, any accurate number is impossible to ascertain, given the impreciseness of the term "rescue" in this context and the fact that the WRB worked in cooperation with so many other organizations.[103] In spite of this, the WRB represents the most systematic and concerted effort by the US government to aid imperiled Jews in Europe.

The Oswego Camp and ambivalent sanctuary

Reflecting the president's decision to offer sanctuary (but not a path toward citizenship) to this small group of refugees, the Fort Ontario Emergency Refugee Shelter fell under the jurisdiction of the War Relocation Authority, the administrative body that oversaw the incarceration of Japanese Americans during World War II. The refugees arrived at the camp in August and remained there until February 1946. Nearly a third were Yugoslavian and a quarter were Austrian. Significant numbers of Poles and Germans were also present. Well more than half of the refugees already possessed close ties with the United States: some held visas, others had applied for them, and more than one-third already had family members living in the country.[104]

Given that the number of refugees was less than 1,000, that they arrived primarily from refugee camps that were located within Allied-occupied portions of Italy, and that this was the only effort by the United States to house refugees from Nazism, the historian Sharon Lowenstein has appropriately referred to the Oswego Camp as a form of "token refuge," that is, one that was designed more to save face rather than to make a lasting impact on the overall crisis. While most press reports were favorable, even this comparatively small humanitarian act generated some opposition. Some Zionists saw it as a threat to their efforts to pressure the British to allow increased Jewish immigration in Palestine. Other critics were concerned that the camp would be the first of many such sites of refuge opened by Roosevelt and sought to block the program's expansion. Some feared that Nazi spies or subversive elements were among the refugees, and others charged the president with acting outside of his constitutional authority. By contrast, there was a high level of support for admitting prisoners of war to the United States. During the war, the United States housed 425,000 POWs, 372,000 of them German.[105]

When interviewed fifty years after the establishment of the camp, many of the former residents who had lived there as children relayed fond memories of their time in Oswego. For example, Irene Danon, who had spent two and

FIGURE 2.7 *Jewish refugee from Tripoli Victor Franc and his daughter.*

a half years in hiding with her family in Yugoslavia before arriving to safety in Italy and then relocating to Oswego, recalled:

> Well, for the best [most] part it was wonderful. I was very, very happy here. These were very good eighteen months. For the first time in four years, we had, we were able to talk to other people without ... fear. We had teachers ... They taught us how to dance and a lot of social activities ... What impressed me the most was when we got into the barracks, there was a box of cereal and it was one of those little individual boxes that you cut in the middle and put the milk into it and I thought, "My God! These Americans are brilliant!"[106]

Eva Kaufmann, whose family also fled to Italy from Yugoslavia, was eight years old when she arrived at Oswego. She described her arrival in Oswego as "feeling like we've come to heaven" after her family's travails in Europe. "We felt safe. We had food and we had a room of our own."[107] The highlight for most children was Eleanor Roosevelt's visit to the camp on September 20, 1945.

Such memories, however, exist in stark contrast to the difficulties that many residents of the camp experienced at the time. They were immediately deloused upon arrival in New York before the two-day train ride to Fort Ontario, a procedure that reminded some of their time in concentration and internment camps in Europe. While family members were housed with one another, they were confined to the camp and unable to leave. The fort was surrounded by a six-foot-high fence with barbed wire that prevented townspeople as well as family members of refugees who lived in the United States from coming into direct contact with them. They also found that their mail was censored by authorities. Conditions in the camp were initially very poor; they lived in wooden barracks with communal toilets and showers, inadequate health care, and many units lacked furniture. Coming most recently from Italy's Mediterranean climate, they were ill prepared for the harsh winter. In addition, they suffered from the psychological trauma of having been hunted and oppressed. Many, therefore, experienced their time in Oswego as internees, although their only "crime" was to have been refugees from Nazism. They had expected that, in coming to the United States, they would at last be able to live in freedom. Most did not realize that they were to be confined to a camp and would be unable to seek employment, travel, or move freely in and out of the camp. Such conditions led to very high levels of stress among the refugees. Eventually, after repeated protests and organizing by the refugees, the War Relocation Authority made work opportunities available, allowed for a measure of self-governance, arranged for the educational needs of the children, provided medical facilities, and permitted residents of the camp to gain passes to go into town.[108]

At the end of the war, most wished to remain in the United States and to become citizens. As the news of the war's aftermath reached American audiences, and they were exposed to pictures of the horrors of the concentration camps, sympathy for the Oswego refugees grew. As part of a public campaign led by groups such as the AJ Congress, the AFSC, and the National Catholic Welfare Conference, many prominent Americans advocated on their behalf, and thousands wrote to the government arguing for their right to become citizens. In late December 1945, more than seven months after the cessation of hostilities in Europe, President Truman signed a directive that allowed the residents of the camp to remain in the United States and gave them preference under current immigration law. Even this special dispensation was subject to quota regulations. As Lowenstein explains, these refugees had to fit within the quotas of their particular national groups, and to leave the country and then reenter at Niagara Falls in order to be officially counted as immigrants.[109] By early February 1946, the last remaining residents had left the camp and it was shuttered.

***

The monumental effort that was required in order to give shelter to such a small number of refugees illustrates the tremendous obstacles facing advocates for refugees. They had to overcome more than a decade of Americans' anti-immigrant sentiments, governmental efforts to prevent refugees from finding sanctuary in the country, and the limitations imposed by the war itself. In spite of many calls for the country to set aside its differences and unify during wartime, the World War II years in America were a difficult time for many racial, religious, and ethnic minorities. Although Jews were better off than most other ethnic minority groups, they too were constrained by systematic racism that pervaded nearly every aspect of society. Their situation would change, as we will see in Chapter 3, only in the postwar years, when American Jews of European descent moved more decisively into the ranks of the white middle class. This move would profoundly shape the way that they contended with the immediate aftermath of the Holocaust and their new status, by default, as the largest existing Jewish population in the world.

3

Jewish refugees and displaced persons in postwar America

In 1943, the philosopher Hannah Arendt published a short essay entitled "We Refugees" in the New York–based *Menorah Journal*.[1] At the time, Arendt was still a relatively new arrival in the United States who wrote primarily for German émigré publications. This essay was her first attempt in English to come to terms with her status as a European exile from Nazism. Born into a secular Jewish family near the German city of Hanover, Arendt had studied philosophy at the University of Marburg and Heidelberg University, but as a Jew she was prohibited from obtaining an academic position following the Nazi takeover of power. Following a brief arrest by the Gestapo, she left Nazi Germany in 1933 and spent the rest of the decade in Paris. After the 1940 invasion of France, she was registered as an "enemy alien" as a result of her German birth (although Germany had revoked her citizenship in 1937). Since she was a Jew, she was imprisoned for a short period in the Gurs concentration camp. With the assistance of Varian Fry and the Emergency Rescue Committee, she managed to escape France, arriving in the United States in 1941.[2]

After the war, Arendt became involved with an effort to salvage the intellectual legacy of European Jewry. She was among a small group of scholars from the United States who sought to identify new homes for millions of books and documents that had been seized by Nazis who intended to found a Jewish museum following the extermination of European Jewry.[3] In the 1950s, she became one of the great theoreticians of totalitarianism and the intellectual roots of Nazism and Stalinism. Her reporting on the 1961 Jerusalem trial of Nazi leader Adolf Eichmann, which was subsequently published as the book *Eichmann in Jerusalem*, remains one of the most widely read and contested accounts of the Holocaust.

Although when she wrote "We Refugees" the war and Holocaust were ongoing and the full extent of the genocide was not yet fully understood, Arendt anticipated many of the difficulties that were to be faced by Jewish refugees and Holocaust survivors who settled in the United States after the war's end. Central to her concerns were the many unrealistic demands placed on Jewish refugees. In particular, she spoke of the difficulty that "newcomers" like herself experienced when they were expected to embrace their new homes fully while they were still coming to terms with the trauma they had so recently experienced:

> We lost our home, which means the familiarity of daily life. We lost our occupation, which means the confidence that we are of some use in this world. We lost our language, which means the naturalness of reactions, the simplicity of gestures, the unaffected expression of feelings. We left our relatives in the Polish ghettos and our best friends have been killed in concentration camps, and that means the rupture of our private lives.[4]

Arendt's essay gives voice to uncomfortable truths regarding the way that many Holocaust survivors and refugees from Nazism experienced their reception in the United States. It reveals the widespread sense that although their American Jewish hosts publicly and repeatedly offered "official proclamations of hospitality and good will," the new arrivals were not particularly welcome to dwell on their recent experiences:

> In order to forget more efficiently we rather avoid any allusion to concentration or internment camps we experienced in nearly all European countries—it might be interpreted as pessimism or lack of confidence in the new homeland. Besides, how often have we been told that nobody likes to listen to all that; hell is no longer a religious belief or a fantasy, but something as real as houses and stones and trees. Apparently nobody wants to know that contemporary history has created a new kind of human beings—the kind that are put in concentration camps by their foes and in internment camps by their friends.[5]

Arendt attributed this discomfort with the experiences of refugees such as herself to the fact that Nazism had created a new category of people who existed outside of all systems of state authority. As an exile living in America without a passport or citizenship, and therefore without any rights at all, Arendt was suddenly among those who had no identification other than that of being a Jew. To be a Jew without documentation in the world at that moment meant, she argued, that one was simply a "human being." Yet to be a human being in an age in which people were defined by their "passports or birth certificates, and sometimes even tax receipts" meant that she in fact had no status at all and was condemned to be an outcast.[6] She was, in a sense, thrown back to premodern times, when prior to emancipation, European Jews were not accepted as members of the states in which they lived, were treated as perpetual foreigners, and were subject to the whims of governments and rulers.

In spite of the title of her essay, Arendt resisted being called a "refugee." She begins in fact by stating, "In the first place, we don't like to be called 'refugees.' We ourselves call each other 'newcomers' or 'immigrants.' "[7] Arendt's essay highlights the difficulty with the terminology associated with Jews who had either fled from or suffered under Nazism (or both). "Immigrant" is a term that tends to be associated with voluntary migrants, who are generally expected to make their own way in their newly adopted countries. "Refugees" tends to refer to those who were compelled to flee their home countries in search of safety and require assistance and care during their resettlement. However, the United States had no formal refugee policy either during the Nazi period or in the immediate years following, so most refugees from Nazism were counted under the quotas for immigrants. Complicating matters further is that after the war, a new category emerged: "Displaced Persons" or "DPs," which referred to people who had been uprooted by the war and were unable to return home. As this chapter discusses, after the war, most DPs eventually found new places to settle, but Jewish DPs had a particularly difficult time as there was little understanding that amid the war, Nazi Germany had a particular plan to exterminate European Jewry. Many Jewish DPs had been captives for years and held in concentration camps and killing centers. Only after several decades would these DPs come to be known as "Holocaust survivors."

This chapter addresses the difficult subject of the reception of Holocaust survivors by US military forces in Europe and refugee advocacy organizations in America after the end of World War II. As in the years prior to and during the Holocaust, the issue of race shaped how Jewish victims of Nazism were received by Americans. If racist immigration laws resulted in many Jews being prevented from finding shelter in the United States in the 1930s and first half of the 1940s, suspicions regarding Jewish DPs' inability to assimilate into the United States prevented many from obtaining the help that they desperately needed after the war.

It is common today to encounter expressions of national pride for the role that the United States played in liberating Nazi concentration camps in Germany in the last days of the war. Many films, museum exhibitions, monuments, books, and journalistic accounts hail the role of US soldiers in freeing prisoners from camps such as Buchenwald and Dachau. Scholarship on this subject, however, has complicated this account and demonstrated that the US military was entirely unprepared to assume responsibility for the DPs who would come under its care in the immediate postwar period. The poor treatment that many Jewish DPs—many of whom had spent years in Nazi camps and were severely malnourished and in ill health—received at the hands of the military was in part a consequence of antisemitic stereotypes of Jews held by military leaders, who did not comprehend what these survivors had just experienced. The presence of so many stateless DPs also brought about a new global immigration crisis, as hundreds of thousands of Jews were left with nowhere to resettle. In spite of Americans' increasing sympathy toward Hitler's victims and the strengthening social position of American Jews after World War II, the United States was not inclined to grant special refuge to Jewish victims of Nazism after the war than it had been prior to its start. With mixed results, advocates on their behalf had to wage new battles to open the country's borders and make the case that these survivors of Nazism deserved to find permanent refuge in America. Complicating the matter further was that many of the survivors who did manage to find a new home in the United States saw that their presence often created an uncomfortable situation for established American Jews who were benefitting from postwar opportunities to move into the country's white middle class and who felt their status threatened by an influx of European Jews who required extraordinary assistance.

Jewish DPs in the liberated American sector

In the last days of the war, many US soldiers struggled to comprehend what they saw in the newly liberated concentration camps: tens of thousands of starving captives begging for food, suffering from typhus, and dying of dysentery. Tens of thousands more emaciated corpses lay in the road or in piles. Filth and the stench of death were everywhere. Servicemen found mass graves overflowing with decomposing bodies. There was nothing in their experience of fighting that prepared them for what they had stumbled upon. As the former infantryman Rockie Blunt, who had been present at the liberation of the Ohrdruf concentration camp (a subcamp of Buchenwald), described later:

> Concentration camps were in a category all by themselves. They were of such magnitude that it is beyond comprehension. It is more than the human mind can even conceive of . . . When you first come across it, you look but you don't see. You listen but you don't hear. Your mind closes down. We talked to them and they would cry. They were beyond having a voice. Most of them tried to reach out and just touch you with a fingertip, anything just to ensure in their mind that what they were looking at the other side of the wire—us—was real.[8]

FIGURE 3.1 *US generals Eisenhower, Bradley, Patton, and Eddy inspect a cremation pyre at the Ohrdruf concentration camp on April 12, 1945, after liberation.*

The camps were filled with prisoners from all over Europe. Some had been incarcerated years before the war even began. Some were prisoners of war or slave laborers from Nazi-occupied countries. Others were Jewish survivors of death camps in Poland who had been forcibly marched into Germany during the last months of the war ahead of advancing Soviet forces. In the closing months of the war, these concentration camps swelled far beyond capacity, and starvation and disease were rampant. The survivor Hanna Lévy described camp conditions in a March 1945 entry in her diary that she secretly kept while imprisoned at Bergen-Belsen:

> We all have typhoid fever and are bedridden. They put a special barbed wire fence around our barracks …
>
> I was slowly and consciously dying. My body felt nothing seemed to quietly cease to function. Persistent, only the idea of death was alive in me. Around me, everyone was dying as well, and they continue to die, each one in turn …

> The food doesn't come at all anymore. From time to time, a vat of sour soup. Sometimes we cut a weed and boil it. We pick potato skins out of the trash. Those who have sold themselves still possess something but they have no resistance against the contagion, the agony, or death either. It's a general thing, suspended in the air, imminent for everyone.
>
> No one is in charge of us. The Germans don't show up anymore. We know that their end is near, very near. But so is ours.[9]

Allied troops were unprepared to contend with the extent of the suffering that they encountered, and their arrival initially did little to slow the high death rate among inmates.

At the end of the war, Germany had been divided into sectors run by the Soviet Union, the United States, Britain, and France, bringing nearly seven and a half million people requiring repatriation or resettlement under the supervision of the Allied armies. This staggeringly high number of DPs overwhelmed Allied troops, and the hoped-for assistance from the United Nations Relief and Rehabilitation Administration (UNRRA), which had been formed in 1943 to oversee the postwar repatriation of refugees, was slow to materialize. Over the summer months of 1945, Allied armies were able to return approximately six million people to their homes. But there remained some one and a half million in Allied hands in Germany, Austria, and Italy who either could not or would not return to their homes, largely out of fear for their safety or simply because they had no home to which to return. At least 200,000 of these were Jews.[10]

As Leonard Dinnerstein has argued, the inability of UNRRA to manage the crisis forced the militaries of the Allied governments to oversee the DPs' care and resettlement.[11] Since many former concentration camps were located in the American sector, the US Army became responsible for a particularly high number of Jewish DPs. The army, however, was unprepared to manage this task and relied upon what it knew best: maintaining order and discipline. It established a network of DP camps in former military barracks, in summer camps, hotels, and at times, on the same spot as former concentrations camps. It enacted curfews, identification systems, work details, and strict codes of conduct. By explicit policy, the army did not recognize that the Jewish DPs under its authority had faced any particular hardships different from that of other DPs. Consequently, Jewish DPs were at times housed together with the very men who had contributed to their degradation and humiliation, since some of the DPs were former Nazi collaborators who had come to Germany from the Baltic states to aid the Nazi cause or to escape Soviet reprisals. In some instances, Jewish DPs who were former German or Austrian citizens were treated as POWs. Throughout the summer of 1945, Jewish DPs in particular were often considered a nuisance by US troops, who could not understand why DPs were in such poor condition, why many seemed to be unwilling to work or conduct themselves "properly," or why they were even in Germany at all.[12]

In spite of this treatment, the American sector was one of the safer places in Europe for Jewish survivors, and for more than a year after the war's end more DPs arrived in search of assistance. Many were Polish Jews who, upon returning to their homes, encountered brutal antisemitism. As historians Jan Gross and Irena Grudzińska Gross have shown, not only did Nazis steal Jewish property through legal "Aryanization" schemes, but many ethnic Poles had seized the homes, businesses, jewelry, and furnishings of Jews after they were deported.[13] When surviving Jews sought to restore their lives and livelihoods, they often were met with hostility and violence from those who had taken their property. The deadliest act of violence against Polish Jewish survivors occurred on July 4, 1946, in the town of Kielce. Prior to the war, approximately 24,000 Jews had lived in the town, representing one-third of the total population. Almost all were murdered in the Holocaust. After the war, about 200 Jewish survivors either returned or newly settled there, a majority of them living in a building owned by the local Jewish committee. A false allegation that Jews had harmed a non-Jewish boy spread through the town and sparked a violent attack on the occupants of the building. More than 1,000 ethnic Poles gathered and soon violence erupted. By the end of the day, over 40 Jews had been killed and dozens more were wounded. To many of the remaining Jews in postwar Poland, the Kielce pogrom was the final piece of evidence to demonstrate that they had no future in that country. Over the course of the next three months, as many as 90,000 Jews left Poland in the hopes of reaching the relative safety of DP camps in Germany. In response to this influx, on April 12, 1947, the US military barred the migration of any more refugees into the American sector.

As reports of the mistreatment of Jewish DPs made their way to the United States in the summer of 1945 (in particular into the pages of the New York daily newspaper *PM*), concerned leaders within the Jewish community began to petition their representatives in Congress for assistance. Several members of Congress, as well as Secretary of the Treasury Henry Morgenthau Jr., lodged protests with the War Department, State Department, and President Truman. By late June, Acting Secretary of State Joseph Grew appointed Earl Harrison, the US representative to the Intergovernmental Committee on Refugees, to investigate the situation firsthand.[14] During his three-week trip to Europe, Harrison and his associates (which included some members of the War Refugee Board) had full access to DP camps and toured approximately thirty different sites.

The report that Harrison submitted to the president in late August was damning.[15] It did not hesitate to criticize the US military's treatment of the

DPs. Although it acknowledged many DPs' gratitude in being liberated, the report noted that given their subsequent treatment, "liberation" should be understood in military terms only. Having experienced the most vicious treatment at the hands of Nazis, Jewish DPs now found themselves "neglected by their liberators." Harrison understood that, despite what US military policy maintained, the situation facing Jews was remarkably different from that of other DPs. Not only had they endured unprecedented amounts of violence and brutality at the hands of Nazis, most had no home to which they could return. Most were stateless and desperate for information on the possible whereabouts of family members from whom they had been separated. He reported that three months after the fall of Berlin, many DPs were still confined to the same concentration camps from which they had ostensibly been freed. Although they were no longer beaten, threatened with execution, and forced to engage in slave labor, they still lived under armed guard and behind barbed wire, and had little, if any, personal freedom. They live, he declared, "like prisoners or criminals or herded sheep." As late as the end of July, many DPs still wore their striped prison clothes, while others wore discarded uniforms of SS guards. Having suffered years of malnutrition at the hands of the Germans, they continued to be underfed and receive substandard medical care.

In contrast to the military, Harrison placed the needs of Jewish DPs at the center of his concerns and argued that the military's refusal to recognize them as a distinct group was the cause of significant further suffering. He stressed that since Nazis had treated Jews for years in a manner so different from others, "a group has been created which has special needs." He wrote:

> The first and plainest need of these people is a recognition of their actual status and by this I mean their status as Jews. Most of them have spent years in the worst of the concentration camps. In many cases, although the full extent is not yet known, they are the sole survivors of their families and many have been through the agony of witnessing the destruction of their loved ones. Understandably, therefore, their present condition, physical and mental, is far worse than that of other groups.[16]

Harrison also stressed that most Jewish DPs did not want to return to their countries of origin. The majority, he reported, wanted to go to Palestine for either ideological or practical reasons. Many wished to come to the United States but were prevented by the immigration barriers still in effect. He concluded his report with a series of recommendations. These included making the needs of Jewish DPs the first priority for the military and aid groups, facilitating their repatriation or resettlement (in particular to Palestine), identifying adequate short-term housing and care, employing them to assist in administering the camps themselves, installing civilian control over the camps, and providing tracing services so that DPs could reunite with their families.

Within days of receiving the report, President Truman ordered General Eisenhower to make significant reforms and address the concerns in Harrison's report. Truman also called upon newly elected British prime minister Clement Attlee to allow for 100,000 Jews to resettle in Palestine. Eisenhower's public response, reprinted fully in the *New York Times*, was in turns defensive and contrite. He "freely admitted that there is need for improvement" and reported that many improvements in housing had been instituted and DPs were now being given preference over German civilians. He also insisted that the magnitude of the task facing the military was daunting. With so many different population groups under US military control, adequate housing was extraordinarily difficult to secure. He took greatest offense at Harrison's "assertion that our military guards are now substituting for SS troops," which he called misleading, and he defended the need for security against the "depredation and banditry" that existed within the camps. He closed his letter by stating that Harrison both ignored the challenges the military was facing and dismissed its many successes in saving Jewish lives and repatriating many former prisoners.[17] Harrison deemed Eisenhower's public response "generally misleading" and argued that Jews in Germany should not be forced to live in camps while Germans were freely able to live in homes. "What difference does it make what kind of camps they are in?" he argued. "The point is that they shouldn't be in any camps at all."[18] (General Patton too was hostile toward DPs, especially Jewish ones. After reading Harrison's report, he wrote in his diary that "Harrison and his ilk believe that the Displaced Person is a human being, which he is not, and this applies particularly to the Jews who are lower than animals."[19])

Following Harrison's recommendation, the US military established separate facilities for Jewish DPs. In late December 1945, Truman directed that preferential treatment be given to DPs (without specifying Jewish DPs) under existing immigration laws and also allowed the more than 900 refugees at the Fort Ontario camp to leave the United States and be readmitted as immigrants. In his directive, which permitted 40,000 DPs to enter the United States under the quota system, he noted that during the war years very few Europeans had immigrated to the United States: "In the fiscal year 1942, only 10 per cent of the immigration quotas was used; in 1943, 5 per cent; in 1944, 6 per cent; and in 1945, 7 per cent. As of Nov. 30, 1945, the end of the fifth month of the present fiscal year, only about 10 per cent of the quotas for the European countries has been used." The president asserted that "common decency and the fundamental comradeship of all human beings require us to do what lies within our power to see that our established immigration quotas are used in order to reduce human suffering."[20]

The DP camps ended up lasting far longer than anyone had imagined when they were first established in 1945. Most non-Jewish DPs were able to return to their countries of origin or find countries in which to resettle. However, many Jewish DPs languished while the leaders of the United States and Great Britain sought to find them permanent homes. In the meantime, DPs organized themselves into groups that were divided along linguistic, political, and cultural lines. Collectively, Jewish DPs began to consider themselves *sheyres hapleyte*, a Yiddish term meaning "the surviving remnant," and held annual congresses to represent their needs and plan for the future. Increasingly, DPs were given a role in administering the camps, and they established courts, schools, hospitals, cultural and sports organizations, and welfare committees. They sought to rebuild their lives while still living in the camps, and many married and had children.

Advocacy for Jewish survivors

The way in which the American public became aware of the assault on European Jewry was initially shaped by the carnage encountered by US troops during the final military campaigns against Germany. In the last year of the war, the Allied forces attacked Germany from multiple sides. Soviet armies drove from the east and US, British, and Canadian forces raced to Berlin from the south and west. The Soviets were the first to reach the major killing centers in Poland such as Majdanek, Belzec, Sobibor, Treblinka, and Auschwitz. However, the photographs and films that became widely distributed in the United States were from those concentration camps that had been liberated by the Allies. In the last days of the war and throughout the summer of 1945, camps such as Buchenwald, Bergen-Belsen, Dora-Mittelbau, Flossenbürg, Dachau, and Mauthausen became household names. The descriptions and images of liberated inmates were circulated widely and profoundly shaped the early public perceptions of Nazi crimes. A headline in *Life* magazine from May 7, 1945, stated "Atrocities: Capture of the German Concentration Camps Piles Up Evidence of Barbarism That Reaches the Low Point of Human Degradation" and featured a full-page photo of a young boy walking down a road past dozens of corpses.[21] Other photos showed the charred remains of bodies hastily burned by evacuating SS guards.

Many Americans who were moved by the plight of Jewish DPs pressed for solutions to allow them to find permanent residence in the United States. But this task proved to be a difficult one and took several years to accomplish. There was still little public or governmental support for altering the 1924 legislation that favored Northern Europeans over other immigrant groups. Even among many of the strongest proponents for DPs, which included labor

FIGURE 3.2 *Young boy dressed in shorts walks along a dirt road lined with the corpses of hundreds of prisoners who died at the Bergen-Belsen extermination camp, near the towns of Bergen and Celle, Germany, April 20, 1945.*

leaders and several members of Congress, few wished to make permanent changes in the law in order to help a single population group. The close association of eugenics, white supremacy, and antisemitism with Nazism had not fully discredited racial ideologies in the postwar United States, where they continued to shape ideas about who should have the right to settle in the country, receive government support, and have the full protection of the law. Adding to DPs' difficulties was the rapidly growing anxiety brought about by the Cold War with the Soviet Union, which led many to associate Jews from Eastern Europe with communism and provided yet another justification for those seeking to tighten US borders.[22]

Given this uncertain climate, American Jewish communal leaders often assumed a cautious approach to their advocacy for Jewish DPs, similar to the way that many Jewish organizations advocated for German Jewish refugees prior to the war. Some Jewish groups, namely, those that were Zionist in their orientation, resisted efforts to bring Jewish DPs to the United States, and instead advocated for greater Jewish migration to Palestine as part of a nascent Jewish state. Meanwhile, a highly visible group in the campaign to raise public awareness and convince Congress to support the DPs, the Citizens Committee on Displaced Persons (CCDP), was hesitant to reveal its Jewish backers—it was founded, supported, and often staffed primarily by the American Jewish Committee and the American Council for Judaism—and took great pains to downplay the fact that the DPs who needed the most help were Jews.

Advocates adopted a multipronged approach that included scholarly research, congressional testimony, journalistic accounts, and radio dramas. In each of these various forms, they sought to challenge so-called patriotic groups and conservative lawmakers who cast DPs as a threat to the country's racial, ethnic, and political stability by presenting Holocaust survivors in ways that were nonthreatening to US citizens, positioning DPs as merely another group of immigrants in a long history of people coming to the United States to escape tyranny. To bolster their cause, advocates enlisted prominent figures. A 1947 report by the Committee for the Study of Recent Immigration from Europe entitled *Refugees in America*, for example, was sponsored by Eleanor Roosevelt, Earl Harrison, Senator Robert F. Wagner, *Nation* editor Freda Kirchwey, labor leader David Dubinsky, reformer Dorothy Canfield Fisher, and the writer Thomas Mann, as well as famous philanthropists, heads of major religious organizations, Hollywood stars, and political activists.[23] This lengthy and well-researched study authored by Yale sociologist Maurice R. Davie examined the reception and progress of refugees from Nazi Germany since 1933. It recognized that many refugees had had a difficult time adjusting to their new country, but showed that within a short period of time, they were able to adapt to their new status. It reported that the vast majority of them (96.5 percent) fully identified with the United States and had no intention of ever returning to the country of their birth. Many immediately sought to begin the naturalization process. The report concluded that

> the weight of the evidence pro and con … demonstrates that by and large the refugees have shown unusual adaptability, that in a short period of time they have gone a long way toward becoming a part of the nation, that they presented little or no problem to the American community, and that they have had a beneficial effect upon this country out of proportion to their numbers.[24]

Studies such as *Refugees in America* helped to provide the substance to testimony given to Congress during debates about the fate of the DPs. Advocates argued that the United States must do its "fair share" and that it would benefit financially from such immigration. In testimony given to the Immigration Subcommittee of the Senate Judiciary Committee in September 1948, Irving M. Engel of the AJ Committee argued that there was sufficient evidence to demonstrate that the ethnic diversity of the United States was a sign of the country's strength and that it was necessary to revise US immigration policy in such a way as to give immigrants of all stripes a chance to become "good Americans."[25] Engel argued that at the core "Americanism"—as articulated by Presidents Washington, Jefferson, and Lincoln—rested upon the values of tolerance and acceptance of racial, religious, and national differences. He concluded, "It is with grateful recognition of the blessings bestowed on our land through past waves of freedom-seeking pilgrims that we urge a refashioning of our immigration laws so that they will more adequately reflect the true ideals of America."[26]

The story of the DP Kurt Maier was featured prominently in the campaigns. Born in Czechoslovakia in 1911, Maier was an acclaimed pianist who was living in Prague in the spring of 1939, when the country was seized by Germany.[27] For a short while, he was able to continue performing and teaching, but he found himself increasingly shunned by non-Jewish friends, patrons, and students. In early December 1941, Maier, along with thousands of other Czech Jews, was deported to the Theresienstadt camp. Maier and his mother spent more than two and a half years there; he worked in the camp's musical band, and his mother mended clothes.[28] In October 1944, he was transported to Auschwitz (his mother, who had been deported there several months earlier, was murdered upon her arrival). Maier was eventually assigned to play in one of the camp orchestras that accompanied prisoners as they marched to their work details. Maier was transferred several more times, first to Sachsenhausen, then Ohrdruf, and finally he was sent on a forced march to Buchenwald, just ahead of the advancing US Army. After the camp was liberated on April 11, 1945, he spent several weeks recovering from typhus under the care of American doctors. On account of President Truman's directive that gave DPs preference under the existing immigration quota system, he arrived at the United States in late July 1946.[29]

Maier's story was perfectly suited for the needs of campaigners in the United States. He spoke English well as a result of having performed for many English-speaking tourists prior to the war. He had a sister in the United States who was able to sponsor his entry and ensure that he would not become a public charge. He was affable and able to tell his story well. To correspond with the 1947 Passover holiday, a refugee aid agency known as the United Service for New Americans sponsored a widely distributed radio broadcast titled *Out of the Wilderness* that told the stories of five DPs, including Maier. In late summer 1947, *New Yorker* reporter and former war correspondent Daniel Lang told Maier's story in an article titled "Displaced," which located the story of the DPs squarely within the American tradition of providing sanctuary to people escaping persecution:

> One of the oratorical flourishes that almost every politician uses when addressing a group of foreign-born citizens is to hail America as the haven

> of the oppressed. He tells of the coming of the Pilgrims; of the German Revolution of 1848 . . . of the flight of the Irish from their potato famine; of the exodus of Russians in the time of the Czars . . . In another year or so, when enough of a new group of immigrants have landed here, the politician will be able to add a modern category, the D.P.s, or displaced persons.[30]

Lang's portrait of Maier emphasized the pianist's deep gratitude to his liberators. It also highlighted his early dreams of coming to America, describing how prior to the war, Maier's sister in New York would send him postcards and photographs of interesting sites, including one of the Empire State Building. Although these were taken away from him when he arrived at Auschwitz, their memories sustained him for a time. Later, the American planes that he saw over Auschwitz, and then again while imprisoned in concentration camps in Germany, came to represent for him a sign of hope for the future.

The following year, Lang's article was dramatized for radio. These radio stories sought to appeal to the most noble of American ideals: freedom, refuge, tolerance, and equality for all. The refugees interviewed spoke of their longtime desire to come to the United States and their commitment to American values and work ethic. The broadcasts frequently likened the refugees to the Pilgrims. For example, a broadcast entitled "Plymouth Rock 1949" was played on over 900 stations around the country.[31] Another program redefined the term "DP," recasting them as "delayed pilgrims," as if they had suffered not from racial persecution and genocide but from religious intolerance. In the show, an unnamed refugee thanks America for providing him and his fellow DPs with a new home and declares, "We are born today, for a second time." In spite of these overt Christian motifs, the program made no effort to mask the fact that some of the DPs were Jews, although this was downplayed in other broadcasts.

With a Republican sweep of Congress in November 1946, the work of the CCDP and its allies became more difficult. Advocates adopted a strategy of promoting the admission of 400,000 DPs from Europe, in order to downplay the fact that 100,000 of them would likely be Jews. Over the next two years, the CCDP lobbied members of Congress, promoted letter-writing campaigns, organized a mass media campaign across newspapers, magazines, and radio, and sponsored the film *Passport to Nowhere*, all the while downplaying the fact that many of the DPs in most need of help were Jews. Many national organizations and newspapers eventually endorsed the CCDP's proposal, but due to nativism, anticommunism, and anti-immigrant sentiments among the members of Congress, no action on their behalf was taken. Like the legislatures of most other countries where survivors sought refuge, members of

Congress used the argument that DPs coming to the United States would not be productive members of society and were likely to become public charges.

The legislation that Congress eventually passed in mid-1948 barely addressed the true extent of the DP crisis. Furthermore, its approach to immigration was marked by antipathy toward Jews and Soviet communism. Instead of focusing on DPs still in Allied-controlled camps, the Displaced Persons Act primarily concerned the admission of agricultural workers (which generally excluded Jews) and refugees from Baltic states (many of whom were escaping Soviet rule) and limited the total number of visas to just over 200,000 outside the quota system. It explicitly prohibited the admission of DPs who arrived in the American sector after December 22, 1945, which meant that many Jewish survivors who fled Poland after the pogroms in Kielce were prevented from consideration. The bill also gave special consideration to the ethnic Germans who had been expelled from Soviet-controlled territory. In spite of a large outcry against the proposed legislation by Jewish and non-Jewish groups alike, with deep reluctance Truman signed the bill, an act that negated his December 1945 directive to provide preferential treatment to DPs under immigration laws.[32]

Truman, however, was able to maneuver around many of the discriminatory aspects of the legislation by appointing commissioners who were sympathetic to the plight of Jewish DPs and willing to interpret the law in the most flexible manner possible. The newly formed Displaced Persons Commission had to overcome numerous obstacles put in place by Congress, as well as painfully slow administrative processes and the byzantine requirements of the legislation.

Standing at odds with the efforts by many elected officials to prevent Jewish DPs from entering the country are the attempts by government officials to recruit Nazis to the United States for their scientific knowledge to fight the Cold War. As the work of several investigative journalists has shown, even prior to the end of the war, the United States was already laying the groundwork for the postwar struggle against communism.[33] The most controversial of all efforts to recruit and provide sanctuary for Nazis went by the code name Operation Paperclip. Directed out of the Pentagon and over the strong objections of the State Department, the program brought as many as 1,600 German scientists—many of whom were former Nazis—to the United States to work on some of the most controversial military projects of the Cold War. As reporter Annie Jacobsen has written, "Operation Paperclip left behind a legacy of ballistic missiles, sarin gas cluster bombs, underground bunkers, space capsules, and weaponized bubonic plague."[34] In spite of President Truman's directive that forbade the recruitment of figures who were closely associated with the Nazi Party, members of the US intelligence service regularly offered positions to scientists who were involved in of the regime's most murderous programs. The US military hid their Nazi pasts (which were paper clipped to their new government files—hence the name of the program), provided them with salaries and housing, and made it possible for their wives and children to join them in America. Very few scientists were prevented from participating in the program because of their past association with the Nazi regime. Even chemists from the IG Farben conglomerate received sanctuary in the country. During the war, IG Farben had held the patent on the murderous gas Zyklon B and built an industrial complex at Auschwitz that relied on the slave labor of tens of thousands. One of the most notorious recruits was Wernher von Braun, the engineer credited for designing the German V-2 rocket, the first long-range guided ballistic missile and which was used extensively by Germany against England. Other beneficiaries of Operation Paperclip had served directly with Hitler, Himmler, or Göring. Many had actively participated in the murder of European Jews. A few had even faced trial at Nuremberg.

Although Operation Paperclip was a military secret, word of the project soon got out. In 1946, there was a brief campaign against the project, which had support by Albert Einstein, Eleanor Roosevelt, Norman Vincent Peale, A. Philip Randolph, and Rabbi Stephen Wise.[35] Protests, however, were insufficient to bring Operation Paperclip to a halt. Within eighteen months of the end of World War II, the priorities of the Cold War outweighed any remaining moral or legal qualms over colluding with former Nazi enemies.

With the election of an overwhelmingly Democratic Congress in the fall of 1948, hopes ran high for an amended DP Act that would be more generous in terms of the number of refugees allowed into the United States and more flexible when it came to recognizing the needs of Jewish survivors. However, the strongly isolationist and antisemitic senator from Nevada Pat McCarran managed to block substantive reform for well over a year.[36] Reflecting Cold War priorities, McCarran put forward a bill that would give preference to ethnic Germans expelled from Soviet-controlled lands in Eastern Europe. Eventually, more liberal voices prevailed during what was a bruising fight on the Senate floor. The final bill passed by both houses in June 1950 allowed for an additional 100,000 DPs over the 1948 Act to enter and included other groups of refugees as well, such as expelled ethnic Germans, members of the Polish Anders' Army, and European Jews who had found refuge during the war in Shanghai, bringing the total number of persons allowed to enter the country under the terms of the act to 415,000. In his statement about the amended bill, Truman affirmed his commitment to the way in which DPs strengthened the country:

> The countrymen of these displaced persons have brought to us in the past the best of their labor, their hatred of tyranny, and their love of freedom. They have helped our country grow in strength and moral leadership. I have

every confidence that the new Americans who will come to our country under the provisions of the present bill will also make a substantial contribution to our national well-being.[37]

The struggle for this amended act had been so contentious that nationwide sympathy toward DPs diminished further, and those responsible for overseeing the new arrivals' resettlement found themselves working in a much less friendly atmosphere. In all, Dinnerstein estimates, "fewer than 100,000 Jewish DPs reached the United States as a result of the Truman Directive and the two DP acts."[38] In total, approximately 140,000 Jewish DPs arrived between 1946 and 1954 (a number that includes those who entered via the existing immigration quota system).[39] Most were selected because at least one family member had professional skills that would make them "useful" to the country. Following the passage of the 1950 legislation, most DP camps emptied out and many of the remaining DPs found homes in the United States, Canada, and Western and Central European countries. A majority settled in Israel after the founding of the state in 1948. In a bitter turn of history, some were provided with the homes of Palestinian Arabs who were forcibly expelled during Israel's war of independence.[40] Approximately 2,000 DPs remained in camps by 1953. The final DP camp at Föhrenwald was shuttered in 1957.

To Hannah Arendt, the very existence of such a category of "displaced persons"—people who were stateless and therefore without the protections or rights that only governments can provide to citizens—was yet another sign of the failure of democratic societies to pose an effective challenge to mid-century totalitarian regimes. In her 1951 magnum opus, *The Origins of Totalitarianism*, which she wrote in the midst of the DP crisis, she argued that the problem of these new stateless people was entirely without precedent in the world:

The first loss which the rightless suffered was the loss of their homes, and this meant the loss of the entire social texture into which they were born and in which they established for themselves a distinct place in the world. This calamity is far from unprecedented; in the long memory of history, forced migrations of individuals or whole groups of people for political or economic reasons look like everyday occurrences. What is unprecedented is not the loss of a home but the impossibility of finding a new one. Suddenly, there was no place on earth where migrants could go without the severest restrictions, no country where they would be assimilated, no territory where they could found a new community of their own. This, moreover, had next to nothing to do with any material problem of overpopulation; it was a problem not of space but of political organization. Nobody had been aware that mankind, for so long a time considered under the image of a family of nations, had reached the stage where whoever was thrown out of one of these tightly organized closed communities found himself thrown out of the family of nations altogether ...

Their plight is not that they are not equal before the law, but that no law exists for them.[41]

The American Jewish community and postwar mobility

Into what sort of Jewish community were Holocaust survivors entering? How welcoming of an environment were they to find? One scholar of this period has referred to the late 1940s and 1950s as a "lull between two storms" for American Jewry, situated between the war and Holocaust of the 1940s and the racial violence and upheavals of the 1960s.[42] It was a time in which Jews in America experienced an unprecedented decline in antisemitism (although housing discrimination and quotas at universities still existed in some places) and almost no antisemitic violence. In the two decades following the end of World War II, the American Jewish community found itself enjoying many of the fruits of its efforts over the previous half century to be accepted into the white middle class. Like Italian Americans, Irish Americans, and Polish Americans, Jewish Americans had once been among the "in between" races, but by the 1950s they were broadly thought of as white, if still distinctively Jewish. They were able to partake of the dramatic postwar economic expansion, which allowed them to rise in socioeconomic status.

The anthropologist Karen Brodkin has demonstrated that two acts of Congress were instrumental to Jews' new socioeconomic and racial status: the Servicemen's Readjustment Act of 1944 and the Housing Act of 1949.[43] The GI Bill, as the first of these is known, allowed nearly eight million former World War II veterans (just over 50 percent of the total) to attend college, university, or training programs, as well as receive low-cost mortgages, affordable business loans, or unemployment compensation. The Housing Act was designed to reduce urban blight, facilitate new suburban construction, and bring millions of American families into the middle class via low interest, long-term housing loans. It doubled the number of homeowners in the United States over the subsequent two decades. For American Jews, these two pieces of legislation were utterly transformative. Nearly two-thirds of all Jewish men whose parents had largely been members of the working class or small business owners now began to join the professions, entering fields such as medicine, law, real estate, and finance.

With their new wealth and with the financial assistance of the Federal Housing Authority, many Jews joined the wave of white city dwellers who moved to the outskirts of the city or into new suburban communities where they had access to better schools, jobs, and resources. In New York City alone, 1.24 million people, most of whom were white, left for the suburbs after the war. At the same time an influx of African Americans, Puerto Ricans, and other nonwhite immigrant groups numbering nearly the same maintained the city's overall population.[44] As Jews left Manhattan for the outer boroughs, the Jewish population of Queens nearly quadrupled in size between 1940 and the mid-1950s. In some Queens neighborhoods, two-thirds of all residents were Jewish.[45]

While these legislative acts helped lower the racial barriers to Jewish integration into the white middle class in the postwar decades, they also kept African Americans in poverty and segregated into poor urban neighborhoods, further deepening the racial divide between blacks and whites. Although the GI Bill technically applied equally to all Americans, racism within the military during the war years led to 39 percent of black soldiers being dishonorably discharged (as opposed to 21 percent of white soldiers), thus rendering them ineligible for benefits.[46] And since historically white universities were no more inclined to admit African American students after the war as they had been before, the GI Bill had a much less positive effect on the African American population as a whole. Given that administration of the GI Bill was left to local—and therefore typically white—authorities, African American veterans were systematically excluded from its benefits. In the words of one study of the bill's effects, "Written under Southern auspices, the law was deliberately designed to accommodate Jim Crow."[47] Furthermore, the Housing Act of 1949 was intended to reduce urban blight, but it did nothing to address the widespread practices of racial discrimination in lending, the redlining of neighborhoods, restrictive covenants, and the need for new urban housing projects. As a consequence, white Americans, including most Jews, could leave the city should they choose, while most African Americans were, by default and design, forced to stay.[48]

Even after Jews moved into the middle class and became part of the white majority, they maintained their prewar affinity toward the Democratic Party and remained deeply liberal, especially in domestic politics. Hasia Diner has noted that "with the exception of the dwindling Jewish far left, Jews subscribed to a political vision that emphasized a belief in progress and a commitment to Western values, to America, and to the idea that people of good will could together eradicate prejudice and foster a common culture that tolerated difference."[49] Later a Jewish conservative critic of liberalism would famously complain that Jews "earn like Episcopalians and vote like Puerto Ricans."[50] The reasons for the persistence of this political stance have been disputed, but some scholars have speculated that it was born out of loyalty toward President Roosevelt for the New Deal, which helped many poor urban

Jews, and for pushing the country to enter World War II and the fight against Nazism. By the mid-twentieth century, the Democratic Party became responsive to Jewish immigrants' desire to become full Americans.[51]

American Jews' newly achieved status led some community leaders and Jewish thinkers to fear that young Jews would assimilate fully into the mainstream and no longer identify with their religious or ethnic heritage. In a 1948 study entitled *Crisis, Catastrophe and Survival: A Jewish Balance Sheet, 1914–1948*, Jewish demographer Jacob Lestschinsky attempted to calculate the lives lost in the Holocaust and to identify the key issues facing Jewry in the generations to come.[52] As a Jewish nationalist from Eastern Europe who had long sympathized with Zionism and Yiddishism, Lestschinsky had always viewed Jews as a separate people who were historically, culturally, and religiously distinct from other nations. He was focused primarily on the future tasks awaiting the Jewish people, yet he was also deeply pessimistic and argued that the recent cataclysm had accelerated a process of prewar Jewish decline to such an extent that it was unclear if the Jewish people could ever recover.

Writing in New York City for the World Jewish Congress's Institute of Jewish Affairs, Lestschinsky was worried for the Jewish future. Numerically speaking, the Holocaust had reduced the number of Jews in Europe to the levels of well more than a century earlier. In 1840 the number of Jews in Europe was 3.95 million and by 1939 it had risen to 9.5 million (even accounting for the more than 2.5 million who had emigrated out of Europe in this period). By 1947 the number of European Jews had been reduced to 3 million, with the vast majority who remained living in the Soviet Union. With nearly 6 million Jews (a number inflated by approximately 1 million), the United States in 1948 was home to over 50 percent of the world Jewish population, which totaled just over 11 million. Lestschinsky argued that the impact of the destruction would last generations and that the "biological restoration" of world Jewry would be painfully slow, if it was even possible, as the birth rate among Jews in Western countries was significantly lower than what had been that of Jews in Eastern Europe. He further noted that while the Nazi genocide had brought about a radical change in the composition of world Jewry, it also accelerated a "process of disintegration of Eastern European Jewry" that "was unmistakably under way everywhere" prior to the war. By this, Lestschinsky meant that in spite of its rapid population growth over the past century and the development of many new secular Jewish national and cultural movements (such as Zionism and Yiddishism), Jews had in fact been becoming more secular and acculturating into their host societies.

The most significant effect of the Holocaust, Lestschinsky argued, was that the "center" of the Jewish people had shifted from Europe to the United States. He feared that this new reality did not augur well for the future. For most of its millennia-long history, Jews tended to live and work separately from non-Jews and the two populations only tended to engage one another during moments of commercial activity. European Jewry had lived in enough cultural, religious, geographic, and commercial separation from non-Jews to maintain their distinctiveness and forge their own national destiny. As he put it:

> The Jewish populations [in Eastern Europe] ... were firmly rooted in their countries of domicile. They had lived there for hundreds of years in a way of life distinctly their own; they had built a system of institutions which derived directly from the vast heritage of their past; they were therefore inspired by faith in their ability to withstand the assault of the non-Jewish environment and to develop their national identity more fully.[53]

By contrast, the United States was a society "with a very high potential for assimilation," which gave Jews the opportunity to intermarry and become part of the majority. By living in a democratic society that did not legally, socially, and economically exclude them from full participation, Jews faced a new threat of disappearing as a distinct people. Without the European Jewish population, which in spite of its own increasing rate of assimilation had served as a well-spring for Jewish cultural, spiritual, and national creativity for Jews worldwide, the community in the United States was simply not strong enough to assume the mantle of leadership that had been thrust upon them: "From so closely-knit an ethnic entity, the Jews have been transformed, in their countries of immigration, into disunited individuals, who lose their own language in the course of one or two generations and are able to transmit to their children only a meager cultural heritage which becomes easily dissipated in the foreign environment."[54] The one hope, according to Lestschinsky, was the nascent Jewish state in Palestine (not yet founded when his study was published in early 1948). He looked optimistically to the Jewish community there as providing a communal response to the destruction of European Jewry, but recognized that at only 6 percent of the world Jewish population, its influence was largely spiritual and ideological, rather than numerical or economic.

Lestschinsky did not accurately predict the future course of world Jewry. Two decades later in the United States, the rise of "hybrid" identities among many of those who were of the "in between races" a generation or two earlier allowed Jewish Americans to exist side by side with Italian American, Irish Americans, and Polish Americans who could proudly proclaim their allegiance both to their adopted country and the Old World. He also did not anticipate just how rapidly the Jewish community in Israel would grow, outpacing the United States in the early twenty-first century to become home to the largest Jewish community in the world. Nevertheless, by expressing concern over the "dangers" of cultural assimilation in the United States, he anticipated a significant portion of the agenda of Jewish communal leaders, who over the next several decades expressed fears that the Americanization of Jews would mean the end of Jewish communal identity.

Indeed, in the postwar period American Jews lost much of the cohesiveness they had maintained prior to the war. Increased rates of intermarriage led some Jews to disaffiliate with Judaism and its communal institutions, as Lestschinsky had feared. Greater dispersion weakened many of the familial, economic, and ethnic bonds that had existed for several generations. However, other Jews—in particular second- and third-generation Americans—underwent something of a renewal and deepened their ties in part because of their high rates of concentration and proximity to urban areas.[55] As Jews moved to the suburbs they were financially able to move their institutions with them. The sociologist Samuel Heilman depicts this period as a time of "starting over" for American Jews, in which they created a Judaism replete with communal institutions, educational programs, and organizations that were fully compatible with middle-class American values.[56] As David Kaufman has shown, the phenomenon of the "shul with a pool"—synagogues that were as much Jewish community gathering sites as centers of worship—became ever more widespread in the postwar era.[57]

Identifying their Jewishness as a matter of religious preference rather than racial or ethnic particularism, Jews in the postwar period sought to reintroduce themselves as fully compatible with American society. In an article in *Life* magazine in 1950, Rabbi Philip S. Bernstein, who had been a leader in the campaigns on behalf of DPs seeking to resettle in the United States, sought to explain for readers "what the Jews believe."[58] In this essay, which was soon expanded to a full-length book, Bernstein presented Jews in strictly religious terms—and nonthreatening ones at that. Beginning his essay by declaring that "the Jew has no single organized church," he emphasized American Jews' loyalty to the United States. Bernstein then surveyed the central tenets of Jewish faith and practice and showed how they were compatible with American religious traditions. He ended the work by explaining why Jews had rejected Jesus's message, depicting that rejection as a consequence not of Christ's own teachings, but that of his followers, who used it as a tool to persecute Jews in subsequent centuries. In a similar vein, a 1952 essay in *Look* magazine by Rabbi Morris N. Kertzer sought to answer the question, "What is a Jew?"[59] In an attempt to "set the record straight," Kertzer sought to minimize any lingering anxiety that Christians might feel about Jews by stressing their common belief in the Old Testament and the fact that Judaism was not a proselytizing religion. Kertzer went further than Bernstein to stress Jewish compatibility with the United States. Adopting a question and answer format, his essay asked, "Is an American Jew's first loyalty to Israel or America?" and then responded unequivocally that "the only loyalty of an American Jew is to the United States of America—without any ifs, ands, or buts."[60]

The Jewish community into which Holocaust survivors arrived, therefore, was one that was increasingly focused on its future and optimistic about the days ahead. While some leaders and scholars agonized about the weakening of Jewish identity through assimilation, most Jews felt comfortable about the compromises they had made in order to be *both* Jewish *and* American. The arrival of 140,000 Jewish DPs between 1947 and 1954 was, then, something of a "mixed blessing" both for the community and the DPs themselves. While DPs were generally welcomed and very often had their immediate needs provided for, many also received the message quite explicitly that they needed to adapt quickly to their new homes and forget the past. As Hannah Arendt described,

> As soon as we were saved—and most of us had to be saved several times—we started our new lives and tried to follow as closely as possible all the good advice our saviors passed on to us. We were told to forget; and we forgot quicker than anybody ever could imagine. In a friendly way we were reminded that the new country would become a new home; and after four weeks in France or six weeks in America, we pretended to be Frenchmen or Americans.[61]

Shifting narratives of American Jewish silence

In recent years, scholars have significantly revised a long-standing assumption about how the American Jewish community contended with the legacy of the Holocaust in the immediate postwar years. For decades, it was commonly accepted and frequently asserted—by scholars, survivors, and members of the Jewish community—that until the early 1960s, most American Jews consciously avoided talking about the Holocaust—to one another, to society as a whole, and, as the quotation by Arendt suggests, to survivors in particular. According to this understanding, many Jews felt a strong sense of shame about European Jews' destruction as well as their alleged passivity during the war, while others felt partly responsible for not having taken a more active role to stop the murder of Jews overseas. Still others were worried that paying too much attention to the destruction of European Jewry would only highlight increasingly discredited notions of Jewish "difference," threatening their newly attained status within the American mainstream. Some have also suggested more simply that this relative silence was a consequence of the lack of comprehensive histories of the Holocaust, which began to appear only in the 1960s.[62]

This self-imposed silence, as the common narrative asserts, was shattered in the 1960s. Events in 1961, including the dramatic coverage of the trial of Adolf Eichmann in Jerusalem, the Hollywood film *Judgment at Nuremberg*, and the release of historian Raul Hilberg's comprehensive history of the Holocaust, *The Destruction of the European Jews*, raised American Jewry's consciousness about the Holocaust and began a long period of soul searching. As well, the 1960s was a time when many white Americans began to explore their own particular ethnic histories, which led many to proudly assert new hybrid identities as Polish American, Irish American, Greek American, Italian American, and so on.[63] For Jews who had relinquished so much of their particularism in the quest to assimilate into American culture, the Holocaust (along with new affinities toward Israel) soon became increasingly central to a newly refashioned Jewish American identity, one that had become largely divested of any conspicuous religious and racial differences.[64] By the end of the decade, Holocaust commemorations, memorials, and educational efforts were more frequent in Jewish communities.

As the historian Hasia Diner and others have amply demonstrated, however, this account of American Jewish silence does not easily square with the historical record.[65] In particular, Diner's richly documented study shows that from some of the earliest reports of mass violence against European Jews, American Jews responded with a mixture of anxiety, sadness, and a desire to commemorate the tragedy. Moreover, they responded publicly and reverentially, in memorials intended both for the Jewish community itself and for the larger public. From the early 1940s onward, and with growing conviction, clarity, and assertiveness, American Jewish organizations sought to commemorate, memorialize, and impart lessons of the Holocaust in ways that corresponded to their needs at the time. For example, American Jews reimagined Passover *haggadot* (ritual texts that tell the story of the Jews' emancipation from Egyptian slavery in the biblical era) to enshrine the memory of the Holocaust into an annual commemoration. They sought, with varying degrees of success, to create physical memorials in urban centers and in Jewish cemeteries, synagogues, and community centers. Organizations raised funds to support Jewish communal welfare at home, in Europe, and in Israel in the name of the Holocaust. From sermons and the recitation of new prayers to the creation of new education curriculum in Jewish schools, remembering the Holocaust quickly became an obligation assumed by many American Jews.

Those Jews in America who had direct ties to Europe felt the destruction of the Holocaust most acutely, and soon after the end of the war, many began the task of documenting, commemorating, and memorializing their former communities. For example, members of Jewish hometown societies in America, known in Yiddish as *landsmanshaftn*, produced *Yizher bikher* (memorial books) to commemorate destroyed Jewish communities in the absence of gravestones or religious burials. Such works, which number in the hundreds, are typically in Yiddish or Hebrew and contain reflections, photos, sketches, and lists of residents. As the scholar Jonathan Boyarin has noted, "The scope of the genre is unprecedented and commensurate with the Jewish disaster in the Holocaust."[66] Scholarly and cultural organizations of Eastern European Jews quickly focused their efforts on the task of documenting the historical record of their people and recovering their remaining cultural artifacts. The Yiddish Scientific Institute (YIVO), which had relocated its headquarters to the United States soon after the outbreak of the war in Europe, immediately mounted exhibitions, published several of the earliest historical and popular accounts of the genocide, and was central in the effort to save vast archives of the recently destroyed Jewish communities. In 1946, YIVO's director, Max Weinreich, published the widely read *Hitler's Professors*, a condemnation of the German scientists and scholars who provided their expertise to the Nazi regime.[67] The following year, the labor leader, Yiddish journalist, and editor Raphael Abramovitch edited the bilingual Yiddish/English photographic collection *Di farshvundene velt/The Vanished World*, which offered a pictorial history of Eastern European Jewry in the years before World War II.[68]

Although recent scholarship has set out to reverse the conventional narrative about American Jews' "silence" in the postwar period, significant issues remain for historians to consider. Chief among them is the fact, as explained by Hannah Arendt in "We Refugees," that many Holocaust survivors and refugees from Nazism in the United States received the message after the war that their experiences were not valued and that they would be better off staying silent about it. This impression abounds in survivor memoirs. For example, Ruth Kluger writes about this phenomenon as beginning soon after her liberation. In her memoir of the Holocaust, she recounted that even US soldiers refused to acknowledge her and her mother's story of escape from the Christianstadt forced labor camp:

> My mother determined to try out her English, walked up to the first American uniform in view, a military policeman directing traffic, and told him in a few words that we had escaped from a concentration camp. Since I knew no English, I couldn't understand his answer, but his gesture was unmistakable. His put his hands over his ears and turned away. My mother translated. He had had his fill of people who claimed they had been in the camps. They were all over the place. Please, leave him alone![69]

Auschwitz survivor Vladek Spiegelman, whose son Art wrote the Pulitzer Prize–winning graphic memoir *Maus*, told him at the start of his project, "It would take *many* books, my life, and no one wants anyway to hear such stories."[70]

It may be, in fact, that both narratives of the American Jewish response to the Holocaust are correct in their own way. As Diner and others have shown, many individual Jews, Jewish communities, and organizations *did* speak passionately and consistently about the Holocaust in the postwar years and earnestly sought to convey their heartbreak, outrage, and determination to prevent such acts in the future. At the same time, however, many survivors who came to the United States were marginalized, told to forget the past, and found that their stories were ignored. The contrast between Holocaust commemorations and survivors' experiences might have been a reflection of the reality that the American Jewish community needed to make sense of the Holocaust on its own terms and through its own voices and did not want this process challenged by the lived experiences of survivors, which did not neatly fit with how postwar American Jews perceived themselves. This might explain why, as the following discussion describes, Jewish welfare organizations took a deeply paternalistic stances toward the resettlement of Jewish DPs after the war and often ignored their most pressing psychological needs. This also might help illuminate why some of Americans' first encounters with the Holocaust occurred through rather anodyne accounts that affirmed their sense of self rather than challenge it, such as Anne Frank's *Diary* or its Broadway play version.

American Jewish philanthropy and resettlement efforts

Efforts to assist DPs both in Europe and after their arrival in the United States were spearheaded by Jewish relief organizations and paid for almost entirely by private funds donated by the American Jewish community. Lucy Dawidowicz notes that Jewish Federations raised $57 million in 1945, and $131 million the following year, to assist DPs both at home and in Europe.[71] One agency established to assist refugees was so large that it was second only to the American Red Cross in terms of budget.[72] In spite of this philanthropy and the highly positive image regularly put forward in the press and by agency publications, Jewish DPs entering the United States often did not get the support they needed but rather received assistance according to what agencies paternalistically determined was best for them. In her study of hundreds of case files, historian Beth Cohen has shown that the organizations most responsible for assisting the resettlement of DPs, such as the United Service for New Americans (USNA), the New York Association for New Americans, and Jewish Family and Children's Services, systematically approached their work in such a way that treated the survivors as simple immigrants looking to resettle in a new homeland, favored the goals of rapid resettlement above all, and often disregarded their most pressing physical, psychological, economic, and religious needs.[73] As Ruth Kluger recounts, the idea that survivors were simply immigrants of another stripe often led to her and her mother being condescended to by prewar refugees of Nazism, who insisted that they become self-sufficient quickly (as they had done) and not ask for too many handouts. As she writes, "They were proud of having weathered so much hardship and of the elbow grease they had demonstrated. The wives had earned a pittance cleaning houses. We had spent the same time as slave laborers, not earning anything, but that was a different story and didn't count."[74]

Although the newly arrived DPs faced many difficulties in the resettlement process, organizational pronouncements regularly touted their progress. In the fall of 1947, for example, William Rosenwald, USNA's honorary president and national chairman of the United Jewish Appeal, claimed that DPs were adjusting quickly to their lives in America and "thousands are already usefully employed and self-sustaining."[75] USNA's occasional publication, *New Neighbors*, published between 1948 and 1952, reinforced the notion that DPs were fully capable of transitioning quickly to life in the United States. This narrative was clearly a strategic move to counter those critics who argued that these survivors of the Holocaust were too scarred, too enfeebled, or too unassimilable to become Americans. Each issue of *New Neighbors* was filled with success stories of DPs quickly adjusting to their new ways of life. Photographs featured a group of thirty-seven children "just off the boat from European DP camps" visiting the circus, wearing cowboy hats, and learning to eat hotdogs. Another showed a photo of a three-year-old saluting the American flag while wearing a USNA pin. The front-page story of the September 1949 issue features a photograph of a young boy eating an enormous piece of cake under the headline "Born in a Concentration Camp, He Lived to See Coney Island." There was a particularly strong focus on DPs settling in places other than New York, especially in the American South and West. The May–June 1948 edition, for example, featured stories about DPs settling in Dallas, Texas, where they became "completely self-supporting" and "solid citizens" who took up English, began the process of naturalization, and quickly melted into the surrounding society. One striking photo in the May 1949 issue features a group of DPs, among them an Auschwitz survivor, a refugee who found shelter in Shanghai, and two brothers who hid with the Polish underground, donating blood at a Red Cross center.[76]

The pleasant public face of the resettlement project, and its claims of the DPs' easy assimilation, belied the difficulties many refugees actually experienced. As Beth Cohen describes,

> The newcomers' voices in the agency files make it clear that it would be false to conclude that self-maintenance equaled adjustment. Hardly. The

'HOT DOG!' SAY DP CHILDREN ENJOYING DAY AT THE CIRCUS

TASTE OF AMERICA. 37 children, just off the boat from European DP camps, had the first carefree good time of their lives when they were treated to an afternoon at the circus by William Rosenwald, Honorary Chairman of United Service for New Americans and National Chairman of the United Jewish Appeal, and Samuel Hausman, Chairman of the United Jewish Appeal of Greater New York. Mr. Rosenwald is shown assisting famed clown Emmett Kelly in a lesson on eating a hot dog, for the entertainment of Mr. Hausman and the youngsters. *(See story of UJA on page 8.)*

FIGURE 3.3 New Neighbors, *United Service for New Americans, Inc. Vol. 1 No. 2 (May–June 1948): 12.*

road was bumpy and fraught with dangers to which the caregivers were all too blind. Moreover, it was less a fresh beginning than a piecing together of a path that had been irrevocably shattered in Europe. In the agencies' rush to close the refugees' cases, this was forgotten.[77]

The organizations and case workers assigned to assist DPs reflected the strong tendency toward conformity and social acceptance that was prevalent

BANNER OCCASION: The stars and stripes form a symbolic and stirring framework, in this intentional double exposure, as three-year old Shirley Weitzman salutes the U. S. on her arrival with her family aboard the Gen. Heinzelman. The DP ship arrived in New York while the Annual Meeting, which took place January 14-15, was in progress.

FIGURE 3.4 New Neighbors, *United Service for New Americans, Inc. Vol. 3 No. 2 (February 1950): 5.*

throughout the United States in the postwar period. The emphasis on quick and seamless assimilation also stemmed from a deep concern that refugees might jeopardize the newly achieved status of the established Jewish community. This was most apparent in the desire of the organizations to avoid housing the majority of newly arriving refugees in New York City. They were fearful that the presence of so many needy Jews would spark an antisemitic backlash and threaten the status of all Jews in the city. Thus even though most DPs wished to remain in New York (and approximately 60 percent ultimately did), refugees were not often given much input into where they would be housed, and resettlement programs sought to disperse them across the United States. DPs ended up in forty-six states, often in cities which were far away from major Jewish centers, such as Cheyenne, Denver, and Tulsa, and the USNA petitioned even smaller communities with just a handful of Jews to help absorb refugees. Instead of settling into life in New York City—historically a welcoming home for new migrants with the largest concentration of Jews in the country and the greatest number of social services—many survivors found themselves in communities that they felt "dumped" into and that, in turn, often felt put upon to support them.

FIGURE 3.5 New Neighbors, *United Service for New Americans, Inc. Vol. 2 No. 4 (September 1949): 5.*

Many DPs arrived without resources, identifiable work skills, or much knowledge of English. Many were also suffering from the physical and psychological traumas they had experienced during the Holocaust. About one-third arrived entirely alone, while others had very young children, new spouses, or other family members accompanying them. Technically, the Hoover-era LPC proviso was still in effect, and agencies had to secure affidavits testifying that these new migrants would not require public assistance. However, many of the new arrivals required tremendous amounts of financial help. Many sponsors did not fulfill their obligation to assist DPs, putting further stress on relief groups.

When DPs arrived in the United States, they were often first taken to a reception center where they would typically stay for a few weeks up to a few months. There, DPs met with case workers, who were tasked with locating them opportunities for occupational training, homes, and medical care. Many DPs required extended care and treatment, but agencies were under directives to provide no more than one year of support, by which time DPs should be self-sufficient. After the end of the one-year adjustment period, most cases were marked "closed" regardless of whether the person had successfully managed to become self-supporting. As Cohen states, "From 1950 on, getting the refugee working and off relief became the primary goal and the standard by which the agencies judged their success."[78] Case after case reveals that when the needs of refugees did not square with the goals of the resettlement agencies, refugees often found themselves bullied and pressured into taking up permanent residences before they were ready or assuming occupations that did not correspond to their education or experience. Tensions between case workers and clients often escalated dramatically. At times, when refugees did not follow orders to take any available work, they found themselves at risk of having all of their support revoked. Many formerly well-paid professionals were pressured to take up jobs where they had to perform menial or unskilled labor.

As historian Rebecca Kobrin has shown, DPs who were women often had much more difficult experiences than men. For men, the process of Americanization meant becoming the family's chief breadwinner. It allowed them eventually to obtain vocational or professional training and to find careers. For women, however, it meant transforming themselves in such ways so as to conform with American postwar notions of motherhood and femininity. In many instances, it required sacrificing one's career goals in order to satisfy social service agencies' expectations for women.[79] Professional women, therefore, often suffered a double blow. Kobrin demonstrates that "it was in fact female doctors and dentists who suffered the greatest losses, both professionally and personally, by immigrating to the United States."[80] They were regularly denied the retraining options available to their male counterparts and were expected to place the needs of their families over that of their careers—demands not placed upon men. If women complained about their loss in status and the unfair expectations placed upon them, they were regularly told to forget the past and adapt to their new circumstances.

Resettlement in comparative perspective: DPs in Canada and Israel

That survivors faced difficulties in adjusting to their new lives was not unique to the United States. In Canada, where 35,000 survivors and their children resettled from 1947 to 1955, society as a whole was not particularly disposed toward welcoming these refugees from the Holocaust. As in the United States, Canadian policy favored young immigrants who were able to contribute economically to the country and would not require public assistance, while survivors with illnesses or disabilities, the elderly, or those without occupational skills were denied entry visas.[81] The extant Jewish community expressed an ambivalence similar to that of their US counterparts, and, numbering only 170,000, was ill-equipped to meet these new immigrants' needs in a sustained way. After being received with a display of generosity, most survivors found Canadian Jews to be unprepared to provide the much-needed long-term support. Social service agencies were unaware of and unable to deal with the psychological and physical trauma that the survivors had experienced, nor were agencies particularly attuned to the many obstacles that survivors would face while resettling in their new home. Many newcomers found themselves initially placed in occupations that barely paid subsistence wages and in housing that was overcrowded or otherwise inadequate. For years, survivors were left feeling as if they were permanent outsiders, even among other Jews. Many responded to this marginalization by forming their own independent networks of support.[82]

Although by the late 1950s many survivors had reestablished themselves and were integrated into the larger Canadian Jewish community, attitudes toward newly arriving survivors still had not significantly changed. The writer Eva Hoffman, for example, who was born in Cracow soon after the war to Jewish parents who had hidden during the Holocaust, departed Poland with her parents and younger sister and arrived in Montreal in the late 1950s, settling in Vancouver after an arduous trip across the country. As she describes in her memoir, *Lost in Translation*, the Hoffmans had not been DPs, but were among those relatively few Jewish families who were able, for a time, to rebuild their lives in Poland after the war. Eva's mother and father, who had lived near the city of Lvov, had lost nearly every member of their families during the war and yet were able to maintain a middle-class existence. The persistence of antisemitism in Poland—on one occasion, Eva's father was told that "the best thing Hitler did was to eliminate the Jews," and on another Eva herself was attacked by a gang of schoolchildren—and the increasing repression by Soviet authorities convinced the Hoffmans that they should emigrate.[83]

Although they had high expectations of their adopted country, the Hoffmans found life in Canada to be very difficult. In spite of her parents many skills, they were never able to achieve financial stability. Even more difficult to contend with were the attitudes of the more established Vancouver Jewish community, who looked upon the new arrivals as a burden. Their first hosts, in the name of making the Hoffmans self-sufficient, put them out after only a week—before they had any opportunity to learn English, find work, or locate new housing. For young Eva, assimilation to Canadian society was deeply invasive. Without asking her permission, a well-meaning older woman who had herself emigrated from Poland several years before forcibly shaved her armpits in an effort to make her conform to contemporary standards of beauty. Others pressured her regularly to present herself in feminine ways. Without any means to resist, she and her mother felt they had no choice but to assent. Eventually, the family was able to buy a tiny house, a "minimally furnished cell of the American Dream," and work as scrap dealers in order to make ends meet.[84] Although her parents considered themselves a "success story," they never fully recovered their former way of life and never quite lived up to the expectations of postwar Canadian Jewish society.

In Israel, the situation for survivors was often even more difficult. By the early 1950s, the number of Holocaust survivors who had immigrated to Israel totaled 400,000. The 1950 Law of Return allowed all Jews to gain citizenship automatically. Although Israel was exceptional in that it welcomed unlimited numbers of Jewish refugees, their reception in the new state was decidedly mixed. Prior to the creation of the state, in the 1930s, Zionist leaders in Palestine had negotiated a plan with German officials under the Haavara Agreement, which allowed for 60,000 Germans Jews to emigrate. These were mostly healthy Jews who possessed some resources and were willing to invest their energy into building up—rather than require assistance from—the new society, even if they were not necessarily ideologically Zionist. The Jewish survivors who arrived in Israel after the war, by contrast, were often in dire straits, weakened by their experiences and without resources, energy, or, in some cases, a commitment to Zionism. Nevertheless, between the end of World War II and the founding of the state, Zionist leaders were desperate to bring Jews—regardless of their physical condition—to Palestine, a task they viewed as necessary both to the survival of the Jewish people and to the establishment of a state. As Segev states, achieving a Jewish majority was vital, "Everyone understood that, without them [survivors], there was no chance of achieving statehood."[85] Through the Brihah ("Flight" in Hebrew) movement, as many as 150,000 Jewish DPs, most of whom were from Eastern European countries, traveled clandestinely to Palestine, with much of the financial support provided by the American Joint Distribution Committee.

Israel's material needs in its first years were great and its capacity to absorb such a large number of survivors was severely constrained. The resources expended in the absorption of the refugees, as a consequence, were utterly insufficient to the need. When refugees arrived, they often found themselves alone and without support in a society that was ashamed of them. Their traumatic experiences of defeat, capture, and death did not correspond with the new heroic image that young Israelis were fashioning for themselves in their new nation. As Segev put it, "The sabra ["native"] represented the national ideal, and the Holocaust survivor its reverse."[86] A widespread derogatory term for survivors was the Hebrew word *sabon*, meaning "soap," a reference to the false rumor that Nazis had used the fat from Jewish corpses to make soap during the war.[87] Finding housing was particularly challenging. Orphans were often sent to Jewish collective agricultural settlements, known as *kibbutzim*, where they were raised to be Israelis. Tens of thousands were required to live in tents in immigrant camps for months until homes could be found. It would be several years before Israel would come to terms both with the legacy of the Holocaust and its initial treatment of survivors.[88]

***

It also would take many years before attitudes toward Jewish DPs would change in the United States, and for DPs to be considered as "Holocaust survivors" who found their experiences valued, their testimony taken seriously by scholars and jurists, and their presence respected. As the next chapter will demonstrate, Americans initially came to be aware of the Holocaust not through the firsthand experiences that were recounted by the survivors in their midst. Rather, the growing awareness of what eventually came to be known as "the Holocaust" was shaped by the firsthand accounts, popular films, historical studies, and criminal trials of the two decades following the war.

4

America confronts the Holocaust, 1945–1960s

While American Jews were coming to terms with the consequences of the Holocaust, Americans as a whole were likewise learning about the catastrophe. Since few Americans experienced the Holocaust directly, they came to learn about it indirectly, particularly through published firsthand accounts, film and television, historical scholarship, and reports on the highly publicized trials of Nazi Party officials.

Examining these four sites of representation, this chapter charts the gradual development of awareness about the Holocaust in postwar America. It discusses how this understanding helped to create a climate of sympathy for what European Jews had suffered and helped facilitate American Jewry's incorporation into the white middle class. It looks at how the publication of diaries and memoirs by Jews who had experienced the Holocaust themselves or who had returned to Europe immediately after the end of the war often gave a human face to the tragedy and personalized for Americans a catastrophe that felt too large to otherwise comprehend. The chapter then explores how the film and television industries sought to portray the Holocaust, recognizing that they were often constrained by the commercial demands of the marketplace and a reluctance to put the suffering of Jews at the center of a work. As a result, the treatment of Jews was more often alluded to than confronted directly. A third means by which Americans came to learn about the fate of Jews under Nazism was through academic scholarship. Although Holocaust studies is today a thriving interdisciplinary field, until the early 1960s, there were very few scholars who felt that it was a subject worthy of research and those who did were usually ones who had in one way or another experienced Nazism directly. Undoubtedly the most comprehensive effort in the postwar era to explain the full suffering of Jews in the Holocaust to the world was the 1961 trial of the Nazi leader Adolf Eichmann. The fourth and final section in the chapter discusses both the Eichmann trial, held in the state of Israel, and the Nuremberg trials, which took place six months after the end of the war, and were in many respects the first attempt to establish a formal record of Nazi crimes against civilians.

As this chapter will also demonstrate, it took a great deal of time for our contemporary understanding of the Holocaust to coalesce. While there was no "conspiracy of silence" around the Holocaust in the first years after the war, few were rushing to talk about it. Archival records had to become available. People who had been traumatized needed time to speak. Artists, filmmakers, and scholars had to develop ways to represent it to broad audiences. The Holocaust seemed, and in many ways was, an event entirely without precedent. The extreme methods of killing, their scope, the overwhelming numbers of victims and perpetrators alike were staggering. When looking at this period, we discover that there was not one single moment when Americans became aware of the Holocaust. Instead, there was a gradual unfolding awareness that was punctuated by particular cultural events that seem to "introduce" the Holocaust to American audiences time and time again.

Firsthand accounts

Soon after the Holocaust—long before it was ever referred to by that name and well before most Americans fully comprehended that Hitler's plans included the murder of all Jews—several books appeared that provided accounts of Jewish life under Nazi rule. Some of these were written by Polish Jews who had found refuge in the United States during the war years and then returned to their native country to report on the condition of the surviving remnant in Poland. One such work was by Jacob Pat, a member of the Jewish Labor Committee and a Yiddish cultural activist. Pat traveled back to Poland in the winter of 1946 and met with the survivors of once-vibrant Jewish communities and heard story after story of the tragedies that had befallen Polish Jews. The following year, he published a report of his travels, first in Yiddish and then in English translation, under the title *Ashes and Fire*.[1] This work was one of the first detailed accounts of the fate of Polish Jews to appear in the United States, and it described the horrors of life in the ghettos, the Warsaw Ghetto uprising and the Jewish resistance movements, and the death camps at Chelmno and Auschwitz. Pat had encountered survivors around the country and was impressed at their many attempts to rebuild Jewish life in the postwar era. With the support of the Jewish Labor Committee, Pat was able to distribute relief funds to Jewish communities seeking to reestablish businesses, cooperatives, cultural projects, and welfare programs in Poland. Although the ferocity of many ethnic Poles' anti-Jewish violence after the war convinced large numbers of Jews that there was no longer a future for them in Poland,

Pat's work introduced to American readers a portrait of a tenacious people seeking to return to their lives.

Another work in this vein is that of the journalist Samuel L. Shneiderman, who returned to Poland soon after the war and found it unrecognizable. Shneiderman was no stranger to reporting on war—in the 1930s he had covered the Spanish Civil War for Polish newspapers—but he was shocked by what he witnessed when he flew into Warsaw in 1946. As he wrote in *Between Fear and Hope*:

> Finally we came above the ruins of the Polish capital. The empty shells of its bombed house and its gaping naked chimneys were flooded with sunlight. The green patches of parks helped me to orientate myself to the city where I had spent the best years of my youth but, though the plane was now flying very low, I was unable to recognize a single street.[2]

He devoted considerable space in his account to his time in Kielce, having arrived there immediately after the July 4 massacre. He was one of the first journalists who sent dispatches about the pogrom back to audiences in the United States. For much of his subsequent career, Shneiderman would dedicate himself to portraying, through both his writing and documentary filmmaking, the Yiddish world that the Nazis destroyed.

Books like *Ashes and Fire* and *Between Fear and Hope* reached only relatively small audiences. It was Mary Berg's *Warsaw Ghetto: A Diary* that initially captured the attention of large numbers of sympathetic American readers. Berg, who was born in 1924, wrote her diary while she was incarcerated in the ghetto from the time of its creation in October 1940 until late July 1942, on the eve of the deportations that brought as many as 250,000 Jewish prisoners to their deaths in the Treblinka killing center.[3] Because Mary's mother was a US citizen (she had moved to Poland in her youth and then married and had two daughters), Mary and her family had access to better housing and food than the vast majority imprisoned in the ghetto and did not face the same daily struggle to survive, although they were still trapped within its walls and the misery of life there was all around them. On the eve of the July 1942 deportations, they, along with other inmates who possessed foreign citizenships, found themselves transferred to the Gestapo-run Pawiak prison located inside the ghetto. They eventually learned that they were to be transferred to an internment camp in France, where they arrived in early 1943. Mary and her family spent the next year in the Vittel camp, which the Germans had established in the Vosges mountains near the German border as a "model" camp—housed in a repurposed luxury hotel, with sufficient food, recreational activities, and access to postal services—in order to show to critics that they were treating the prisoners in their custody well. In late winter 1944, Mary and her family were released from Vittel, having demonstrated that they possessed papers that would allow them to emigrate to the United States. They arrived in New York in March. Two months after their departure, approximately 250 prisoners in Vittel who did not possess valid foreign papers were deported to Auschwitz and murdered.[4]

Soon after disembarking in New York, Mary met Samuel Shneiderman, the author of *Between Fear and Hope*. In her suitcase, she carried twelve spiral-bound notebooks filled with diary entries that dated from her first days in the ghetto. It is unclear why Shneiderman was on the docks that day, but their meeting was fortuitous. Working together, they transformed her diary, which she had written in a Polish shorthand in order to protect the privacy of those about whom she was writing, into Yiddish prose. Two months later, the diaries were published in installments in the Yiddish newspaper *Der morgen zshurnal* (The Jewish Morning Journal). Soon, excerpts in translation began to appear in English- and German-language periodicals in the United States. By February 1945, less than a year after her arrival in New York, and while the war was still under way, a full English-language translation was published. It was reviewed widely and favorably. Berg achieved a bit of celebrity status, and used it in public campaigns against Nazi aggression. With her family, she led a demonstration at New York's City Hall on behalf of Polish Jewry. She was interviewed in

FIGURE 4.1 *Portrait of Miriam Wattenberg (Mary Berg).*

newspapers. She also participated in radio interviews, including one with the famous journalist I. F. Stone, who included her in a discussion entitled "Forum for Democracy" which focused on the subject of "war criminals, crime and punishment." During this discussion, Berg called for those responsible to be punished for their acts.[5]

American readers were struck by Berg's unflinching eyewitness account of life in the Warsaw Ghetto. Explaining that she was one of the relatively fortunate ones who was afforded a protected status on account of her mother's citizenship, Berg recounted the suffering of the masses around her. She described starving people begging for scraps of rotting food, the murder of a young man who had been rounded up for labor service, random shootings by German guards at the ghetto's exits, the devastating consequence of a typhus epidemic, and perhaps worst of all, the round-up of Jews (what Berg called "deportations and street pogroms") at a rate of 3,000 persons per day to be sent the ghetto's *Umschlagplatz* (departure point). These deportees were told that they were being sent to labor camps in the east. (In reality, they were brought to Treblinka, where they were murdered.) She discussed the suicide of ghetto leader Adam Czerniakow as well as the complicated role of the Jewish Council and the Jewish Police. While confined in the Pawiak prison, she was able to witness some of the most wretched scenes of violence. In August 1942, in the midst of the deportations, she wrote:

> Behind the Pawiak gate, we are experiencing all the terror that is abroad in the ghetto. For the last few nights we have been unable to sleep. The noise of the shooting, the cries of despair, are driving us crazy. I have to summon all my strength to write these notes. I have lost count of the days, and I do not know what day it is. But what does it matter? We are here as on a little island amidst an ocean of blood. The whole ghetto is drowning in blood. We literally see fresh human blood, we can smell it. Does the outside world know anything about it? Why does no one come to our aid? I cannot go on living; my strength is exhausted. How long are we going to be kept here to witness all this?[6]

Within a few years of her diary's publication, Mary Berg spurned the spotlight. In the words of one journalist, "Berg [had] published her diary as a call to action" and was not interested in the spotlight for her own self-enrichment.[7] After 1950, there were no further printings of her diary until 2007, and Berg faded from public view. For decades, very little was known of Berg and her whereabouts, though occasionally there were speculations about the reasons for her silence. Some held that she was haunted by guilt for surviving owing to her mother's US passport.[8] When the scholar Susan Lee Pentlin sought out Berg to discuss reissuing her diary, Berg's response points to perhaps another reason why she rejected being an icon of the Holocaust. Berg replied angrily to Pentlin, stating that the constant focus on the Nazi Holocaust was distracting from the genocides happening in the present: "instead of continuing to milk the Jewish Holocaust to its limits ... do go and make a difference in all those Holocausts taking place right now in Bosnia or Chechin [Chechnya] ... Don't tell me this is different."[9] Mary Berg largely got her wish to be left alone. She lived much of her life in York County, Pennsylvania, in near-total obscurity, running an antique shop and living under her married name, Mary Pentin. Her identity was discovered only after her death in 2013, when a collector bought her scrapbook and photo albums at an auction and realized that they held materials related to Berg's diaries, including newspaper clippings, photographs, telegrams, and invitations for speaking engagements. The items, including photos taken of Mary, her family, and friends in the Warsaw Ghetto, are now part of the collection at the United States Holocaust Memorial Museum.[10]

Berg's *Warsaw Ghetto* was quickly outshone by the 1952 English-language publication of Anne Frank's diary, which prompted a frenzy of interest among readers and became a worldwide sensation. Since Frank's diary was first published in Dutch in 1947, it has been translated into more than seventy languages and is one of the most widely read books in the world. It has been the basis of two Hollywood films, a Broadway play, television and radio dramas, documentaries, memorials, and a museum, and has been the subject of several thousand books. There are two separate foundations in Europe as well as a center in the United States whose mission it is to promote the spirit and message of Frank's diary and to research every facet of her interrupted life. For many Americans, Anne Frank's diary is the first, and perhaps only, account that they read about the Holocaust.[11]

Although both Frank and Berg turned to diary-writing as a form of consolation in order to contend with the difficulties of their confinement—Berg in 1939, when she was fifteen years old, and Frank in 1942, when she was thirteen—the two diaries differ dramatically from one another. Berg's diary is an often harrowing account of daily life in the Warsaw Ghetto and is notable for her close proximity to the murder and mass deportations of Polish Jewry. When Anne Frank was writing her diary, she was insulated from the direct violence of the Holocaust (although later, of course, she faced its full horror whereas Berg escaped it). Her diary is an account of the eight residents hiding in a secret annex in Amsterdam, where over a period of two years Frank and those with whom she hid did not leave the building even a single time. As a result, her diary contains little firsthand information about the larger situation European Jews were facing. Rather, it is remarkable for its portrayal of life in hiding and is filled with descriptions of the negotiations and disputes that occurred between the annex's residents over their increasingly scarce resources and the rising danger from outside. Unlike Berg's, many of Frank's entries describe sentiments that might ring familiar to young readers: her yearning to be free from the rules of her home, her tense relationship with her mother, and her occasional romantic interest in a boy named Peter who was also hiding in the annex. It was these features of the work, in contrast to Berg's stark portrayal of life in the ghettos, that not only made Anne Frank's diary accessible to American readers, but also, through its theatrical and cinematic renderings, helped to facilitate the universalizing of her experiences and to aid by extension, American Jewry's acceptance into white society.

The broad sketch of Anne Frank's short life is well known. She was born in 1929 to a German Jewish family. In 1933, the Franks emigrated to the Netherlands to escape Nazi rule and Otto Frank established a franchise of a company that sold spice and pectin, which was located in a warehouse on one of Amsterdam's famous canals, known as the Prinsengracht. In the spring of 1940, the Germany army conquered the Netherlands, and Jews were subjected to increasingly harsh treatment that included segregation, the theft of their property, and incarceration in transit and labor camps. On two occasions, in 1938 and 1941, Otto Frank attempt to secure visas to the United States for his family, but to no avail. (In fact, on December 1, 1941, he was granted a visa to travel to Cuba, but it was limited only to him and it is unclear whether the news of it ever reached him. In any case, with the outbreak of war the following week, the visa was canceled when Germany declared war on the United States.)

For Anne's thirteenth birthday on June 12, 1942, her father gave her a diary in which she began writing immediately. On July 6, the Frank family went into hiding in the warehouse, in a set of rooms that Otto had arranged with the help of sympathetic members of his staff. Joining the Franks were four Jewish friends of the family who were likewise threatened. For the next twenty-five months, Anne wrote regularly in her diary, which, by the time of her capture, had extended into several notebooks. It remains unknown to this day how the authorities came to learn that the Franks and the others were in hiding, but in August 1944, the annex was raided by the police and the inhabitants were arrested and sent to the Westerbork transit camp in the north of Holland. The following month, they were transferred to Auschwitz, where they were put to hard labor. At the end of October, Anne and Margot were sent to the Bergen-Belsen concentration camp. Both died in March 1945, only a few weeks before British forces liberated the camp. With the exception of Otto Frank, all of the residents of the secret annex were murdered in the Holocaust.

Upon returning to Amsterdam after the war, Otto was given Anne's diary by a former employee who had held on to it after the family's arrest. He discovered that Anne had begun revising her diary in late March 1944 upon hearing a radio broadcast from the Dutch government in exile asking those in hiding to record their experiences. In one of her diary entries that month she declares, "I want to publish a book entitled *Het Achterhuis* after the war," and speculates as to whether her diary would assist her in that task.[12] Like Mary Berg, once Anne Frank learned of the possibility that her private thoughts might be published, she quickly came to recognize herself as an author whose work might make a positive impact on the world. As the writer Francine Prose, author of *Anne Frank: The Book, The Life, The Afterlife* states, Frank revised her work for publication at a furious pace, adding to some earlier entries while cutting others, inventing new dialogue and giving pseudonyms to the four residents of the Annex who were not her family members, averaging several pages a day.[13] After Otto Frank learned that Anne, his other daughter Margot, and his wife Edith had all been murdered, he decided to respect Anne's intentions and saw her diary into publication. Working over a period of several months, he stitched together what became known in Dutch as *Het Achterhuis* (literally, "the house behind") out of Anne's original diary, her revisions, and some fictional stories that she also composed while in hiding and which were based on life in the annex. As was the case with many influential books on the Holocaust, publishers initially rejected Frank's diary, but it was eventually printed and was quickly recognized as an important wartime account. Soon, translations in other languages appeared. In November 1950, a short piece in the *New Yorker* by the journalist Janet Flanner (writing under the pen name Genêt) aroused interest in the work in the United States. It appeared in English in 1952 and quickly became a bestseller, helped in part by two separate reviews in the *New York Times* and an introduction by Eleanor Roosevelt, who characterized it as "an appropriate monument to her fine spirit and to the spirits of those who have worked and are working still for peace."[14]

Otto Frank's rendering has been the source of a significant deal of criticism over the years. He has been accused of distorting Anne's intentions, of deracinating the Frank family in order to minimize their Jewishness, of downplaying her sexual longings and curiosity, of universalizing the family's particular experience to such a degree as to divest it of any real significance, and of doing so in order to profit off of his daughter's death.[15] Eleanor Roosevelt's introduction, which provided nearly the entire context of the diary for its American readers, makes no reference to the reason the Franks and others were in hiding, the Nazi mass murder of Jews, or Anne's death. An early popular edition depicts only a young girl as seen from behind who is wearing a black armband with a yellow Jewish star. A very short epilogue summarizes the fate of the residents of the annex.

Above all it was the popularized versions of her diary—most notably a Broadway play and a Hollywood film—that were most responsible for turning Anne from a deeply perceptive and sensitive chronicler of her family's circumstances to a comparatively de-Judaized and overly Americanized young girl. As Prose writes, "On stage and screen, the adorable was emphasized at the expense of the human, the particular was replaced by the so-called universal, and *universal* was interpreted to mean *American*—or, in any case, *not Jewish,* since *Jewish* was understood to signify a smaller audience, more limited earnings, and, more disturbingly, subject matter that might alienate a non-Jewish audience."[16] Overseeing the transformation of the book into a play was an arduous task for Otto Frank. Not only did it involve negotiating between competing playwrights whose disputes became public, but it also involved transforming the diary into a performance that would be welcomed by theatregoers. The final version depicts an Anne who was almost entirely removed not only from her Jewishness, but also from the intelligence, sensitivity, and sexuality that characterizes the diary. Instead, audiences were presented with a young girl who flitted across the stage, made pithy speeches about Hollywood stars, was enthralled in puppy love, and sought to cling to her childhood rather than strive—as the diary attests—to be accepted seriously as an adult. These adaptations of Frank's diary were wildly popular. The play remained on Broadway for twenty months before touring the United States, and it received both a Tony Award and a Pulitzer Prize. In 1959, the film version appeared and won three Academy Awards.

One consequence of these adaptations was that for millions of Americans, the Holocaust was divested of its real suffering and became instead something they could relate to. Anne and her struggles were made ordinary and identifiable. The shocking images that first identified the Holocaust for Americans—the pictures of camps like Buchenwald with its starving prisoners—were replaced by the beatific face of Anne, whose death was understood but never portrayed. Some later commentators have expressed very strong objections to the ways in which Frank's diary has been appropriated for universal causes and for the sake of profit and mass appeal. One leading Jewish writer has even speculated whether it might have been more "salvational" had "Anne Frank's diary burned" rather than misappropriated.[17]

At the time of the play, however, very few American Jews objected to its de-Judaizing of the Franks. Rather, the concern of several contemporary critics was its portrayal of Anne as much more childish and more in love with Peter than the impression conveyed by the diary.[18] In fact, the popular renderings of the diary were largely in line with the wishes of many Jews to be embraced by the American "mainstream." The dramatic versions of Anne's *Diary* successfully validated Jewish suffering in the Holocaust without threatening American Jewry's move into the white middle class.

In the postwar years, the Holocaust also became the subject of a small number of fictional works. Some, like John Hersey's award-winning 1950 novel, *The Wall,* which tells the story of the Warsaw Ghetto through the device

FIGURE 4.2 *Susan Strasberg and Joseph Schildkraut in the Broadway production of* The Diary of Anne Frank, *1955.*

of a diary written by the fictional Noach Levinson, received great acclaim. This deeply sympathetic work written by a child of Christian missionaries, spoke to the suffering and heroism of Polish Jewry and did so in a way that emphasized the dignity of the Jewish inhabitants of the ghetto as they gradually became aware of their impending murder. In subsequent years, other literary works appeared, both fictional and real—and some which bridged the two genres. The author Leon Uris published two works, *Exodus* in 1958 and *Mila 18* in 1961, both of which depicted Jewish heroism during the Holocaust and expressed the belief, shared by a growing numbers of Jews, that the establishment of the State of Israel was necessary to ensure Jews' protection. Other works, such as Elie Wiesel's 1961 *Night*, Jerzy Kosiński's 1965 *The Painted Bird*, and Jean-François Steiner's 1967 *Treblinka* brought what seemed to be either first-hand or deeply researched knowledge of extreme Nazi violence, brutality, and sadism to readers. As it turns out, each of these three works—which blur the lines between memoir and fiction—became the subject of controversy in later years, as the veracity of the accounts was called into question and the authors were accused of attempting to profit off of Jewish suffering.[19]

Film and television

For many years after the war, Hollywood did not portray the specific experiences of Jewish victims. Instead, Americans' own experience tended to be at the forefront of most films that contended with World War II. Although it was known by that time that the Nazis had murdered millions of Jews, the killing was often understood within the framework of crimes committed in the context of German aggression. There was little comprehension of it then as a genocide that ran parallel to the war, even as it was intertwined with it. Typically, wartime films that addressed the threat of Nazism, such as the 1944 film adaptation of the German author Anna Seghers's novel *The Seventh Cross*, made little reference to the fate of Jews.[20] Starring Spencer Tracy, *The Seventh Cross* is the story of an attempt by prisoners in a fictional concentration camp in Germany to escape and avoid capture. The hero of the work is the non-Jewish communist George Heisler, who must rely on a secret network of anti-Nazi sympathizers to survive. In the film, Jews are mentioned only in passing as one victim of Nazism among many. One of the seven prisoners is Jewish and Heisler receives help from a Jewish doctor, but the focus of the film is the universal suffering caused by Nazism and the importance of a united resistance to fascism.

The exception to Hollywood's general avoidance of Nazis' campaign against Jews is the little-known B-movie *None Shall Escape*, which was released in February 1944 just as the knowledge of Nazi crimes in Poland was garnering widespread attention.[21] This film stands alone in its depiction of the particular suffering of Polish Jewry. Taking as its cue President Roosevelt's warning that those responsible for war crimes would be punished, the film is set in a post-war international court where a fictional Nazi leader named Wilhelm Grimm, played by the Canadian actor Alexander Knox, is being tried for war crimes committed in a Polish village that had been under his authority. The film is told via a series of flashbacks portraying the testimony of three witnesses: a local priest, Grimm's brother, and his former fiancé, who collectively recount Grimm's transformation from a lowly village schoolteacher of German into a disaffected and wounded veteran of war, then into sexual predator, and finally, into a fanatical Nazi ideologue. Although the film presents an overly convivial portrait of Jewish-Polish relations, at its climax is the forced deportation of the village's Jewish population. Grimm explains to his nephew that "there must be fewer mouths to feed," intimating that they are being sent to their deaths and not simply relocated. As Jews are being loaded onto trains, the town priest, Grimm's former fiancé, and the village rabbi try to intervene. "Before God and man I protest this crime against humanity," the priest declares. The village rabbi is permitted to give a speech in which he is expected to calm the population. Instead, he makes an impassioned speech defending the eternal Jewish commitment to reason and justice in spite of the oppression Jews have faced:

> Let us prepare ourselves to face the supreme moment in our lives. This is our last journey. It doesn't matter if it's long or short. For centuries, we have sought only peace. We've submitted to many degradations believing that we would achieve justice through reason. We've tried to take our place honestly, decently, alongside all mankind to help make a better world. A world in which all men live as free neighbors. We have hoped and prayed, but now we see that hope was not enough!

The rabbi then urges their resistance in the universal fight against injustice:

> Tolerated! Is there any greater degradation than to be tolerated? To be permitted to exist? We have submitted too long. If we want equality and justice we must take our place alongside all other oppressed peoples, regardless of race or religion. Their fight is ours. Ours is theirs. We haven't much time left. By our actions we will be remembered. This is our last free choice. Our moment in history. And I say to you let us choose to fight! Here! Now!

At that, the rabbi lunges at a German soldier and the village Jews begin to throw themselves at their guards. Several men run down the ramp from the train and on Grimm's order, machine gunners cut them down and then turn their guns to the men, women, and children still on the train, killing them all. The rabbi, however, rises to meet Grimm and says, "We will never die. But you, all of you" at which point Grimm shoots him. He survives long enough to say the Mourner's Kaddish over his dead brethren.

None Shall Escape was nominated for an Academy Award and Columbia Pictures invested in a strong marketing campaign for it, but it was not well received by critics or audiences. As the historian Thomas Doherty has shown, the film's conceit of a trial for war crimes was too soon for most moviegoers, who were unable to imagine postwar justice while the war was still ongoing. Faced with the film's lack of success, "Hollywood backed off" and refrained from making any more wartime pictures about Nazism.[22]

For many Americans, it was through newsreels, rather than feature films, that they first witnessed the horror of Nazi concentration camps.[23] Newsreels were highly scripted and often sensationalistic short films that presented news and information about current events. Until the widespread adoption of television into homes in the early 1950s, newsreels were the main source of visual information for Americans. They were shown in cinemas, either as stand-alone features or as part of larger programs. During World War II, newsreels produced by the US government, the US military, and private studios were shown regularly around the country. Often, they contained a strong propaganda element, with the goal of bolstering popular support for the war effort and, briefly, for the effort to bring Nazis to justice. The first impressions that many Americans had of German atrocities were shaped in large measure by these newsreel images of the concentration camps liberated by US, British, and Canadian troops in April and May 1945. These pictures turned American audiences into a type of witness to Nazi crimes, but they also distorted many Americans' understanding of what actually had occurred in that they led viewers to believe that the camps liberated by Western Allies were the scenes of the majority of Nazi violence rather than the killing centers of Poland.

One of the first newsreels about the concentration camps was entitled *Nazi Atrocities* and was released by the US Army in April 1945.[24] The film includes footage of starving prisoners who had been held in camps in Hadamar, Ohrdruf, Paderborn, and Holzen. It described medical experiments performed on prisoners and showed execution sites and burial pits with burned corpses. The film identifies the newly liberated prisoners by their nationalities—mainly Russian, Polish, and Germans—and refers to the mass executions of political prisoners. In another portion of the newsreel, US soldiers compel German civilians (and one military officer) to tour the camp at Ohrdruf and view the atrocities carried out by their government. Later that year, a film by the US Office of War Information entitled *That Justice Be Done* pressed the case for the need to prosecute the perpetrators of war crimes. It begins with a pair of quotations: Thomas Jefferson's statement that he has "sworn upon the altar of god eternal hostility against every form of tyranny over the mind of man," followed by Hitler's declaration of his right "to remove millions of an inferior race that breeds like vermin."[25]

Another powerful example of this new genre of film was *Death Mills*, made by the German director Hanuš Burger and supervised by the Austrian-born Jewish filmmaker Billy Wilder, who had been living in the United States since 1934. In 1945, Wilder returned to Germany, where he had at one time worked as a journalist, in order to make a film that was to be shown directly to German civilian audiences. Produced by the Psychological Warfare Department of the US Department of War, the film, known in German as *Die Todesmühlen*, aimed to confront Germans with the atrocities committed in their name, and often with their participation and complicity.[26] It included clips from newsreels and showed many of the atrocities US troops uncovered as they made their way across Germany. It begins by displaying the aftermath of the massacre at Gardelegen, where just two days before the arrival of US troops, German soldiers had murdered over a thousand prisoners of war by forcing them into a barn that they then set on fire. It goes on to show footage from several camps, including Buchenwald, Dachau, Auschwitz, Mauthausen, and Bergen-Belsen.

As with many such works, no particular mention of Jewish victims is made, and the film even portrays the murdered in overtly Christian terms. It closes by contrasting the cheering masses of Germans at the Nuremberg rallies staged by Nazis before the war and the sober expression of defeated Germans confronting the destruction wreaked by their military. The narrator ends by holding ordinary Germans responsible for the destruction:

> Yesterday, while millions were dying concentration camps, Germans jammed Nuremberg to cheer the Nazi Party and sing hymns of hate. Today, these Germans who cheered the destruction of humanity in their own land, who cheered the attack on helpless neighbors, who cheered the destruction of Europe, plead for your sympathy. They are the same Germans who once "heiled" Hitler. Remember: if they bear heavy crosses now, they are the crosses of the millions crucified in Nazi death mills.

The following year, Orson Welles's fictional film *The Stranger* brought documentary footage of Nazi crimes to a wide audience. Starring Edward G. Robinson, Loretta Young, and also Welles, it tells the story of a United Nations War Crimes Commission investigator's attempt to track down a former Nazi criminal in a small New England town where he was living under a new identity. In the course of the film, the investigator tries to convince the Nazi's new American wife that her husband is in fact the war criminal Franz Kindler. In order to make his case and to shake her belief in her husband's innocence, he shows her (and the audience) actual newsreel footage of a concentration camp—taken from Billy Wilder's *Death Mills*. It was the only time that portions of Wilder's film were shown widely in the United States. Although *The Stranger* did not win any awards, it ended up being one of Welles's most commercially successful films.

In general, postwar Hollywood productions tended to shy away from overtly Jewish subjects; at most, a film might have one or two Jewish characters, noticeable largely by their last name and or a passing reference. This reflected the general reticence on the part of many Jewish Americans not to call attention to themselves or their own particular plight, and a preference to emphasize their compatibility with the societal norms of white Americans. One exception to this tendency was Elia Kazan's 1947 film adaptation of the novel *Gentleman's Agreement* by Laura Z. Hobson, which had first appeared in serial form in *Cosmopolitan* magazine in 1946.[27] Although it made no reference to the recent genocide of Jews in Europe, *Gentleman's Agreement* spoke directly to the postwar prevalence of antisemitism in the United States and overtly pressed the case for Jews to be considered among white Americans. Starring Gregory Peck as a non-Jewish muckraking reporter named Philip Schuyler Green, the film depicts his efforts to expose antisemitism by posing for six months as a Jew named Phil Greenberg. After changing his identity, he regularly encounters bigotry and prejudice, including from physicians, a soldier, a hotel manager, and even his own love interest. He also discovers that some of the people around him are passing as non-Jews, having changed their names to avoid discrimination. At the end of film, his exposé "I was Jewish for Six Months!" shocks his readers and is embraced as a major step toward combatting prejudice. The message of the film, echoing the hopes of many Jewish Americans, is that Jews are like other white Americans and that any seeming difference is entirely superficial.

Gentleman's Agreement won several Academy Awards. It also was the subject of a great deal of concern and criticism both prior to its production and after its release. While Kazan was debating whether to take on the film, he was approached by representatives of the AJ Committee as well as other members of the film industry with their concerns that the film would exacerbate, rather than alleviate, antisemitism by calling attention to the problem. After the film's release, it faced criticism from those who were concerned about a film regarding antisemitism that told from the point of view of a non-Jewish character rather than a Jewish one. As the scholar Eric Sundquist has also noted, in 1949 the author and social critic James Baldwin criticized the film for promoting a message of assimilation into whiteness over one of tolerance over differences.[28]

After 1947, Hollywood was largely silent on the questions of Nazism and antisemitism for more than a decade until the 1959 release of *The Diary of Anne Frank*. In 1960, Otto Preminger's film *Exodus*, which was adapted from Leon Uris's novel and starred Eva Marie Saint and Paul Newman, told a heroic fictional tale of European Jewish refugees who make their way to Palestine and establish the State of Israel. Throughout the film, Holocaust survivors make the case that as a result of their brutal suffering at the hands of German Nazis, Jews deserve the protection of their own state in what they considered to be their ancestral homeland. This film was one of the first successful attempts to link the suffering of European Jews with the founding of Israel.

Perhaps no film had as much impact in the first decades after the Holocaust as the 1961 *Judgment at Nuremberg*. It appeared in the same year in which the Nazi leader Adolf Eichmann stood trial in Jerusalem for his crimes and the political scientist Raul Hilberg published his monumental study of the Holocaust, *The Destruction of the European Jews* (both of which are discussed below). Taking the war crimes trials that occurred in Germany in 1946 as its setting, this fictional work by the American Jewish director Stanley Kramer made the case for the necessity of bringing war criminals to justice. More importantly, it introduced a younger generation of filmgoers to the horrors of the Nazi regime. The film stars Spencer Tracy (who had played the lead in *The Seventh Cross*) as Chief Trial Judge Dan Haywood, who is alone among the American judges in insisting on the importance of trying four Nazi-era German judges and prosecutors who are accused of war crimes.

The film is exceptional in many regards. As a courtroom drama, it did not recreate the scenes of deportations, mass violence, and executions that would later become commonplace in film. Instead, like *The Stranger*, it replayed actual newsreel footage of mass graves as evidence of Nazi crimes against humanity. As a film told primarily from the point of view of the Allied victors, it boldly contends with the issue of American complicity with eugenics and systemic racism in the early twentieth century. It even raises questions about the morality of the American use of the atomic bomb on Hiroshima and Nagasaki. It was the first time a film directly addressed the mass murder of Jews and discussed Nazi murder techniques at length, including the various ruses that had been employed to compel victims to enter gas chambers. In one of the most poignant scenes, the prosecuting attorney shows images of naked corpses piled up in mass graves at the Bergen-Belsen concentration camp and declares that the dead comprised "members of every occupied country in Europe. Two-thirds of the Jews of Europe ... exterminated. More than six million ... according to reports from the Nazis' own figures. But the real figures, no one knows."

Appearing more than fifteen years after the end of the war, the effect of *Judgment at Nuremberg* was enormous. It was nominated for nearly a dozen Academy Awards, winning two of them, and is widely thought of as one of the most important films of all time. It was also deeply critical of the Allied system of justice. Near the end of the drama, the defendants' attorney predicts that within five years the Nazi judges and prosecutors who were sentenced to life terms would be free. After the film's closing scene, a postscript informs the audience, "The Nuremberg trials held in the American Zone ended July 14, 1949. There were ninety-nine defendants sentenced to prison terms. Not one is still serving his sentence."

It was not until two decades after the end of the war that Hollywood released a film that both contended fully with the impact of the Holocaust and placed a Jewish character at its center.[29] Whereas *Gentleman's Agreement* was the story of a non-Jew's exposé of antisemitism in America and *Judgment at Nuremberg* revealed the horror of Nazi crimes from the perspective of a non-Jewish New England lawyer, the 1965 release of Sydney Lumet's *The Pawnbroker*, starring Rod Steiger, tells the story of a Jewish Holocaust survivor's psychological trauma.[30] In the film, which is based on a book of the same title by Edward Lewis Wallant, the protagonist Sol Nazerman, a former concentration camp survivor, is a bitter, callous pawnbroker in the New York City neighborhood of Harlem. In the 1960s, Harlem was widely seen as a neighborhood in crisis. Home largely to African Americans, it was one of the

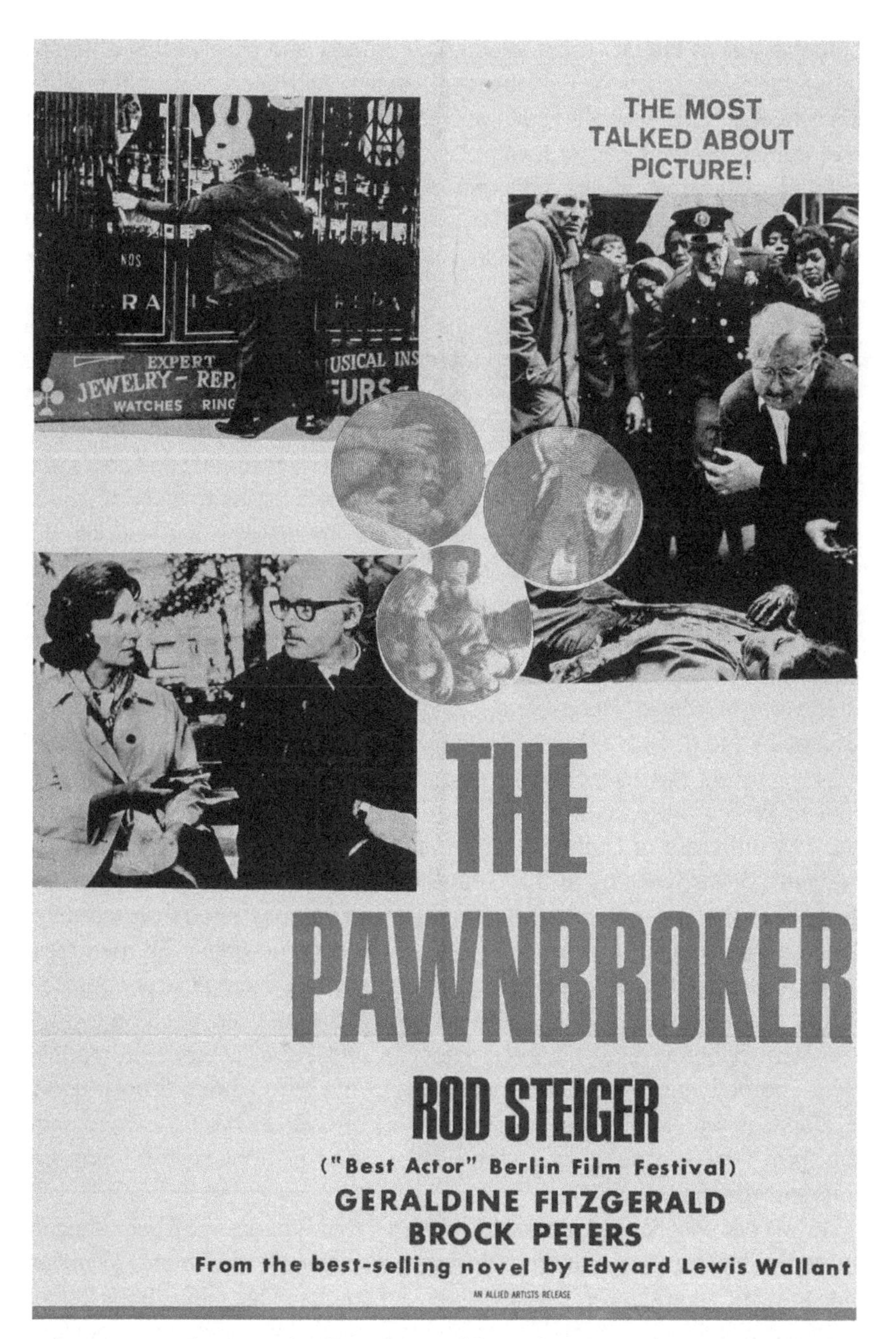

FIGURE 4.3 The Pawnbroker, *directed by Sidney Lumet.*

communities in the city most affected by poverty and policies that enforced urban racial segregation. For decades, Harlem had been one of the major centers of African American cultural creativity and of the political struggle for civil rights, including the growing black nationalist movement. In the white popular imagination, it was a dangerous place, and this image was solidified by what became known as the Harlem Riot of 1964, which broke out that summer after an off-duty white police officer murdered a fifteen-year-old black teenager, James Powell.

In the film's Harlem, Nazerman runs his pawnshop both dependent on his clientele for his own livelihood and utterly contemptuous of them, referring to those who come to his shop as "scum" and "rejects." The pawnshop itself is literally filled with cages, which not only protect the merchandise but also keep Nazerman physically separated from most human contact and serve as a constant reminder of his earlier imprisonment. He explains to a social worker who tries to assist him that he no longer has any feelings or emotions. But over the course of the film, he is forced to confront the pain from which he thought he had successfully closed himself. It is revealed, through a series of flashbacks, that Nazerman's wife was forced into sexual slavery by the Nazis—which a guard compelled him to witness—and that both of his children were murdered. His experiences during the Holocaust, the film shows, caused him to give up all hope in humanity and to embrace the stereotype of the miserly old Jew as a defense mechanism against the world around him.

The Pawnbroker was a groundbreaking film. It dramatized for audiences the raw brutalism of Nazi aggression, and perhaps most influentially, it put Nazism's Jewish victims at the center. The film had a clear social message that linked the suffering of racial minorities and demonstrated how racial violence is reproduced. Nazerman, having once suffered under German racial laws, replicates that suffering from his more privileged status as a white Jew in the United States. As his name implies, Nazerman can become himself the Nazi, depending on his circumstances and social context—something which he only may realize at the very end of the film. As film scholar Judith E. Doneson writes, "The Jew [Nazerman] is portrayed as having learned nothing from the Holocaust, while the viewer, from his 'objective' standpoint, understands the lesson."[31]

It was not only on the big screen, however, that Americans visually encountered the Holocaust. As Jeffrey Shandler writes in *While America Watches*, the arrival of televisions into many American homes in the early 1950s helped establish a "national viewership" for the Holocaust.[32] Whereas newsreel footage tended to focus on what we might think of as journalistic accounts of the liberation of concentration camps and the condition of their inmates, television, which came of age only in the early 1950s, tended to focus on the aftermath of the Holocaust. Such stories often gave particular emphasis to how well survivors—still then widely called "DPs"—were transitioning to their new lives in the country of their liberators, the United States.

No moment on television better exemplifies this tendency than a 1953 episode of the hit television show *This Is Your Life*.[33] A typical episode would surprise a member of the live studio audience with an emotionally uplifting tour of vignettes from their personal history, which would be followed by a reunion with distant friends and relatives from the guest's past. At the end of most episodes, host Ralph Edwards would make an appeal for a worthy cause and announce a charitable gift by one of the show's sponsors. Episodes tended to be light-hearted affairs featuring celebrities, such as actors, writers, performers, and sports figures. Especially in its early years, more "everyday" guests were featured, including disabled war veterans. The show's genesis was in fact tied to World War II: in the immediate aftermath of the war, General Omar Bradley wanted to help injured service members readjust to civilian life and he turned to popular radio personality Edwards to create a show about family reunification. *This Is Your Life* quickly became one of NBC's most popular shows, and eventually prompted a dozen international versions.

The May 27, 1953, episode stood out from most others in a dramatic way. The evening's surprise guest was Hanna Bloch Kohner, the wife of well-known Hollywood talent agent Walter Kohner. She was also a Jewish survivor of Auschwitz and three other Nazi concentration camps. In keeping with the show's focus on stories of success in the face of adversity and emphasis on American patriotism, Edwards began by expressing his surprise at the contrast between Bloch Kohner's appearance and the images of DPs that were widely circulated after the war:

> May I say, Mrs. Kohner, that looking at you, it's hard to believe that during seven short years of a still-short life you lived a lifetime of fear, terror, and tragedy. You look like a young American girl just out of college, not at all like a survivor of Hitler's cruel purge of German Jews. These, as well as happier events in your life, we will relive with you, in just a moment. But so intense is your story, that our sponsor, Hazel Bishop, wants to devote full time to it without interruption.

That Bloch Kohner was chosen as that show's featured guest seems, by all appearances, to have been a legitimate surprise to her. She took the news quite well and quips that her family should win an Academy Award for never revealing their participation in the months-long preparation.

For the next half hour, *This Is Your Life* viewers became witnesses to Hanna's seven years of persecution under Nazi rule in Vienna; her incarceration in the Auschwitz killing center; the murder of her father, mother, and husband; her separation from her brother; and her eventual liberation and arrival to the

United States. Following the show's format, the episode was punctuated with visits from family and friends, and throughout, Edwards maintains a respectful but light-hearted approach to the reunions. Hanna presented herself to be a willing participant in the television drama, even as painful moments were recounted. Edwards describes, for instance, that the April 1938 German invasion of Austria occurred as she was preparing to marry her fiancé, Walter Kohner. When Edwards speaks of the October German takeover of the Czech Sudetenland, where Hanna was then residing, the music turns to the ominous Nazi anthem, the Horst-Wessel-Lied. Hanna looks briefly at the camera, bites her lip, and then looks downward as he describes the arson of the local synagogue where she and Walter once worshipped. We subsequently learn that Walter received a visa to come to the United States before they could marry and that he was unable to secure a visa for her. The wait within the quota system by then was several years long, leaving Hanna trapped in Europe.

Hanna then moved to the Netherlands, near Amsterdam. Edwards describes the May 10, 1940, German invasion of Western Europe as "that fateful day, [when] the Nazis swarm into the low countries, putting a merciless end to your dreams." Without many options, she met and married a young German refugee named Carl Benjamin. In 1943, the two were arrested and sent to the Westerbork transit camp, where Hanna spent the next eight months and where she met fellow prisoner Eva Hertzberg. Eva, who in 1953 was living in Hollywood, was brought out on stage to describe their "trip" to the Theresienstadt concentration camp. When the host Edwards notes that en route, Hanna could see her hometown through the train's grill work, Hanna interjects that "it wasn't a nice homecoming." Soon after, she was sent to the extermination camp at Auschwitz, where her parents and husband were murdered. Edwards makes a point to mention that upon her arrival she was forced to take a shower and that "some showers had regular water, some had liquid gas, and you never knew which one you were sent to." In late 1944, Hanna was sent to the Mauthausen concentration camp in Austria. There, she was sick but wanted to work in order to get more food and avoid being killed. "Down to 73 pounds!" exclaims Edwards, "Ill with a fever of 103 degrees! ... Ready to collapse."

But on May 7, 1945, she was liberated by US troops—"V for Victory!" Edwards shouts. The viewers are then introduced to one of her liberators, who had sent a message to her fiancé Walter. We learn that Walter eventually was able to find her in Amsterdam after the war. He proposed the next day and they were soon married. Edwards then declares, "Your dreams come true at last, you sailed for America in July 1946." Finally, near the end of the half-hour broadcast, Edwards brings out his biggest surprise: Hanna's brother Gottfried, whom she had not seen in over a decade and who was living in Israel. The last time they had spoken was in Auschwitz, where they had been able briefly to exchange messages. Edwards concludes Hanna's story by declaring, "Out of the darkness of terror and despair a new life has been born in a new world for you, Hanna Kohner. This is your life!" He then presents her with several gifts from the show's sponsor, the cosmetics company Hazel Bishop, including a film of that evening's episode and a projector on which to watch it, a 14-carat gold bracelet with charms representing different moments from her life, and a jeweled lipstick case. Edwards then thanked the show's sponsors and made a request for donations to the United Jewish Appeal, a philanthropic organization providing support to Jews worldwide, including many Holocaust survivors.

This episode of *This Is Your Life* has prompted a range of responses from observers. Many find it disturbing for its effortless co-optation of Hanna Bloch Kohner's experiences—including the murder of her first husband and her mother and father—for their entertainment value. Others see it as heartbreaking for the pain and loss that she endured during the war. For others, the episode remains uplifting for its celebration of the fact that she was able to rebuild her life so successfully in the United States after the war. At the time of the episode's airing, Hanna Bloch Kohner was, for many Americans, their first encounter with a survivor of the Holocaust. They were presented with a story that was a tragedy but had a literal Hollywood happy ending.[34] As Jeffrey Shandler has noted, not only did *This Is Your Life* bring the Holocaust to American living rooms, it also was essential in transforming the image of DPs into *survivors*, as individuals who could serve as a paragons for morality and virtue.[35]

The Holocaust and historians

Whereas popular accounts of the Holocaust appeared soon after the war, academic scholarship on the Holocaust materialized more slowly. Today, Holocaust studies is a well-established field of academic research, with many centers dedicated to it across the United States and around the world, but in the initial postwar era few scholars studied the genocide that had just occurred. The immediacy and enormity of the murder, the scale of the devastation to the Jewish community, and the lack of organized archives contributed to the time lag between the end of the Holocaust and the appearance of the first historical accounts by scholars. By the 1960s, however, scholarly works began to inform popular accounts and shaped how many Americans began to understand both the Holocaust and the various ways that Jews had responded to it.

The few who did conduct research in the late 1940s and 1950s often found that their work was not taken seriously by their peers. When Raul Hilberg, who wrote one of the earliest comprehensive studies of the Holocaust, was a graduate student and told his academic adviser that he wanted to focus on the subject of Nazi policy toward European Jews, his adviser famously warned him, "It's your funeral."[36] Nevertheless, there were historians who persisted in documenting and chronicling the destruction that had occurred. In fact, even in the midst of the Holocaust itself, some European Jewish scholars—like so many diarists—took upon themselves the responsibility of chronicling Jewish life under German occupation and detailing the destruction process. According to one oft-repeated account, the renowned Jewish historian Simon Dubnow, who at age eighty-one was murdered in Riga, Latvia, is said to have pleaded to the Jews around him, "Yidn, shraybt un farshraybt!" (Yiddish: "Jews, write and record!"). Most significantly, the Polish Jewish historian Emanuel Ringelblum founded a secret archive with colleagues while they were imprisoned in the Warsaw Ghetto. Named Oyneg Shabes (which literally means "joy of the Sabbath," a reference to the fact that its members tended to meet on the Jewish day of rest), Ringelblum's organization enlisted the help of hundreds of ghetto inhabitants—representing the full range of occupations, religious affiliations, and political persuasions—to record everyday life under German rule. The aim of the archive was to establish a record of Nazi crimes. They also hoped to get verifiable information on the murder of Polish Jewry out into the world as events were unfolding. The archivists collected oral testimonies of ghetto inhabitants, essays, memoirs, diaries, newspapers, official records of the Jewish government and underground movements, children's schoolwork, advertisements, photographs, artwork, songs, rumors, jokes, and nearly every piece of ephemera they could find. When it became clear that the Nazis were deporting the inhabitants of the ghetto to their deaths in the Treblinka death camp, Ringelblum and his colleagues deposited the material in metal milk cans and boxes, which they buried in various places around the ghetto. Ringelblum and most of the members of Oyneg Shabes were murdered in the Holocaust, but after the war three surviving members were able to excavate many of the materials, which are now available in Warsaw for researchers. One of the now-famous milk cans is on display at the United States Holocaust Memorial Museum.[37]

One of the first historians to study the Holocaust after the war was Philip Friedman, himself a survivor. Until his death in 1960 he composed—in Yiddish, Polish, and English—several of the foundational historical studies of the mass murder of Polish Jews, including the first comprehensive examination of the Auschwitz death camp. Born in 1901, Friedman received formal training as a historian in Lwów (then in Poland, and now the city of Lviv in Ukraine) and Vienna, and researched the socioeconomic history of Polish Jewry. Just before the start of the war, he returned to Lwów and hid outside the Jewish ghetto that Nazis had created in that city. He survived the war, but his wife and daughter were killed.[38] In fall 1944, soon after the Soviet liberation of the city, Friedman and a small number of colleagues who had also survived immediately began the task of documenting the genocide. According to Jacob Pat in *Ashes and Fire*, "These Jewish historians began writing the new history. At that time they were obsessed with only one idea ... 'To avenge our martyrs, to draw up and document the great indictment.' "[39] Friedman's team, which called itself the Central Jewish Historical Commission, soon began to assemble survivor testimonies; German, Polish, and Yiddish newspapers published under Nazi authority; and "German posters, anti-Jewish regulations, passports, identity cards, maps and plans of Ghettoes and concentration camps, and whole cartons full of letters."[40] Within a year after the liberation of Lublin, the commission had gathered over 7,000 files of materials; soon it had formed branches in more than half a dozen cities and had thirty employees. The commission assumed responsibility for locating and excavating the Oyneg Shabes archive buried under the rubble of the Warsaw Ghetto.

After believing initially that he might have a future in Poland, Friedman and his new wife, the scholar Ada June Eber-Friedman, felt compelled to leave due to the persistence of antisemitic violence and the increasing ideological pressure the new Soviet regime placed on his work. In summer 1946 they traveled to Germany so that Friedman could testify in and act as a consultant to the Nuremberg International Military Tribunal. For the next two years, they lived mostly in Germany, where Friedman continued his scholarly work and also helped organize a 1947 conference in Paris dedicated to coordinating the many efforts under way to gather historical evidence and survivor testimonies.

In 1948, with the assistance of Friedman's former teacher and Columbia University historian Salo Baron, the couple received visas to come to the United States. For the next dozen years, Friedman worked at Columbia as a research fellow and taught classes on Jewish history. According to historian Roni Stauber, Friedman was motivated by the need to understand the tragedy from a "psychological, social, and historical" point of view as well as by a desire to communicate what had occurred to the larger world.[41] In those years, he lectured widely on the Holocaust and published dozens of articles on many aspects of the Holocaust in addition to two book-length studies, one on the topic of Christian rescuers and another on the 1943 Warsaw Ghetto uprising. Among his greatest contributions was coediting a comprehensive bibliography of all known scholarship on the Holocaust, which became an indispensable guide for future researchers.[42] His groundbreaking work not only helped launch Holocaust studies as a scholarly discipline, but also made the case for the necessity to understand the genocide as a Europe-wide phenomenon and to maintain the centrality of the experience of Nazism's victims. On account of these efforts, Salo Baron referred to him as the "father of the Jewish Holocaust literature."[43]

Friedman also contended with a number of methodological questions of how best to study the Holocaust and sought to establish standards for conducting such research. He was among the first scholars, for example, to insist on the necessity of incorporating survivor testimony into the historical record.[44] Friedman and other early historians of the Holocaust saw their work as part of the larger course of Jewish history and not distinct from it, as some scholars would later insist.[45] However, in spite of their efforts to document the genocide and make their work broadly available, much of what they compiled went unrecognized within the wider historical profession for many decades. As the historian Lucy Dawidowicz later explained, this may have been less a result of the relative obscurity of the academic journals in which these scholars were able to publish their research, and "more likely because the subject matter was still too traumatic for historical consideration."[46]

The historical studies that first exerted the greatest influence on our understanding of the Holocaust were those by scholars who based their work not on survivor testimony and eyewitness accounts but on Nazi documents that the Allies had collected at the end of the war. Many professional historians initially tended to favor such documents because of their presumed objectivity, in contrast to the subjectivity that is inherent in personal accounts. As well, many historians felt that the most pressing issue was to uncover exactly how the Nazis carried out the murder of millions rather than document the experience of Jewish victims.

Most prominent among the first professional scholars to write on the Holocaust was Hilberg, a professor of political science at the University of Vermont. Born in 1926 to a Jewish family in Vienna, Hilberg was still a child when his family was evicted from their home following the Nazi takeover of Austria in March 1938. A year later, they fled the country and, after spending four months in Cuba, arrived in the United States on September 1, 1939, the same day that Germany invaded Poland. He was drafted into service near the end of the war and because of his knowledge of the German language, he served with a unit that was tasked with examining captured enemy documents. While stationed for a few weeks at the former Nazi Party headquarters in Munich, Hilberg identified a large number of crates as comprising part of Hitler's private library.[47] This discovery, along with learning of the murder of twenty-six close members of his family during the war, prompted him to abandon his earlier studies in chemistry for political science and to dedicate his life to investigating the Holocaust.[48] He wrote in his memoir about his decision, "Briefly I weighed the possibility of writing a dissertation about an aspect of war crimes, and then I woke up. It was the evidence that I wanted. My subject would be the destruction of the European Jews."[49]

As a student at Columbia University in the late 1940s and early 1950s, Hilberg studied Jewish history with Salo Baron and, to a lesser extent, with

Philip Friedman.[50] Unlike his mentors who had focused on Jewish victims, however, Hilberg was primarily interested in the actions of the perpetrators. While writing his PhD dissertation, Hilberg began to work with the government's War Documentation Project, which was tasked with organizing, cataloging, and researching the vast amount of German documents captured by the US military at the end of the war. These materials occupied several miles' worth of shelf space and had been kept classified until the early 1950s. Many of the researchers associated with the project were, like Hilberg, former refugees from Nazism and some, including Gerhard Weinberg and Henry Friedlander, became among the most highly regarded historians of World War II and the Holocaust.[51] The project's holdings were vast and contained such items as German operational plans for the invasion of Western Europe and Poland, Nazi Party materials, records related to the July 1944 plot to assassinate Hitler, and the files of major Nazi leaders like Joseph Goebbels and Alfred Rosenberg.[52]

These documents formed the basis of Hilberg's dissertation, which, after being rejected by many publishers, was eventually published in 1961 as *The Destruction of the European Jews*.[53] Although a small number of works describing themselves as complete histories of the murder of European Jews had appeared, none were as comprehensive as Hilberg's. What set *The Destruction of the European Jews* apart was its apparent totality. Long before the coining of the term "Holocaust," or acceptance of the idea that there had been a specific campaign to murder all Jews, Hilberg understood that the Nazi plan was to kill every Jew in Europe. His study was the first to examine the genocide as related to but distinct from the war effort, and it made the case (later refined and revised by other scholars) that the Holocaust could be understood as having moved through definable stages: the classification of populations into Aryan and non-Aryan, the expropriation of Jewish assets, the concentration of Jews in camps and ghettos, their deportation, and finally, their destruction. As one scholar put it, Hilberg's book "was in fact the first scientific attempt to find out how a highly civilized, 20th century nation succeeded in setting aside all juridical, administrative, psychological and moral obstacles, in order to almost completely destroy a population."[54] Chief among the book's merits is its highly detailed descriptions of Nazi administrative rule—with its many competing authorities, bureaucratic organizations, and jurisdictions—and its financial arrangements. It demonstrates convincingly that the murders were not committed by a small handful of sadistic killers but were made possible by the participation of a significant percentage of the German population.

When *The Destruction of the European Jews* appeared, the work was initially overlooked, with the exception of a few, mostly praiseworthy reviews in academic journals and a brief mention in the *New York Times*. It had been published by a small independent press (at Hilberg's own expense) that had little ability to market it internationally. It took nearly a year for the first truly engaged review to appear in a mass-circulation publication. Written by the Oxford historian Hugh Trevor-Roper and appearing in the widely read American Jewish magazine *Commentary*, the review hailed the work as a "careful, analytic, three-dimensional study of a social and political experience unique in history."[55] Over the following years, the book began to garner greater attention and many reviews then appeared in academic journals and popular media.

In spite of the accolades it received, Hilberg's work was also subject to a great deal of criticism, even prior to its release. When looking for a publisher, he submitted the manuscript to Yad Vashem, Israel's Holocaust memorial and research institute, which rejected the work in part because it relied almost exclusively on German-language material and did not use Yiddish- and Hebrew-language sources. Moreover, the reviewers at Yad Vashem were especially concerned with the book's depiction of Jewish responses during the Holocaust. Since the book was an analysis of the perpetrators, discussions of Jews were limited largely to the role that their leaders were compelled to play in the extermination process. This left a portrait of Jewish behavior as almost entirely passive and even at times complicit with Nazi actions. Hilberg defended his approach by asserting that "the destruction of European Jewry was fundamentally the work of German perpetrators, and hence it is to them that we must devote our primary attention."[56]

The book in fact begins by stating that "the German destruction of the European Jews was a tour de force; the Jewish collapse under the German assault was a manifestation of failure."[57] This depiction, which appears throughout the work, led many critics to interpret Hilberg as blaming Jews themselves in part for their own murder. He had referred to European Jews as "blind" to their position vis-à-vis their Christian neighbors and argued that their inability to see Nazism as a fundamentally new sort of threat led them to rely upon previous—and therefore ineffectual—methods of contending with attacks on the community, such as looking for ways to placate and accommodate their oppressors. His study overlooked, or was unconcerned with, the wide range of responses by Jews to violence throughout their history, including many instances of Jewish armed response.

Although the reviewers at Yad Vashem who had rejected his work were likely influenced by their organizational mission to memorialize both the Jewish martyrs *and* heroes of the Holocaust, critics outside of Israel also voiced concerns.[58] It was clear that Hilberg's work touched a nerve among postwar Jewish communities. Given the enormity of the genocide, many Jews felt a measure of shame and humiliation at what they perceived to be their defeat in the face of the Nazi onslaught. There were sufficient incidents of what appeared to be Jewish acquiescence to Nazi demands, including Jewish leaders' seeming cooperation with Nazi orders, to reinforce the view that European Jews had done little to save themselves. In the interpretation of some Jews (both survivors and Jews who had not experienced the Holocaust), European Jewry had gone to its death "like sheep to the slaughter"—an allusion to a biblical lament that was repeated for many decades after the war.[59]

In the fall of 1962, six month after it published Trevor-Roper's review, *Commentary* magazine published a long rebuttal to Hilberg's book by Harvard historian Oscar Handlin, who criticized him for "defaming the dead and their culture by complet[ing] the process of destruction begun by the Nazis."[60] Handlin charged Hilberg with accepting the "the picture of the meek, abject Jew, cringing in his cowardice" that had been a staple of Nazi antisemitic propaganda. Another prominent critic of Hilberg was Lucy Dawidowicz, who later authored *The War against the Jews: 1933–1945* in part as a response to *The Destruction of the European Jews.* Above all, however, the reception of the Hilberg's study was shaped by Hannah Arendt, who, as will be discussed below, made liberal use of it in her controversial journalistic account of the 1961 Israeli trial of Adolf Eichmann.

In spite of the many debates surrounding *The Destruction of the European Jews*, and perhaps in part because of them, Hilberg's 1961 work continues to influence Holocaust studies until the present day. Teachers and scholars often still think in terms of his three major categories of perpetrator, victim, and bystander, even as they revise or challenge them, and discussions of Jewish resistance often take as their starting point his contentious descriptions of this era. It remains a widely consulted work for anyone trying to comprehend the complex organizational structures of the Nazi administration. More importantly, it helped to launch the study of the Holocaust as an academic field. Within a decade of Hilberg's book, dozens of major scholarly and popular works had appeared in several languages and the Holocaust increasingly became viewed as a discrete topic for study. All, in one way or another, are indebted to Hilberg's efforts to bring the full history of the Nazi genocide to a wider American audience.

The Holocaust on trial

In addition to firsthand accounts, films and television, and scholarly work, many Americans came to understand the horror of the Holocaust through reports on the trials of major German war criminals conducted by the Allied governments in Nuremberg, Germany, which lasted from November 20, 1945, to October 1, 1946, and the trial of Adolf Eichmann, which was held by Israeli authorities in Jerusalem in 1961. Not only did these trials illuminate the extent of Nazi crimes against Jews and other civilians, but they also kept Nazi crimes against Jews in the news for many years after the end of the war. At the time, both trials were the subject of great debate, including the question of whether it was appropriate for them to be held at all. In the case of the Nuremberg trials, critics argued that such trials were without precedent and a form of unfair "victor's justice." Detractors of the Eichmann trial argued, by contrast, that Nazism's victims should not stand in judgment. Rather an international body, or even Germany itself, was better equipped to adjudicate Eichmann's crimes. However valid these criticisms might be, both the Nuremberg and Eichmann trials served what the historian Lawrence Douglas has argued were "didactic exercises" whose pedagogic value should not be overlooked. Although there remain significant questions as to whether they were the most appropriate method of dispensing justice, these trials unquestionably shaped how many millions of people understood Nazi crimes.[61]

As early as 1941, Roosevelt and Churchill gave their support to a resolution by the governments-in-exile that one of the major aims of the war should be the prosecution of war criminals. On November 1, 1943, the USSR, Britain, and the United States released a joint statement, entitled "Declaration on German Atrocities in Occupied Europe," in which they promised to punish German leaders for crimes against civilians. This action was taken in response to wartime reports of Nazi atrocities that were making their way to the Allied leaders as their troops retook territories that had been under German military control.[62]

A number of Nazi leaders were able to avoid capture at the war's end, and others, like Hitler, the SS leader Heinrich Himmler, and the Minister of Propaganda Joseph Goebbels had committed suicide. Nevertheless, many prominent Nazi leaders had been captured. The Allied governments, however, disagreed over how to treat the defeated German leadership. The Soviet Union favored a quick and decisive solution: execute them and tens of thousands of lower-ranking officials. Many British officials, chief among them Winston Churchill, likewise proposed the summary execution of German leaders and the immediate imprisonment of others without trial.[63] The United States rejected the idea and insisted that Americans would expect judicial proceedings after the war. Further, the US government argued, orderly trials were a necessary step toward rebuilding Germany's civil society.

In August 1945, the Allies formally established the Constitution of the International Military Tribunal, which allowed for the trial and punishment of major war criminals. The tribunal established that "crimes against peace," "war crimes," and "crimes against humanity" were within its jurisdiction.[64] Six months after the end of the war, in November 1945, the tribunal held its first trial, known as the Trial of Major War Criminals, in the city of Nuremberg, Germany. Nuremberg was chosen for its symbolic value: it had been the site of the annual extravagant Nazi Party rallies and this was where the antisemitic Nuremberg Laws were passed in 1935. In spite of widespread destruction in the city, its Palace of Justice was spared and provided an ideal venue for such a trial.

Initially, twenty-four Nazi leaders were charged with conspiracy to commit crimes against peace, war crimes, and crimes against humanity. Among them were the Nazi Party leader Hermann Göring, the leader of occupied Poland Hans Frank, Minister of the Interior Wilhelm Frick, Deputy Führer Rudolf Hess (who was captured after his failed 1941 attempt to broker a separate peace with Britain), former chancellor Franz von Papen, the racial theorist Alfred Rosenberg, the architect and organizer of slave labor Albert Speer, and the antisemitic publisher Julius Streicher. In the end, twenty-one accused stood before the tribunal. Tried in absentia was Nazi Party Secretary Martin Bormann, who was thought at the time to have escaped in the last days of the war but later was discovered to have died in the final days of the siege of Berlin. The head of the German Labour Front, Robert Ley, took his life just prior to the start of the trial. The industrialist Gustav Krupp von Bohlen und Halbach was declared medically unfit to stand trial and released.

Each of the four Allied powers sent one judge and one alternate. The chief prosecutor for the United States was Supreme Court Associate Justice Robert H. Jackson. His appointment by President Truman was a signal both to the other Allied powers and to the German people of the importance the United States was placing on the trial. On being appointed, Jackson threw himself into the case, and his opening statement at the trial was hours long and by all accounts deeply compelling. In it, he gave special attention to the fate of European Jews under Nazism:

> The most savage and numerous crimes planned and committed by the Nazis were those against the Jews ... The persecution of the Jews was a continuous and deliberate policy. It was a policy directed against other nations as well as against the Jews themselves. Anti-Semitism was promoted to divide and embitter the democratic peoples and to soften their resistance to the Nazi aggression ... Of the 9,600,000 Jews who lived in Nazi-dominated Europe, 60 percent are authoritatively estimated to have perished. Five million seven hundred thousand Jews are missing from the countries in which they formerly lived, and over 4,500,000 cannot be accounted for by the normal death rate nor by immigration; nor are they included among displaced persons. History does not record a crime ever perpetrated against so many victims or one ever carried out with such calculated cruelty.[65]

Although most of the evidence presented in the trial comprised documents (approximately 700,000 of them) seized by the Allies, film, too, played an important role in the proceedings. The courtroom itself was erected in such a way as to accommodate the screening of several films that were to be shown by the prosecution. Nine days into the trial, a work by the famous Hollywood director and producer John Ford was shown to the court. Entitled *Nazi Concentration Camps*, it depicted footage taken by US and British film-makers as they toured recently liberated camps in Germany. It was the first time that many in the court had ever viewed such images, and they were shocked. *The New York Times* reported the next day that members of the audience muttered "Oh God—Oh God!" and "Why can't we shoot the swine now?" and that the judges, stunned by what they saw, immediately left the court for the day at the film's end.[66] As the historians Daniel H. Magilow and Lisa Silverman have argued, such use of film in a trial was without precedent. Its impact was so profound that it had a "foundational influence" on the way in which the Holocaust would come to be understood.[67]

For the next several months, judges were presented with a mountain of evidence depicting Nazi crimes. They also heard eyewitness testimony, including from some who were Holocaust survivors, such as Marie-Claude Vaillant-Couturier, a member of the French Resistance who had spent eighteen months in Auschwitz. Also testifying was the Jewish poet Abraham Sutzkever, who had spent two years in the Vilna Ghetto and escaped in order to join partisan fighters in Lithuania. In spite of being asked to sit, Sutzkever insisted on giving his testimony standing. Years later, he wrote, "I spoke standing as if I was saying kaddish for the dead."[68]

In March of 1946, the defense presented its case, arguing that primary responsibility for any war crimes should be placed on the Nazi Party's most senior leaders, who had escaped justice by committing suicide or going into hiding. Others asserted that German actions during the war were no worse than those committed by Allied forces, such as the USSR's murder of Polish officers at Katyn and the United States' submarine attacks on merchant ships. Some argued what became known as the "Nuremberg defense" in which they declared that they were only following orders and therefore could not be held responsible for their actions. Few acknowledged any culpability. The court adjourned on September 1 and the verdicts were handed down a month later. Of the twenty-one defendants to have appeared before the court, eighteen were found guilty and three were acquitted. Of the eighteen, eleven were sentenced to death by hanging. Martin Bormann was also convicted in absentia and sentenced to death. Göring committed suicide in his cell the night before his execution. The remaining ten were hanged on October 16.

Twelve more tribunals were held in Nuremberg's Palace of Justice (the last of them held in 1949), but under the sole authority of the US military. Growing conflicts between the Allies made further collaboration impossible. The International Military Tribunal was, in the words of historian Michael R. Marrus, "a last act of the Allied coalition against Nazi Germany" as the "Cold War storm was gathering."[69] In all, more 200 defendants were brought before the court, including those held in the famous Doctors' Trial, which exposed to the world the Nazi plan for medical killing and the Judges' Trial, which revealed the complicity of Germany's judicial system with the Nazi regime.

In spite of the criticisms leveled against the proceedings at the time, the legacy of the trials has been profound. The "Nuremberg defense" was widely discredited, and today war criminals are not permitted to pass blame for their actions on to their superiors. The Nuremberg trials served as a model for subsequent war crime trials, such as the Tokyo Trials of 1946, which tried Japanese leaders for conspiracy to wage war and for crimes against humanity. They also informed the creation of the International Criminal Court at The Hague and the framework for the 1948 Genocide Convention of the United Nations and the Universal Declaration of Human Rights. In the 1950s and 1960s this notion of universal human rights would serve as the basis of many civil rights leaders' appeals to the international community for help in ending racial oppression in the United States. Finally, although it was not the intention of the prosecutors, the Nuremberg trials also had the effect of putting the murder of Jews at the very center of discussions of Nazi crimes.[70]

After the Nuremberg trials, no country had the ideological commitment or political will to track down and punish Nazi criminals, many of whom had gone into hiding. The Cold War between the United States and the Soviet Union had diverted American interest toward fighting new enemies. With Germany divided since 1949, US leaders were no longer invested in punishing West Germans but instead were far more concerned with stopping them from falling under Soviet influence. In West Germany, it was against the country's constitution to prosecute former Nazis for actions that were legal at the time in which they were committed. This meant that most perpetrators tended to escape being brought to trial entirely. Additionally, very few jurists wished to revisit German actions during the war years and break the general silence that surrounded the murder of European Jewry. The State of Israel, which was founded in 1948, was likewise reluctant to pursue justice for Holocaust victims and, over the course of the 1950s, focused its judicial energies instead on establishing the Jewish nature of the state and its legal structure. When, in 1950, the Knesset (parliament) passed the Nazi and Nazi Collaborators (Punishment) Law, it was done less out of a sense of commitment to see Nazi leaders face their crimes than out of the belief that *not* to have such a law on the books was unimaginable. As Tom Segev argues, it was "a declarative law, enacted because of a widespread feeling that it was 'inconceivable' not to enact it," and was not a reflection of any commitment to pursue Holocaust-era criminals.[71]

Nevertheless, when in May 1960, the Israeli secret service received a tip from the German prosecutor Fritz Bauer that the Nazi leader Adolf Eichmann was alive and hiding in Buenos Aires, Argentina, they organized an operation to bring Eichmann to Israel and to prosecute him under the 1950 law. They kidnapped Eichmann outside his home, interrogated him, and smuggled him out of the country on an Israeli airline. Eichmann, who had had been living under the name Ricardo Klement, quickly admitted his true identity to his captors and agreed to be brought to trial in Israel.

Although Eichmann never attained a position within Hitler's inner circle or oversaw any of the major killing facilities, and while he achieved a military rank equivalent only to that of a US lieutenant colonel, he was in fact the most prominent Nazi official who dealt regularly with European Jewish leaders. He had been responsible for overseeing both the emigration (before the war) and forced deportation (during it) of Viennese, Czech, Polish, and Hungarian Jews. To many Jewish survivors, Eichmann was *the* face of the Holocaust, and he was often mentioned during the Nuremberg trials. In January 1942, he was tasked with preparing the minutes for the Wannsee Conference, during which the murder of Jews was coordinated under the central command of Reinhard Heydrich, chief of the Reich Main Security Office. According to one oft-repeated account, Eichmann stated near the end of the war that he would "leap laughing into the grave because the feeling that he had five million people on his conscience would be for him a source of extraordinary satisfaction."[72]

When Prime Minister David Ben Gurion announced that Israel had arrested Eichmann and that he would be judged according to Israeli law, reaction around the world was mixed. Most Israeli Jews agreed that it was Israel's right and responsibility to hold the trial and felt proud of Israel's accomplishment. American Jewish leaders were more skeptical and several publicly voiced their concerns that an international court along the lines of the Nuremberg proceedings—which would presumably be more objective—was a far more appropriate judicial body. Some objected to Israeli's assertion that it was the sole legitimate representative of world Jewry with the authority to act in the best interests of Jews everywhere. Others feared a rise in global antisemitism because of the trial.

The American press was likewise skeptical about Israel's claim that it had the right to try Eichmann. For example, the *Washington Post* published a Reuters story with the headline "Eichmann in Vengeance Trap" and two days later editorialized that Israel had no legal or moral authority to try Eichmann on its own and was itself acting lawlessly.[73] It argued that Israel had no right to act on behalf of world Jewry or "in the name of some imaginary Jewish ethnic entity." Furthermore, it concluded—likely unaware that Bauer had alerted his Israeli contacts of Eichmann's whereabouts precisely because he did not trust his own government to bring Eichmann to trial—that rather than refer the case to an international body, Israel should "let the Germans who spawned this creature bear the shame of dealing with him."[74] Later that year, the *New York Times* published a sympathetic interview with Ben Gurion that provided him the opportunity to answer his American critics. In it, Ben Gurion argued that since Nazi plans to murder all Jews everywhere was unique within history, it was "historic justice that he be tried by a Jewish state. Only a Jewish state can try him, from a moral point of view."[75]

As Segev and other historians have shown, Eichmann's trial, which began in April 1961, served many functions. It was not only a judicial proceeding, but an attempt to teach a new generation of Israeli Jews as well as the wider world about the suffering endured by the Jewish people both during the war and throughout history. A major subtext of the trial was that without a Jewish state, Jews everywhere would always and forever be at risk of extermination. Although the chief prosecutor Gideon Hausner could have built his case against Eichmann based largely on documents seized in the aftermath of the war (as was done in the Nuremberg trials), he called more than 120 witnesses to testify. Only a small number of them had specific evidence to give against Eichmann. The majority of them helped Hausner to tell the larger story of the Holocaust. He called forward survivors from concentration and death camps. He called partisan fighters from the Warsaw and Vilna Ghettos to testify. He found witnesses who had survived mass shootings and sexual violence. Over the four-month trial, the suffering of the Jewish people was told to the courtroom of reporters, who transmitted the story to the world. As Jeffrey Shandler has shown, the government contracted with a New York company to videotape the entire trial for broadcast to the world, even though there was no television network in Israel at the time and Israelis could only listen to the trial via radios.

Videotapes were flown to the United States daily, and American television viewers were, therefore, kept up to date on the trial's progress. Audiences, especially in urban areas, could view nightly half-hour recaps of the trial, along with longer special programs that were regularly aired. It was, in the words of one media critic, "the most sustained and extensive attention that TV ever has accorded a single news story."[76] The trial was also covered extensively in newspapers and magazines across the country. For many Americans, especially younger ones, the Eichmann trial was the first prolonged news story about the Holocaust that they followed. In this sense, Ben Gurion's intention for the trial to be a means by which the world learned about the Jewish suffering during Holocaust was successfully realized.

In December 1961, a panel of three Israeli judges (all of whom were Jews who had been born in Germany) found Eichmann guilty of crimes against the Jewish people and crimes against humanity. The sentence was death. After a failed appeal, Eichmann was executed on June 1, 1962. His body was cremated and his ashes spread at sea.

In spite of the widespread media coverage of the trial as it was being held, the account that has most shaped the way that many Americans, as well as many Europeans and Israelis, now understand it appeared in early 1963. Writing for the *New Yorker*, Hannah Arendt published a lengthy five-part essay entitled "A Reporter at Large: Eichmann in Jerusalem," which she then expanded and published in book form as *Eichmann in Jerusalem: A Report on the Banality of Evil*.[77] Written in the summer and fall following Eichmann's execution, Arendt's work was based on her firsthand observations of the trial, official transcripts and recordings, and some of the first works of historical scholarship on the Holocaust, especially Hilberg's *The Destruction of the European Jews*. Almost instantly, the work was met with outrage by many within the Jewish community, both in the United States and in Israel. Much of the anger concerned Arendt's portrait of Eichmann as not the monster that the prosecutor Hausner sought to present him as, but as someone pathetic and ordinary. Eichmann came across to Arendt not as an extreme ideologue bent on the murder of every living Jew but as a hapless striver who was anxious to impress his superiors and get ahead in the Nazi hierarchy. Although she recognized Eichmann as an antisemite and a believer in Nazism, he appeared to Arendt as a figure who acted fully within the bounds of the society of which he was a part. Eichmann's evil was, therefore, normalized—or rendered "banal"—given the context in which he acted.[78] As a scholar of totalitarian societies, Arendt regarded this form of evil as much more frightening than the common image of Nazis as psychopaths or madmen who had managed to attain power and were motivated by blind hatred. Her representation outraged many readers who assumed, mistakenly, that Arendt was excusing Eichmann for his crimes and portraying him as simply a cog in a great killing machine.

Many readers were also upset with her condemnation of Jewish communal leaders during the Nazi period. In part drawing from Raul Hilberg's study, which appeared just after the trial, she charged many Jewish leaders with having collaborated with Nazi officials. She wrote, "To a Jew this role of the Jewish leaders in the destruction of their own people is undoubtedly the darkest chapter of the whole dark story. It had been known about before, but it has now been exposed for the first time in all its pathetic and sordid detail by Raul Hilberg."[79] She went on to argue that "wherever Jews lived, there were recognized Jewish leaders, and this leadership, almost without exception, cooperated in one way or another, for one reason or another, with the Nazis." She then speculated—without being able to offer any proof—that "the whole truth was that if the Jewish people had really been unorganized and leaderless, there would have been chaos and plenty of misery but the total number of victims would hardly have been between four and a half and six million people."[80] Although she also claimed that Jewish leaders were hardly exceptional

FIGURE 4.4 *Hannah Arendt with fellow journalist.*

in their cooperation, as most Europeans had seen their leaders capitulate to or be rendered defenseless in the face of Nazi authority, her charges were immediately met with condemnation by many who were associated with the trial, such as the prosecutor Hausner and his assistant Jacob Robinson, whose work *And the Crooked Shall Be Made Straight* was a comprehensive refutation of Arendt's charges.

In spite of these criticisms, many have felt compelled to contend with Arendt's understanding of Nazism and her assessment of the trial, and responses to her work on the Eichmann trial constitute an entire body of scholarship in itself, with new studies regularly appearing to condemn or defend her provocative claims. Her account remains unquestionably the most controversial work written on the Holocaust. A recent article in the *New York Times* discussing a new book on the Eichmann trial is titled "Who's on Trial, Eichmann or Arendt?" and highlights the difficulty we have today of separating the actual trial from Arendt's representation of it.[81]

Many factors are responsible for the outsized reception her work. She was the leading philosopher of her time and was known for her deep personal connections to Jewish history, politics, and culture as well as her frequent critical engagement with them. In *Eichmann in Jerusalem*, she published what was, in fact, a deeply complicated argument about the Holocaust in journalistic form, which perhaps resulted in her study not being read as closely as her works of political theory were. At times, she adopts a deliberately provocative tone, such as when she refers to the former German Jewish leader Leo Baeck as the "Jewish *Führer*."[82] She also leveled her criticism from her position of having been a refugee from Nazism and a formerly strong supporter of Zionism. Perhaps most disconcerting to many readers is that she publicly spoke about issues that were in the 1960s a source of great embarrassment to many Jews in both Israel and the United States. In the years after the Holocaust, many Jews struggled with what Hilberg had called "the Jewish collapse under the German assault." Although the incidents of Jewish armed resistance and militarism were few in number and had little effect on Germany's genocidal goals, those that did exist were heavily examined and touted in literature and public monuments. For many Jews, this seeming "collapse" was evidence of Jewish powerlessness and for some, a lack of Jewish self-worth. The fact that Arendt reported on these issues because they had been raised during the trial itself—by the prosecution and even more so by the judges—did little to placate her critics.

***

Awareness of the Holocaust occurred through a variety of media, including popular and scholarly accounts, and widely covered trials of Nazi criminals. If the first postwar images of Nazi crimes tended to depict its victims primarily in universal terms, by the mid-1960s, the particular fate of European Jews increasingly stood front and center. Americans were coming to understand the Holocaust as a crime against Jews that was distinct from the war itself and one that bestowed upon Jews a special status of victimhood. Nevertheless, the Holocaust was not yet fully a part of the American experience. As the final chapter discusses, over the next several decades, the Holocaust grew in importance and became the standard by which other acts of wartime violence and genocide would be compared.

5

America embraces the Holocaust, 1970s–the present

On April 22, 1993, over 8,000 guests gathered just off the National Mall in Washington, DC, to dedicate what would soon become one of the city's most visited tourist sites. The opening of the United States Holocaust Memorial Museum (USHMM) was the culmination of fifteen years of sustained effort to create a national monument to the Holocaust.[1] With its lofty goals—"to advance and disseminate knowledge about this unprecedented tragedy; to preserve the memory of those who suffered; and to encourage its visitors to reflect upon the moral and spiritual questions raised by the events of the Holocaust as well as their own responsibilities as citizens of a democracy"—the USHMM placed the Holocaust prominently within the American experience. At the dedication, President Bill Clinton spoke of the appropriateness of establishing the museum alongside monuments to Thomas Jefferson and Abraham Lincoln, near to where Marian Anderson had sung "My Country 'Tis of Thee" in 1939, and where Reverend Martin Luther King Jr. gave his "I Have a Dream" speech in 1963. The president was even more explicit in asserting that the Holocaust made particular demands on the United States when he stated that those gathered had acted to "bind one of the darkest lessons in history to the hopeful soul of America."[2]

Considering that for several decades, the Holocaust existed at the margins of most Americans' consciousness, how did it move to the nation's geographical and political center by the early 1990s? Why does it continue to serve as a subject of countless books, films, art installations, monuments, educational programs, and legal cases? As in the first decades after the war, there was no single moment that served as the "tipping point" that brought Holocaust awareness to Americans. Rather, there continued to be periodic—if more frequent and potent—political and cultural events over the 1970s, 1980s, and 1990s that challenged Americans to confront the legacy of the Holocaust.

As in earlier decades, the rise of Holocaust awareness in the United States was in part a reflection and consequence of the changing status of American Jewry. As politically and religiously diverse as American Jewry had become in the postwar decades, Jews of European ancestry in the 1970s and 1980s were considered part of white America and benefited from the many privileges and opportunities that such a status bestows. They were now widely acknowledged to be a politically and economically important group, and for many political leaders, recognition of the Holocaust, along with support for Israel, became a way to show respect for Jewish Americans and acknowledge their place within American society. At the same time, Jews were also successful in retaining a distinct group identity that was not widely viewed as being in conflict with being perceived as white. Cultivating a sense of connection to the victims of the Holocaust and preserving their memory became strategies by which many Jews maintained ties to their own Jewishness.

As this chapter will also explain, another part of the answer to why the Holocaust has become so important in the United States is more straightforward, although it is often overlooked. Since the end of World War II, the steady accumulation of knowledge and cultural productions about the Holocaust has resulted in widespread awareness of the fate of Jews under Nazism. The attempts by memoirists, novelists, filmmakers, artists, scholars, teachers, religious leaders, and others to spread consciousness of the Holocaust, and at times its "lessons," were highly effective. What motivated these efforts often varied considerably. Some acted in the spirit of "never again"—a powerful but ambiguous call that was often repeated in the 1980s and 1990s, and whose meaning often varied with the speaker.[3] Some recognized that the Holocaust was a global event with profound implications for humanity and that each country that was in some way involved was also implicated by it. Some viewed Holocaust education as a means by which to prevent genocides from continuing to occur. Others saw in the Holocaust a way to maintain support for the state of Israel. For many American political leaders, memorials and commemorations were relatively safe ways to demonstrate their commitment to Holocaust awareness without questioning current US policies or committing military or economic resources to prevent other genocides or refugee crises. The seeming omnipresence of Holocaust awareness in the last decades of the twentieth century and the first decades of the twenty-first thus reflects both the elevated standing of Jews within American society and a recognition, which developed gradually over decades, of the genocide's magnitude and implications.

American Jewry and Holocaust awareness

By 1960, most American Jews could conclude that, according to their aspirations of the past several decades, they had "made it." Large numbers enjoyed

a middle-class life and expected that their children would contir
Antisemitism in the United States was at historic lows and Arr
was widely accepting of Jews. Their attachment to Judaism wa
It made few personal demands on them and found expression
sional gestures that displayed pride in their heritage.[4]

At this very moment, however, a change was under way. Younger Jews sought new ways to identify with their Jewish heritage. Jewish baby boomers, who were the first generation to take for granted that they were fully American, questioned whether too much had been sacrificed in the name of the "melting pot" ideal. During the next two decades, many in this generation came to believe that there was historical, ethical, moral, and political value in identifying—if only partially—as a distinct minority group, especially one with a history of victimization. Among the cultural resources from which they could draw to shape this new identity were narratives about the Holocaust. Over the next several decades, Holocaust awareness grew to such an extent that it became a core component of modern American Jewish identity and central to promoting the goal of Jewish continuity against the rapidly growing tendency of Jewish assimilation through intermarriage.

This shift toward embracing a particularistic Jewish identity was prompted by a number of factors. One was the civil rights movement, which saw a particularly high level of Jewish participation, especially in the mid-1960s. As historian Edward S. Shapiro notes, "About half of the white civil rights attorneys in the South in the 1960s were Jews, and nearly two-thirds of the white volunteers involved Freedom Summer in Mississippi in 1964 were Jews. Two of them—Andrew Goodman and Michael Schwerner—were murdered."[5] Civil rights activism was often an expression of Jewish self-affirmation: many Jews (especially from the north) supported African Americans' struggle for equal rights not only because of their historic ties to American liberalism, but also as a result of their own identification with the history of Jewish oppression, violence, and death in the Holocaust.[6] In spite of this intense involvement, the strong association of Jews with the civil rights movement did not last long. Jews continued to vote Democratic, but their economic, racial, and social interests were increasingly aligning with the agenda of the party's more moderate wing. As African American activists faced the halting progress of the civil rights movement, some came to reject the integrationist approach typically favored by liberal Jews, and to demand more radical approaches that tended to alienate Jewish supporters. Further, as Cheryl Lynn Greenberg has demonstrated, "Although Jews still expressed less racism than other whites, they nonetheless engaged in the same social segregation of blacks that white Christians had made a tradition."[7] The identity politics emerging in the late 1960s led both Jews and African Americans to look inward rather than toward coalitions. By that time, many Jews also were put off by what they perceived to be antisemitism from black nationalists (which was more a result of occasional comments from some leaders than a characteristic of the wider movement), as well as some civil rights leaders' criticism of Israel's treatment of Palestinians. When civil rights activists began to advance affirmative action solutions to solve persistent racial inequality, many Jews opposed them, believing that they were an attack on the color-blind society for which they had long fought, and that such policies promised Jews (as a group) no tangible benefits.

Another, and more influential, factor shaping how young American Jews related to their Jewish identity and the Holocaust was the onset of apparent crises facing Jews elsewhere in the world. Especially after the 1967 mid-east war, in which, in the eyes of many Jews, Israel emerged victorious from what seemed to be the brink of defeat, Jews across the political spectrum quickly aligned themselves with the young country's fate and saw parallels between the Holocaust and the potential slaughter of Israeli Jews. As well, in the late 1960s and early 1970s, American Jews began to advocate for Jews in the Soviet Union, who numbered over two million. New spikes in Soviet antisemitism meant that Jews regularly faced discrimination, the systematic closing of synagogues and religious schools, and racist representations in the press. Prevented from emigrating, many Soviet Jews publicly protested against the authorities, with some even taking extreme measures, such as when a group of Jews hijacked a plane in a failed attempt to flee the country. The resulting crackdown against Jewish religious activity prompted a strong political campaign among American Jews to agitate on behalf of their right to emigrate. Such campaigns on behalf of Jews in Israel and the Soviet Union provided a means by which American Jews could be active politically, embrace the language of civil rights, and yet not threaten their socioeconomic status within white America.

While the events of the tumultuous era of the 1960s and early 1970s prompted a multitude of reinvigorated Jewish identities, most American Jews had distanced themselves too far from traditional Jewish customs, practices, and languages to "return" to a religious Judaism. The Holocaust increasingly became the justification for Jewish investment in liberalism (or for others, a commitment to conservatism or even the extreme right), in Israel, and in the fate of Soviet Jewry. As Shapiro writes, "For some American Jews, the Holocaust became central to their own image of themselves as Jews. With often only a tenuous relationship to Judaism, they clung to the Holocaust as the core element in their Jewish identity."[8] This overidentification with the Holocaust had its critics, both religious and secular alike, who were concerned with the idea of placing victimization at the heart of Jewish communal identity. Nevertheless, since the mid-1960s most American Jewish organizations—such as synagogues, federations, and schools—have made Holocaust commemoration and education central to their activities, and Jewish writers and artists have contended with the Holocaust in their work in ever greater number. The stature of Holocaust survivors increased dramatically, and some, such as Elie Wiesel, gained international prominence.

By the early 1980s, many Jews also began to reassess the political loyalties and strategies of their predecessors during the war years. They asked and debated questions about American Jewry's own response to the Holocaust: Had American Jews been too passive during the Holocaust? Did they place too much trust in President Roosevelt and the Democratic Party? Should major Jewish organizations have taken more strident action on behalf of European Jewry? Did they do everything possible to rescue Jews facing genocide, or were they too concerned with their own well-being? This reconsideration was a corollary to two debates that were under way. The first of these, which had been an ongoing one in Israel, concerned whether Jews had acted morally or bravely during the Holocaust: Had Jews fought strenuously and heroically enough against their Nazi oppressors? Had some Jews collaborated with Nazism for their own personal gain? As the Israeli historian of the Holocaust Yehuda Bauer put it in an essay that challenged Raul Hilberg's depictions of Jewish powerlessness, "Jewish reaction to Nazi rule is of tremendous importance to Jews and non-Jews alike. The Jew wants to know the tradition to which he is heir. How did that tradition, that whole range of historically developed values, stand up to the supreme test of Hitler's death sentence on the Jewish people? Did Jewish civilization ... simply collapse?"[9] The second debate (discussed in the introduction to this book) occurred among historians—both Jewish and non-Jewish—about whether the US government and particularly Roosevelt had acted strongly enough to stop Hitler or whether the Roosevelt administration had been at best unconcerned with, and at worst acquiescent, in the genocide. While scholars raised the question as early as the late 1960s, the debate around it became more heightened during the 1980s, and was prompted in part by a conservative reassessment of Roosevelt's legacy during the Reagan presidency.

As American Jews began to examine whether their forebears had lived up to their moral responsibility during the Holocaust, the question very quickly became contentious. In 1981, the American Jewish Commission on the Holocaust formed with the goal "to record and publish the truth, as nearly as [they] would determine it, as to what American Jewish leaders did, and what indeed they might have been able to do in all of the circumstances to mitigate the massive evils of the Holocaust."[10] The commission, which had only one professional historian, was composed mainly of rabbis and members of Jewish communal organizations. From the outset, the intentions of the group were clear: expose the faults of American Jewish leaders during the Holocaust and depict them as having been more concerned with petty disputes and their own social standing than with saving European Jewry. In 1984 it released its controversial report, *American Jewry during the Holocaust*, which concluded that American Jewish organizations failed to conduct "a united, sustained campaign for all out mobilization of American Jews and their organizations on behalf of massive rescue."[11] Although the majority of the commission's members did not endorse the report and objected to its one-sidedness and lack of scholarly rigor, it quickly made headlines and seemed to confirm for many Jews what they had suspected: American Jews failed to come to the rescue of European Jews. That same year, a widely viewed documentary entitled *Who Shall Live and Who Shall Die* promoted a similar point of view.

Several studies in this vein would be published across the 1980s, with one of the most provocative and condemnatory accounts, *Were We Our Brothers' Keepers?*, appearing in 1985, a year after the American Jewish Commission on the Holocaust released its report. Written by Haskel Lookstein, a prominent American Orthodox rabbi and a leader in the effort to assist Soviet Jewish emigration, the book argued that American Jewry during World War II failed to live up to its responsibility to defend European Jews imperiled by Nazism. In particular, Lookstein castigated—along with FDR and the American press—the World War II generation of American Jewish leaders for adopting an approach that was far more concerned with putting their self-interest over that of their "brethren" in Europe.[12] His study begins with Jewish organizations' response to the *Kristallnacht* pogrom of November 1938 and continues, chapter by chapter, through the *St. Louis* crisis, the first reports of mass killing of Jews, the Warsaw Ghetto uprising, the establishment of the War Refugee Board, discussions over whether to bomb Auschwitz, and the deportation and murder of Hungarian Jews in 1944. At each stage in the persecution and murder of European Jewry, he argued, American Jewish leaders and organizations failed to use all of their authority to thwart Nazi efforts at genocide. Without providing evidence that such strategies would have changed the outcome of the Holocaust, he criticized American Jewish leaders for not staging more mass demonstrations against Germany and opting, instead, to publish letters of condemnation. He faulted them for not publicly criticizing Roosevelt for his refusal to lessen the restrictions on immigration. He took them to task for aligning their interests too closely with Allied efforts to focus on stopping the war as the best solution to stopping Hitler. Furthermore, Lookstein charged Jewish religious leaders with having been far too indifferent to the crisis. A tragedy of such enormity, he argued, should have, at minimum, prompted changes in Jewish religious behavior. He demanded to know "why, for example, was there not a regular fast day each month or a special prayer circulated by the Synagogue Council of America to be recited at Sabbath services every week?" As Lookstein himself concluded, "The Final Solution may have been *unstoppable* by American Jewry, but it should have been *unbearable* for them. And it wasn't. This is important, not alone for our understanding

of the past, but for our sense of responsibility in the futur
to the book, Elie Wiesel gave sanction to this view and co
ference of the Allies and friends." Calling it "unbelievab
charged American Jewry with "not respond[ing] to the h
their brothers and sisters in nazified Europe."

As we have seen in Chapters 1 and 2, American Jewish leaders,
as they were, in fact had quickly condemned the rise of Nazism in Germany and called upon the president and Congress to take action. While there were many debates at the time on the best strategies for action, very few leaders or organizations were indifferent, as Lookstein charged, to the plight of European Jews. At the same time, they were only able to act within the limits of what seemed possible given the tenuous relationship of groups, such as the AJ Committee and the AJ Congress, to the Roosevelt administration.[14] As the historian Henry L. Feingold has argued of American Jewish organizations, "They failed not from lack of trying. They did not remotely possess the kind of power required to convince an almost totally unreceptive officialdom that something more was involved in the Jewish pleas for action than 'Jewish wailing.' " Although it is possible more could have been done by Jewish leaders, it is not at all clear whether it would have changed the president's approach or whether the still-tenuous status of American Jews would not have been threatened by a more strident display of activism. As Feingold wrote, "Enough was not done and could never have been done in a catastrophe of such magnitude."[15] The problem cannot be so easily characterized, as some critical reports asserted, as "the leaders of the 30's and 40's just didn't care enough."[16]

Holocaust controversies in the news

While events in Israel and the Soviet Union in the late 1970s and early 1980s helped to elevate the significance of the Holocaust for many American Jews, two controversies in the mid-1980s in particular thrust the Holocaust back into the international spotlight. In the first of these, President Ronald Reagan undertook a ceremonial visit to a military cemetery in the German city of Bitburg. Reagan was in Europe to attend an economic summit, and he used the occasion to commemorate the fortieth anniversary of the end of World War II. By all accounts, the trip was a disaster, a consequence of poor planning and even poorer public relations. Contrary to the assumptions of White House planners, there were no US soldiers buried at the Bitburg cemetery, and so the attempt to demonstrate a spirit of reconciliation fell flat. Making matters worse was that among the dead there were forty-nine members of the Waffen-SS, which the Nuremberg trials had found to be a criminal organization responsible for carrying out the mass murder of Jews. When word of president's impending visit was made public, protests erupted immediately. Jewish organizations were incensed that he would pay homage to perpetrators of the Holocaust. Newspapers editorialized that the visit would disgrace the United States and insult the memory of the dead. A majority of senators and congressional representatives signed letters challenging the visit. But Reagan, unwilling to risk insulting German Chancellor Helmut Kohl, refused to cancel the trip. He inflamed the issue further when, a few weeks before his visit, he seemed to excuse the Nazi soldiers for their violence on account of their age and equated their deaths to those of victims, claiming that "those young men are victims of Nazism also, even though they were fighting in the German uniform, drafted into service to carry out the hateful wishes of the Nazis. They were victims, just as surely as the victims in the concentration camps."[17] As it happened, the day after these comments, Elie Wiesel was scheduled to receive the Congressional Gold Medal at a White House ceremony. Wiesel broke protocol and took Reagan to task for comparing Nazi soldiers and their victims and further implored him: "May I, Mr. President, if it's possible at all implore you to do something else, to find a way, to find another way, and another site. That place, Mr. President, is not your place. Your place is with the victims of the SS."[18] But the protests only served to harden Reagan's resolve and he proceeded with the trip, although a compensatory visit to the Bergen-Belsen concentration camp was hastily arranged to occur earlier on the same day. In the end, Reagan's visit to Bitburg on May 5, 1985, lasted a total of eight minutes. He laid a wreath at a wall of remembrance, stood silently during a short trumpet salute, and hurried away.

The following year, another political firestorm occurred over Kurt Waldheim. From 1972 to 1981, Waldheim had served as secretary general of the United Nations and in 1986 he was elected president of Austria. When accounting for his service in the Germany army during World War II, he claimed that he had been on the Eastern front and that after he was wounded in 1942 his military career ended. In the mid-1980s, however, a number of witnesses and researchers challenged his account after discovering that he had joined a Nazi youth organization a month after the annexation of Austria in 1938. He subsequently joined the Nazi paramilitary organization known as the Sturmabteilung. While he likely did not participate directly in any atrocities, the uncovering of his past generated a brief but intense debate in the United States over whether he should be permitted to visit. Ultimately, the US government, enacting the recently passed Holtzman Act, which authorized the United States to expel Nazis who had settled in the United States and to refuse to allow former Nazis to enter, placed him on a watch list that prevented him from visiting. These political events ensured that the Holocaust remained in the news for many Americans and provided the frame of reference for an intensification of cultural, educational, and legal events related to it.

FIGURE 5.1 *President Ronald Reagan lays a wreath on the tomb of German soldiers on May 5, 1985, at a cemetery in Bitburg, Germany.*

The growing awareness of the Holocaust and the increasing political importance of American Jewry in the mid-1970s was also evident in a series of legal processes, especially at the federal level, that sought to rectify past injustices and provide a measure of compensation for Holocaust survivors. After several decades of ignoring the fact that many Nazis and collaborators entered the United States after the war, the Department of Justice began taking steps to identify them, strip them of their citizenship, and deport them. The federal government also sought to locate and recover the stolen property of Holocaust survivors who were living in the United States. Both of these efforts were, in their own way, controversial, and their successes were uncertain.

The most well-known trial of a former Nazi collaborator in the United States is that of John "Ivan" Demjanjuk. This case attracted widespread and sustained attention, and it was widely seen as an attempt by the US government to address its past misdeeds in allowing former Nazi criminals to settle in the country after the war. A series of dramatic missteps kept the trial in the news for decades. Demjanjuk's legal struggles in the United States began in the mid-1970s and continued for more than three decades, and his case highlights the many complexities involved with bringing Nazi criminals to justice so many years after the events in question. Born in 1920 in a small village in Ukraine, Ivan Demjanjuk received little formal schooling and worked from an early age on the family farm.[19] In 1932, Demjanjuk's family, like millions of other Ukrainians, fell victim to starvation due to the Soviet campaign of forced collectivization. As many as three million (some estimate the number to be more than twice as many) Ukrainians died of hunger in this period, which many consider an act of genocide.[20] When he was sixteen, he found work on a collective farm. Pressed into service in the Soviet army following the German invasion of 1941, he was soon wounded; later, in May 1942, he was captured by German forces. According to his account, he was kept as a prisoner of war until its end three years later. After living in several DP camps, he benefited from the 1950 extension of the Displaced Persons Act of 1948, which, as we have seen in Chapter 3, tended to favor non-Jewish victims of Stalinism rather than Jewish victims of Nazism. In early 1952, Demjanjuk, along with his new wife and son, successfully immigrated to the United States, eventually settling in Cleveland, and Demjanjuk worked at a nearby Ford auto plant. He was naturalized as a citizen in 1958 and changed his first name to John.

Suspicions about Demjanjuk's account of his wartime service surfaced in the mid-1970s when a US senator received a list of seventy suspected Ukrainian war criminals living in the country. The list, which included Demjanjuk's name, was sent by an American of Ukrainian descent with communist sympathies, and the list was likely provided to him by Soviet authorities. As Lawrence Douglas has shown, by that time, "the United States was finally beginning to address the disturbing legacy of the Displaced Persons Act of 1948" and to take steps to investigate whether people who had committed war crimes had found sanctuary in the country.[21] In 1979, the Justice Department created the Office of Special Investigations in order to identify and deport Nazis living in the United States. A review of Demjanjuk's visa and immigration records by the Immigration and Naturalization Services revealed that Demjanjuk had listed that he spent the years 1934–43 in the town of Sobibor, Poland. In the years 1942 and 1943, Sobibor was the site of a German extermination camp where an estimated 200,000 prisoners, primarily Jews, were murdered in gas chambers.

FIGURE 5.2 *John Demjanjuk at arraignment, 1988.*

There was no legal mechanism in the United States to prosecute war crimes that had been committed by noncitizens against noncitizens and which had occurred outside of the country's borders. What the United States could do, however, was strip Demjanjuk of his citizenship, deport him, and extradite him to a country in which he could stand trial. It took three years for Demjanjuk's denaturalization case to come to court. Demjanjuk insisted that he was kept as a prisoner of war and then forced to fight the Soviet army near the end of the war. But when his photograph was shown to a number of Holocaust survivors, several identified him as an extremely ruthless guard in the Treblinka death camp—not in Sobibor—known as Ivan the Terrible. The surfacing of an identity card in 1977 seemingly identified Demjanjuk as having been a member of the Trawniki, a group of Nazi auxiliary forces recruited from the ranks of Eastern Europeans fighting for the Soviets and then captured by the Germans. The Trawniki, who numbered in the thousands and were selected as a result of their anticommunist and antisemitic views, helped staff many of the Nazi death camps in the east and were often directly involved in the murder of Jews. After three separate hearings, and in spite of a number of inconsistencies in the government's case (Demjanjuk's defense was even weaker), Demjanjuk was stripped of his US citizenship and extradited to Israel to stand trial in 1986. Many Ukrainian Americans publicly supported Demjanjuk and saw him as a victim of Soviet espionage. Others, such as Pat Buchanan (a prominent far-right political commentator who would later run for president), made antisemitic allegations that Demjanjuk had fallen victim to a Jewish conspiracy.

Israel tried Demjanjuk under its 1950 Law against Genocide and the Nazi and Nazi Collaborators (Punishment) Law. In the trial, which began in November 1986 and lasted until April 1988, many questions, similar to those in the US hearings, were raised about the identification card's authenticity. As in the Eichmann trial, the prosecution relied heavily on survivor testimonies. The weight of survivor testimony claiming that he was Treblinka's Ivan the Terrible was so great that in April 1988, he was found guilty and sentenced to death by hanging. For five years, Demjanjuk sat in an Israeli prison while his case was on appeal. In that time, the Soviet Union collapsed and new archival documents became available that proved that Demjanjuk was in fact *not* Ivan the Terrible. While it seemed clear to all that Demjanjuk had served with German forces, likely as a member of the Trawniki in Sobibor and other camps, it was also clear that he was not guilty of the crimes of which he had been convicted. In July 1993, the guilty verdict was overturned and Demjanjuk was permitted to return to the United States, where a court ruled that government trial lawyers had deliberately failed to disclose evidence that ran counter to its claims that he was Ivan the Terrible. Demjanjuk's citizenship was restored in 1988.

The following year, however, US prosecutors filed new charges against Demjanjuk, claiming that he had been a guard in the Sobibor and Majdanek death camps, as well as in the Flossenbürg concentration camp. In 2001, he was again stripped of his citizenship and was eventually deported in 2009 to Germany for trial. In failing health, he was convicted in 2011 as an accessory to the murder of nearly 28,000 Jews. He was sentenced to five years in prison, which was then suspended for time served. He died in 2012 while his case was on appeal, which, according to German law, left him legally innocent. In spite of its many complications, the Demjanjuk case helped pave the way for subsequent trials of Nazi perpetrators in Germany (and overturned decades of legal precedent). It was, however, the last high-profile trial for Nazi-era crimes in the United States (and in Israel as well).[22] Since its founding in 1979, the Office of Special Investigations had denaturalized and deported more than 300 former Nazis. However, this case, its most prominent, was widely viewed as a fiasco.

Another set of legal cases that kept the Holocaust in the public realm occurred in the mid-1990s, soon after the opening of the USHMM and the release of the film *Schindler's List*. In response to Holocaust survivors' repeated attempts to track money and assets that had been stolen from them, a number of US politicians undertook a public investigation of the role of Swiss financial institutions in the Holocaust. In what became known in the United States as the "Swiss gold scandal," Swiss banks were accused of having provided protection for assets stolen by Nazis during the war and of refusing to relinquish existing accounts to relatives of victims of the Holocaust.

By the time of these investigations, the West German government had been making reparation payments for nearly forty years. Just months after the end of World War II, Chaim Weizmann, then head of the Jewish Agency (and future president of Israel) demanded that the Allied governments insist upon reparations as part of the war settlement. In 1952, West Germany agreed to pay compensation to Holocaust survivors and families of victims in the form of payments to Israel said to be equivalent to the cost of the absorption of survivors as well as funds provided to an umbrella organization of major American Jewish organizations for distribution to survivors who had resettled in the United States. In 1988, the West German government paid an additional $125 million in order to provide small monthly stipends to survivors.[23] As the scholar Norman Finkelstein has argued, however, oftentimes reparation funds did not reach the actual survivors but instead supported the budgets of the organizations themselves and paid the salaries of the many attorneys who brought the cases.[24]

In 1995, the World Jewish Congress took legal action against several Swiss banks for withholding funds of Jews who had been murdered in the Holocaust. The banks had claimed that they could not release funds in the accounts because they had not been provided with death certificates proving that the account owners were deceased, even though most had died in mass shootings or in death camps. Several political figures in the United States became actively involved in pressuring the Swiss government to release the funds to surviving Jewish family members by holding public hearings and threatening economic sanctions. President Clinton lent his support by instructing an undersecretary to testify and to issue a report implicating the Swiss banks. These hearings regularly became an occasion for political grandstanding. According to observers across the political spectrum, the officials and attorneys involved in these efforts were motived at least as much by political or monetary gain than concern for the actual survivors or possible foreign policy considerations.[25] Meanwhile, little attempt was made to investigate the funds left behind in American banks by Holocaust victims. Eventually, threats of boycotts of Swiss products and financial institutions prompted the banks to settle with the World Jewish Congress for $1.25 billion. A subsequent independent audit suggested that contrary to the claims of those prosecuting the case, there was little evidence of an intentional cover-up by the banks. In 1997, the Swiss government established its own fund for needy Holocaust victims and assisted approximately 300,000 persons in sixty countries.[26]

Literature, television, and film

In the 1960s and 1970s, a number of books about the Holocaust became best-sellers and helped to shape Americans' understanding of the Holocaust. The English translation of Elie Wiesel's memoir *La Nuit* appeared in 1960 and was quickly regarded as a groundbreaking text.[27] *Night* describes Wiesel's loss of faith after his imprisonment in Auschwitz. It is notable for its descriptions of Nazi cruelty and brutality, and its economy of style earned it critical praise as a "slim volume of terrifying power" and a "remarkable close-up of one boy's tragedy."[28] *Night* continues to be read and taught widely and is often considered *the* standard survivor account. Since its original publication, the work has been translated into thirty languages, which propelled Wiesel (who passed away in 2016) into the international spotlight. Other books, along with Anne Frank's *Diary*, that brought the Holocaust to broad US readerships included *I Never Saw Another Butterfly*, a collection of poems and artworks composed by children confined to the Theresienstadt concentration camp, Primo Levi's account of his capture and imprisonment in Auschwitz, *If This Is a Man* (later republished as *Survival in Auschwitz*), and Simon Wiesenthal's *The Sunflower*, a reminiscence and ethical investigation of an encounter Wiesenthal had with a Nazi officer while imprisoned in the Lemberg concentration camp.[29] Several novels in the 1970s appeared that helped to usher in a new wave of fictional works related to Nazism and the Holocaust, such as Saul Bellow's *Mr. Sammler's Planet*, William Styron's *Sophie's Choice*, Philip Roth's *Ghost Writer*, and Leslie Epstein's *King of the Jews*.

Film and television have been particularly compelling media for portraying the Holocaust. As we have seen, there were few American-made cinematic representations of the Holocaust in the 1950s and 1960s, although Nazis increasingly became the subject of both major and low budget productions. By the 1970s, filmmakers were contending with the subject with greater frequency, but more often as a plot point or a way to provide a back story for an extremely evil character. The 1976 hit *Marathon Man*, for example, tells the story of the efforts of graduate student "Babe" Levy (played by Dustin Hoffman) to uncover a plot to sell diamonds stolen from Jews during World War II. The antagonist of the film is the fictional Christian Szell, "the White Angel of Auschwitz" (played by Lawrence Olivier), who successfully escaped capture and runs a diamond ring from South America. In one of the film's most harrowing and memorable scenes, Szell performs dental torture on

Levy, reinforcing preexisting notions of Nazis as evil and sadistic, rather than being "ordinary" killers.[30]

More than any film or television show previously, the April 1978 television airing of the four-part miniseries *The Holocaust* impressed upon American an understanding of the murder of European Jewry as a distinct and catastrophic historical event.[31] With an estimated viewership of 120 million (second only to the showing of *Roots*, which a year earlier depicted the history of slavery in the United States), the Holocaust was once again brought directly into Americans' living rooms.[32] Lasting nine and a half hours over four consecutive nights, *The Holocaust* told the story of the fictional Weiss family of German Jews who experienced the worst horrors of Nazi persecution. Each member of the family endures her or his own particular tragedy. Viewers were shown depictions of the forcible deportation of Jews of Polish ancestry, the violence of the 1938 *Kristallnacht* pogrom, sexual violence against Jewish women, the horrors of the concentration camps and the Warsaw Ghetto, mass shootings in Babi Yar, and the extermination of Jews in Auschwitz. The Jewish characters are portrayed as having a variety of responses ranging from passive submission to armed resistance. *The Holocaust* also traced the journey of a member of the SS who ends up becoming a ruthless murderer. To help audiences understand the larger Holocaust, the studio prepared a viewer's guide in advance of the show's second airing in 1979.

While the miniseries, which starred, among others, Tovah Feldshuh, Meryl Streep, Joseph Bottoms, and James Woods, often strayed far from the historical record, it was received both with great acclaim and significant criticism. Writing in *Time*, for example, the critic Frank Rich, declared it "an uncommonly valuable achievement" that "is likely to awaken more consciences to the horrors of the Third Reich than any single work since Anne Frank's diary nearly three decades ago."[33] It won several Emmy Awards and Golden Globes. When it was aired the following year in Germany, as many as 15 million viewers tuned in. Some viewers, however, found the miniseries wanting and even objectionable. A *New York Times* television critic referred to it as "less a noble failure than a presumptuous venture" that resulted in "a sterile collection of wooden characters and ridiculous coincidences." With over 150 speaking roles and ten years of European history to encapsulate, *The Holocaust*, he argued, fell into the category of "plodding, realist dramas" unable to grasp the full horror of the actual event.[34] A group of Polish Americans objected to the portrayal of Polish soldiers as collaborators in Nazi crimes against Jews, insisting that they too had been victims of German aggression. Notably, this objection sparked questions as to whether there should be representatives from the Polish American community on President Carter's Commission on the Holocaust, which was just being established.[35]

The most vocal critic, by far, was Elie Wiesel, who was by then a professor of humanities at Boston University and widely regarded as *the* moral authority on matters related to the Holocaust. Having been permitted to view *The Holocaust* in its entirety prior to its airing, on the morning of the show's premier Wiesel published his own review in the *New York Times* that condemned the series as a gross distortion of the historical record, calling it "untrue, offensive, cheap" and "an insult to those who perished and to those who survived." He objected to everything about the presentation: its name should not have been "The Holocaust," which reduced the historical event to a spectacle; the facts were not researched adequately; Jewish resistance figures appear as caricatures and both Jews and Germans are stereotypes; the film was too explicit and at times even salacious. Above all, Wiesel, recognizing the compelling power of television to shape viewers' understanding of historical events, feared that "the Holocaust [would] be measured and judged in part by the NBC TV production bearing its name."[36] The screenwriter Gerald Green responded the following week. He acknowledged his respect for Wiesel but insisted that Wiesel was hardly the only figure capable of speaking on the Holocaust: "Survivor, sufferer, prophet, teacher, he is an eminent and scholarly figure, and we must be grateful for his contributions. He is not, of course, the only such expert, the Alpha and Omega of the Holocaust. Others have suffered, survived and written." Green then charged Wiesel with acting out of his own self-interest to defend his position as the sole authority to speak on the Holocaust: "Mr. Wiesel objects that we try to tell it all. Why not? Is Elie Wiesel to be allowed a monopoly on the subject, to be self-anointed and only voice of the Holocaust?"[37] A week later, Wiesel responded, somewhat curiously, by reasserting his authority to speak on behalf of survivors:

> Why do I bother answering Mr. Green? Why did I speak up in the first place? Why have I gone against the Jewish establishment, many clergymen and NBC's powerful p.r. apparatus? I respect their motivations, as I hope they respect mine. And mine has to do with one obsession shared by most survivors: to tell what happened, the way it happened. We believe that this is why we survived.[38]

For months after *The Holocaust* was broadcast, the mainstream press as well as publications by religious and civic groups ran articles about its historical accuracy, appropriateness, the moral debates that it raised, the consequences of showing it to German audiences, and its ability to draw attention to other atrocities occurring around the world. As Jeffrey Shandler has noted, the miniseries is remembered today for the discussions and controversies that it generated more than its depiction of the Holocaust.[39] Although it was an elaborate production, it brought no new perspective to our understanding of the Holocaust, nor did it make any significant advances in television production techniques. Rather, the fact of its airing, its massive viewership, its solidifying the name "The Holocaust" for this historical event, and the highly charged debates that it prompted are its greatest legacy.

In spite of the miniseries' success, only a few films about the Holocaust were made in the immediate years following. *Sophie's Choice*, also starring Streep, appeared in 1982, and garnered her an Academy Award for best actress. In it, she plays Zofia "Sophie" Zawistowski, a Polish immigrant living in Brooklyn after the war who is torn between her desire for two men. Over the course of the film, it is revealed that the choice that is the real source of her suffering is one from her past, when she and her two children were deported to Auschwitz after her arrest on suspicion of helping the Polish resistance.[40] Forced by a sadistic Nazi to decide which child would be sent to forced labor and which to the gas chamber, she calculates that her son would have the greater chance of survival, and chooses him for labor. Ever since, she is haunted by the belief that she condemned her daughter to death. Although the film is not about Jewish suffering per se, it depicts many of the horrors of the Nazi death camps. Three years later, in 1985, the French documentary *Shoah*, directed by Claude Lanzmann and lasting nine and a half hours, was screened around the United States and quickly acknowledged as a masterpiece.

In December 1993, the same year as the opening of the USHMM, a Hollywood film profoundly reshaped the way that many Americans understood the Holocaust. Steven Spielberg's *Schindler's List* is unquestionably one of the most viewed and recognizable American films about the Holocaust. It tells the story of the real-life Oskar Schindler (played by Liam Neeson), an ethnic German, industrialist, and war profiteer who becomes sympathetic toward the Jewish slave laborers who work in his enamelware factory after he witnesses the liquidation of the Cracow Ghetto.[41] He successfully manipulates the sadistic Nazi Amnon Göth (played by Ralph Fiennes) and, following the council of his Jewish assistant, the prisoner Itzhak Stern (played by Ben Kingsly), Schindler spends his fortune to protect 1,100 Jews who would have otherwise been sent to their deaths.

The film depicts, in often terrifying scenes, the brutal hunting down and murder of Jews trying to survive the closing of the Cracow Ghetto, the random shooting at Jews for sport, and scenes from Auschwitz in which naked women are brought to a shower installation where, the viewer is led to expect, they will be gassed. Filmed primarily in black and white, *Schindler's List* blurs the lines between documentary and fantasy, and in its final scenes it shows the real-life survivors whom Schindler aided together with the actors who portrayed them placing stones of remembrance on Schindler's grave in Jerusalem. At times, the film deliberately manipulates the emotions of its viewers and audience members often openly wept in the theaters. One of its most memorable scenes depicts a young girl in a red jacket (one of the very few uses of color) walking through the ghetto during its liquidation; later, she is shown to have been killed.

More than an epic film, *Schindler's List* was meant to commemorate Schindler the man and the Jews he saved, as well as retell the history of the Holocaust itself. Very quickly, even before its release, many came to regard viewing the film as an obligatory act of remembrance and a form of "witnessing" the Holocaust. The film was a great success at the box office and during the awards season. Film critics, as overwhelmed as many audience members, broadly praised the film as marking a great cinematic achievement. Scholars, by contrast, have been more mixed in their assessment. Some have expressed concern with Spielberg's choice to make a film about Jewish suffering that places a non-Jew at the center. Others have taken Spielberg to task for brushing over the less flattering facts about Schindler, such as that he joined a German intelligence unit in 1936 and the Nazi Party in 1939. Some were dismayed by the relative passivity of the Jews portrayed in the film. Others still have expressed concerns that Spielberg, by creating a film that elevates the ideals of industry and entrepreneurialism, in effect "Americanized" the Holocaust. To many, the depiction of Nazis as brutal sadists masked the fact that most were motivated not by tendencies toward extreme brutality but by a belief in the rightness of their cause, the benefits that their actions provided them, or out of a sense of duty and obligation. Still others raised concerns about the consequences of making a Holocaust film in which most of the characters the audience becomes invested in survive, given that millions did not.[42] In spite of these criticisms, *Schindler's List* remains an iconic film of the Holocaust. It also vividly demonstrated the moral, pedagogical, and commercial potential of Holocaust films, and prompted the production of many more in its wake.

Memorials and museums

Just as *Schindler's List* represents the pinnacle (thus far) of efforts to create a powerful cinematic testament to the victims of Nazi genocide, the USHMM represents a high point in the creation of Holocaust memorials and museums and has sparked the creation of dozens, if not hundreds, more across the country. But from the museum's beginnings during the Carter administration, the path toward its dedication in 1993 was by no means a smooth one. Over the decade and a half of its planning, implementation, and construction, many observers questioned the appropriateness of a US national memorial to a European catastrophe. Although many monuments to the Holocaust had already been established across the country, some Americans—Jews among them—were worried that a state-sanctioned memorial would only be a painful reminder of Jewish victimization and powerlessness. Representatives of African American and Native American groups wondered why a memorial to a genocide committed overseas was the subject of memorialization when there were no such national monuments in the capital to genocidal acts committed in the United States. Others were concerned that Carter's commitment to recognizing the Holocaust was primarily a political effort to appease American Jewish voters, whose leaders were suspicious of his efforts to foster a peaceful dialogue between Israelis and Palestinians. Some thought Carter's definition of the Holocaust—which was limited exclusively to Nazism's six million Jewish victims—as insufficient and sought to expand it to include Polish, Ukrainian, and other nationalities who also suffered under Nazism. Some disagreed with the mechanism of its funding and insisted that no federal resources be granted (the land was provided by an act of Congress), while others objected to the vigorous efforts to secure private funds, which were required to pay for the museum's construction and the installation of its exhibitions.[43]

After the museum opened, many of these criticisms abated, although new ones have emerged over the years. Some scholars and observers, for example, have questioned various aspects of the museum and the implications of our contemporary culture of commemoration. A number of historians have asked whether the USHMM is a misguided attempt to Americanize what is largely a European tragedy. These critics have argued that the permanent exhibition incorrectly presents a simplistic narrative of loss and redemption by focusing on the United States' seeming refusal to aid European Jews and then overemphasizing its role as liberator of Jewish Holocaust victims. Some have viewed the USHMM's success as a sign of crass commercialism and part of an effort to "sell" the Holocaust. Others have criticized the USHMM for being part of an effort by some American Jewish leaders to use Jewish suffering to garner political, economic, and military support for the State of Israel.

There are also opponents of the USHMM who are motivated by outright hatred and antisemitism. For example, on June 10, 2009, James Wenneker von Brunn, a Holocaust denier and white supremacist active in far-right antigovernment groups, shot and killed Museum Special Police Officer Stephen Tyrone Johns. In von Brunn's car was a note that said in part, "The Holocaust is a lie. Obama was created by Jews. Obama does what his Jew owners tell him to do. Jews captured America's money. Jews control the mass media. The 1st Amendment is abrogated—henceforth."[44]

One question concerning the USHMM that has been raised by friends and skeptics alike and which has persisted to the present day is whether it should

FIGURE 5.3 *Police gather in front of the United States Holocaust Memorial Museum following the June 10, 2009, shooting.*

be limited to memorializing past events or become an institution that would also take an active role in preventing other genocides. Would it be a force for the prevention of mass violence or a comparatively low-stakes means by which political leaders could acknowledge past crimes against Jews without having to take political and military steps to thwart future efforts at mass violence? Would the museum be a call to action or a substitute for action? Genocides in Rwanda and Darfur, which occurred after the museum's opening, brought this question to the fore, as has the more recent (and ongoing at the time of this writing) refugee crisis in Syria. Such questions were in fact raised at the dedication itself. Near the end of his address, Wiesel turned to face President Clinton and challenged him to take steps to stop the Bosnian Serbian forces' ongoing campaign of genocide against Bosnian Muslims:

> What have we learned? We have learned some lessons, minor lessons, perhaps, that we are all responsible, and indifference is a sin and a punishment. And we have learned that when people suffer we cannot remain indifferent. And, Mr. President, I cannot not tell you something. I have been in the former Yugoslavia last fall. I cannot sleep since for what I have seen. As a Jew I am saying that we must do something to stop the bloodshed in that country! People fight each other and children die. Why? Something, anything must be done.

Although Clinton applauded Wiesel's comments, it was more than two years before US forces, acting under NATO auspices, intervened in an attempt to stop the killing. By that time, as many as 100,000 Muslims had been killed and 1 million were displaced. In July 1995, units of the Bosnian Serb Army acting under the command of General Ratko Mladić slaughtered over 7,000 Bosnian Muslims in a genocidal act in the city of Srebrenica. Recent reports have shown that Clinton (along with the British Prime Minister John Major) was likely aware of that the murders would take place as much as six weeks beforehand and did not intervene.[45] As the historian Edward T. Linenthal has remarked, "Clearly, Holocaust memory was to be taken seriously when it was convenient to do so, and ignored when other priorities intruded."[46]

By the time of the opening of the USHMM, at least seventeen states and the District of Columbia were homes to memorials.[47] These included a 1955 monument erected by the New American Jewish Club of Richmond, Virginia, the Illinois Holocaust Museum and Education Center in Skokie, and a gravestone dedicated in 1961, "In Memory of the Six Million Who Perished," in Akron, Ohio, by Branch 587 of the Workmen's Circle, a Yiddish labor-oriented social organization. Projects to establish physical memorials (as opposed to liturgical, literary, ceremonial, and performative memorials, which began during the war and have continued without pause ever since) were initiated almost immediately after the war. The first effort to build a permanent memorial in the United States began in New York City in 1948 and has a complicated history. As the scholar James E. Young has explained, in 1947 the Memorial Committee for the Six Million Jews of Europe considered several proposals for monuments to be built in the city's Upper West Side. In October of that year, on a small parcel of land near to 83rd Street and Riverside Drive, a plaque was laid on what was to be the site of a monument dedicated to the memory of European Jewry. The plaque's text reads, "THIS IS THE SITE FOR THE AMERICAN MEMORIAL TO THE HEROES OF THE WARSAW GHETTO BATTLE, APRIL–MAY, 1943, AND TO THE 6,000,000 JEWS OF EUROPE MARTYRED IN THE CAUSE OF HUMAN LIBERTY." In a ceremony attended by 15,000 people, including Mayor William O'Dwyer, New York Senator Irving Ives, and dozens of survivors from concentration camps, the site was dedicated and two bronze boxes containing soil from camps in Czechoslovakia were buried beneath the plaque. The dedication was also an occasion for a speech by Senator Robert Wagner (read by his son) on the need for the United Nations to make a final resolution concerning the status of Palestine, and portrayed the decision as an opportunity for the new international body to prove its legitimacy and usefulness. "Unless the United Nations equitably determines the Palestine issue," he advised, "it can never hope to be an agency for the complex difficulties arising in an atomic era." He went on to say that "the enforcement by the United Nations of the promises solemnly made to

FIGURE 5.4 *Memorial to Warsaw uprising, Riverside Park Manhattan.*

the Jews will at once establish that body as an organ of international law and morality."[48]

The monument planned for the site, a 50-by-50-foot sculpture, was never built. Preliminary designs were rejected by the city's Arts Commission, and later efforts to fundraise for a replacement broke down when the sculptor passed away. For nearly two decades, the project remained stalled, and attempts in the mid-1960s to place a sculpture by Nathan Rapoport, whose works were by then nearly synonymous with the Holocaust, were rejected by the Arts Commission, in part because the monument was then seen as representing the narrow interests of "special groups" and the committee's approval might set a "highly regrettable precedent."[49] But the plaque remained, although it lay neglected until the early 1990s, when volunteers began to restore the area around it. Since 2001, the site has served as the location of annual commemorations of the Warsaw Ghetto uprising.[50] Other monuments to the Holocaust in the city include the Museum of Jewish Heritage—A Living Memorial to the Holocaust, which opened in 1997 in Battery Park and portrays Jewish history before, during, and after the Holocaust.

In Los Angeles, home to the second largest Jewish community in the United States as well as 30,000 survivors, rivalries that formed between competing groups led to two memorials, one founded well before the creation of the USHMM and the other opening at virtually the same time as it. The first of these memorials has its origins in efforts in 1961 by Holocaust survivors who were seeking a permanent home for the artifacts from their time in the Holocaust that they had managed to save. They hoped to create a memorial site that would serve as both monument and museum. After approaching county officials, they were permitted to build a monument in Pan Pacific Park in the city's heavily Jewish Fairfax district. The project experienced many delays, however, and was not completed until 1991. In the meantime, the group also established a small museum that was housed within the local Jewish Federation building. As Young notes, "For a while, this room was the first and only Holocaust museum in America," and it was visited by thousands of schoolchildren from all over Los Angeles.[51] In 2010, the museum—now called the Los Angeles Museum of the Holocaust—moved to its current home alongside the monument in Pan Pacific Park. In spite of its new location, it has sought to keep to its roots as a modest museum that is rich in artifacts and historical exhibitions.

By contrast, the Museum of Tolerance, which lays two and half miles to the west in the city's Pico-Robertson neighborhood, is very much within the Hollywood vein of high-profile and high-tech attractions that promise to bring "experiences" to visitors. In 1977, Marvin Hier founded a Jewish religious school to which he added a memorial and museum to the Holocaust named the Simon Wiesenthal Center. Hier's organizing skills were exceptional, and his message regarding the importance of Holocaust awareness was convincing to many donors. His project quickly began to outpace the one that had been established by survivors and that was housed within the central organization of the Jewish community. His seemingly brash methods (with no lack of self-promotion) quickly alienated much of the established Jewish community but attracted a great deal of celebrity support.[52] The Museum of Tolerance: A Simon Wiesenthal Center Museum, as the project came to be called, is a massive multimillion dollar structure that promises to deliver a rich multimedia experience that compels viewers to confront the long history of antisemitism, prejudice, and discrimination.[53] It is much less a museum in the conventional sense—there are relatively few archives and artifacts—than it is an entertainment venue that imparts lessons of tolerance drawn from the history of the Holocaust. It is a site for visiting dignitaries, school groups, and tourists to the city. In 2005, Heir became embroiled in what remains an ongoing controversy when the Simon Wiesenthal Center announced plans to build a "Museum of Tolerance and a Center for Human Dignity" in West Jerusalem, Israel, on the site of a Muslim cemetery.[54] Tensions between the two institutions persist even to this day.[55]

In the nearly twenty-five years since the dedication of the USHMM, hundreds of monuments, memorials, and museums to the Holocaust have appeared in the United States. According to a survey by the Jewish genealogical organization Avotaynu, there are over 300 such sites across the country, and they are located in nearly every state.[56] They range from the modest and unimposing, such as memorial gardens or plaques in public spaces, to the substantial, as with Holocaust museums or permanent exhibitions. The motives for creating these more recent museums are numerous and often intertwined. Appearing primarily in a period when Americans began questioning their country's role during the Holocaust, many were constructed as acts of contrition. Several repeat the familiar historical message that the United States initially ignored (at best) the crisis facing European Jewry or (at worst) exacerbated it, before arriving on the scene as liberators at the end of the war. Likewise, for American Jews, the sustained public questioning led to the founding of many public monuments and memorials as a type of compensation for the perceived reluctance of an earlier generation to challenge President Roosevelt more forcefully. As Rabbi Arthur Hertzberg stated in the *New York Times* in 1990:

> And so, in expiation of the sins of the fathers, whose quiet interventions in Washington did little good, this generation of American Jewish leaders is largely confrontationist with enemies and critics. Holocaust consciousness has created a sense of Jews in part of their souls as an embattled bastion in the very America of today that is free and open enough for Jews to enshrine their most painful memory in museums in very public places.[57]

Holocaust studies

Similar to Holocaust films and memorials, scholarship on the Holocaust took several decades to be recognized as a distinct phenomenon. Even by the early 1970s, a decade after Raul Hilberg's *The Destruction of the European Jews*, there were only a handful of historical works on the Nazi assault on European Jewry, and significantly fewer on other groups similarly targeted, such as Roma and people perceived as disabled. It took seven years after Hilberg's 1961 study for another attempt at a comprehensive history of the Holocaust to appear by a scholar in the United States. Although her work was challenged by critics in part for its limited citations (it was intended for a more general readership), Nora Levin's *The Holocaust: The Destruction of European Jewry, 1933–1945* was deeply informed by her comprehensive understanding of the intricacies of Jewish history.[58] Two years later, the historian Karl A. Schleunes published *The Twisted Road to Auschwitz: Nazi Policy toward German Jews, 1933–1939*, which argued—against a common view—that Nazi actions against German Jewry were not premeditated and planned meticulously step by step, but instead developed over time in a nonlinear fashion.[59] In 1975, Lucy Dawidowicz published *The War against the Jews, 1933–1945*, which was, in part, a direct rebuttal to Hilberg's portrayal of Jews as passive victims. Over the subsequent decade and a half, the field of Holocaust studies began to grow, and scholars in the United States participated in many of the debates in the field. These included questions over the place of antisemitism within Nazi policymaking, the extent to which the Final Solution was a goal of the Nazis from the outset of the party's founding or one that developed over the course of the war, how far responsibility for the Holocaust extended (only to Nazi leaders or to "ordinary Germans" as well), and the historical uniqueness of the Holocaust itself. By the mid-1980s, the field of Holocaust studies had grown significantly, so much so that there began to appear books that reflected on the development of the field itself, sparking the subdiscipline of Holocaust historiography.[60]

This increased attention on the Holocaust prompted concern from some quarters. In 1981, for example, the literary scholar Robert Alter cautioned that growing interest in the Holocaust threatened to overshadow other areas of Jewish studies. He was fearful that the new fascination with the Holocaust (which was prompted, he believed, by the seeming threat posed to Israel in the 1967 and 1973 wars), would lead to "serious distortions of the Holocaust itself, and, what is worse, Jewish life ... when the Holocaust is commercialized, politicized, theologized, or academicized."[61] Alter expressed alarm with the growing number of scholarly works that were being published, pointing to three (!) new books on Holocaust literature appearing in that year alone. In spite of his concern, however, over the next decade academic programs in Holocaust studies emerged in many universities across the country, and by the start of the twenty-first century, scholarly works in English were published at a rate of several hundred per year.[62]

In the mid-1990s, research on the Holocaust received an unexpected contribution from an unlikely source. Following the success of *Schindler's List*, Steven Spielberg established a foundation to support filmed interviews with Holocaust survivors with the goal of creating a permanent archive of their testimony. Initially named the Survivors of the Shoah Visual History Foundation, the project videotaped the testimony of over 50,000 survivors from 1994 to 1999, and it quickly became one of the world's largest digital archives and generated a great deal of attention in the press. At the time, many scholars showed great skepticism toward the project. Some were concerned that the interviewers were not properly trained in methods of gathering oral testimony nor in the history of the Holocaust itself. Others were concerned with the inconsistency of the testimonies because of the lack of standardized questions (resulting in some testimonies lasting only a short while, with others lasting several hours). Still others challenged the project over its basic assumption that such an archive of testimonies was inherently valuable. Given assumptions regarding the general unreliability of much eyewitness testimony, especially decades after the event in question, many wondered whether this was not a misplaced use of what are generally scarce resources for academic inquiries.

Over time, however, the archive, now housed at the University of Southern California and called the USC Shoah Foundation: The Institute for Visual History and Education, has become an important center for scholars investigating the Holocaust and other genocides. It also has expanded its mission and houses testimony from survivors and witnesses of other genocides and mass murders, including those in Armenia, Nanjing, Cambodia, Rwanda, and Guatemala. As for the interviews of Holocaust survivors conducted in the 1990s, they have become a highly valuable tool for many researchers, often in ways not imagined at the time of their filming. For example, linguists have turned to the archive to chart the development regional dialects in European languages. Those working in digital humanities have been able to make use of the testimonies, most of which have been indexed by keyword.[63] The many freely available testimonies have also become a resource for teachers all over the world when giving lessons on the Holocaust.

Although most of the scholarly debates about the Holocaust have stayed within the confines of academic discourse, some have made their way to the broader American reading public. One of the best known, as discussed in the introduction, is the role of the US government in the refugee crisis and the Allied efforts to save European Jewry. Since the first books on the subject were published in the 1960s, it has remained a highly contested issue that regularly draws heated opinions on all sides. Another fiercely debated topic that has come to the public's attention regards the complicity of US corporations with Nazism, with companies such as IBM, Ford, General Motors, and the precursors to Koch Industries being taken to task for profiting off of German militarization during the Nazi period.[64] Other debates have concerned the activities of Holocaust deniers, many of whom present themselves as engaging in legitimate academic investigations. In one high-profile case, Holocaust denier David Irving sued (unsuccessfully) Emory University historian Deborah Lipstadt and her publisher for libel in British court over her contention that Irving deliberately misinterpreted the historical record to deny the Holocaust. In a rare case of Hollywood drawing its material from the tribulations of scholars, the story of the 1996 trial is now a feature film.[65]

In recent decades, Holocaust studies has grown dramatically, and today there are very few scholarly approaches outside of the hard sciences that have not made significant contributions to the discipline. It is a dynamic field of inquiry that is not only an amalgam of various academic approaches, but also contains its own vibrant set of terminologies, intellectual demands, and assumptions. It touches upon dozens of languages and nearly every region of the world. The opening of archives in the former Soviet Union has made possible entirely new avenues of investigation as German documents captured by

Soviet forces are increasingly available to researchers. Scholars now regularly take very seriously the diaries, memoirs, and firsthand accounts of survivors and witnesses. They still view the Holocaust as a genocidal event that had Jews at its epicenter, but many also recognize that Nazis utilized the same killing methods on other groups of people in the name of racial purification, such as people perceived to have been disabled and Roma. There is also a widespread recognition that not all perpetrators were Germans, and that Nazis found many sympathizers and willing collaborators among the populations whose countries they occupied. Increasing numbers of scholars are paying attention to questions of gender, recognizing that women and men—whether as victims, perpetrators, bystanders, enablers, beneficiaries, or rescuers—often had vastly different experiences with Nazi violence. Many scholars also strive toward a more integrated understanding of the Holocaust, acknowledging that while it was not identical to World War II, it cannot be understood as separate from it.[66]

Holocaust education

As with scholarship, Holocaust education became widespread only several decades after the end of World War II. In the early 1970s, there were very few university courses taught on the Holocaust; Hilberg's courses at the University of Vermont were among the only available anywhere in the country. In secondary schools, it was a topic that was rarely discussed at all. A 1972 study on secondary education by the historian and survivor Henry Friedlander concluded that "discussion of the Holocaust is bland and superficial" and tended to "skim over the persecution and killing."[67] A few years later he argued that teaching about the Holocaust was necessary to teach "civic virtue" and that "the only defense against persecution and extermination is citizens prepared to oppose the power of the state and to face the hostility of their neighbors to aid the intended victims."[68] By the 1980s, there was less reticence about teaching the subject due to the growing awareness of the Holocaust in American society and the sustained efforts of educators committed to teaching the ethical and moral questions that it raised.

Although both the political left and the political right have been in favor of teaching the Holocaust in secondary schools, such agreement, as the scholar Thomas D. Fallace argues, is less a sign of universal respect for the topic than an indicator of its malleability as a subject.[69] Holocaust education in secondary schools may have had roots in the movement for progressive education in the 1960s and 1970s, but it was during the conservative backlash of the Reagan years that it came into fruition and its content and purpose were often debated among educators, politicians, and school boards. A key disagreement has been about what "lessons" can be drawn from the Holocaust: some insist that the Holocaust should be taught as a unique historical event whose primary lessons regard the history of antisemitism and Jewish victimization, while others seek to impart broader lessons about human nature, hatred, and social justice. In spite of some protests from those who feared that Holocaust education would foster anti-German or pro-Israeli sentiments among students or take away from the study of other genocides, the Holocaust is now taught widely in secondary schools and is addressed, in one form or another, in the public school curricula of thirty-five states and the District of Columbia: several states now mandate the teaching of the Holocaust, either as a subject on its own or as part of curricula on human rights and genocide. Primarily a subject in high schools, it is also presented to middle schools and in some schools at the elementary level.[70]

The case of the educational organization Facing History and Ourselves (FHAO) demonstrates well some of the successes and tensions that have marked Holocaust education in secondary schools. Today, FHAO is among the most prominent organizations dedicated to developing curricula grounded in Holocaust studies. Founded in 1976 by William S. Parsons and Margot Stern Strom, two Boston educators who introduced the study of genocide to students in their middle-school classes, FHAO quickly grew into an organization that gained national recognition. Working in a racially segregated school system, Parsons and Strom were motivated by a desire to link the study of the Holocaust to pressing contemporary issues, such as civil rights, mass violence, and the United States' war in Vietnam. Through an examination of the Holocaust, they hoped to make their students engaged citizens who would participate in, and thus influence, the democratic society of which they were a part. This approach initially brought great success to FHAO and within two years, it was an independent organization developing curricula broadly.[71] In 1980, FHAO was selected as an "exemplary model education program" by the US Department of Education, which made its program available nationally in 1982. Along with teaching the Armenian and Jewish genocides, the curriculum sought to bring students' attention to global problems, such as the proliferation of nuclear weapons that threatens to destroy all of humankind.

FHAO faced attacks by the Reagan administration, which objected to its focus on social justice. It nearly lost the federal government's support when a reviewer for the Department of Education objected to the fact that its curriculum gave different hate groups, such as the Ku Klux Klan, the same amount of space as the Nazi Party and compared its pedagogical methods to that of Hitler, Goebbels, and Mao Zedong.[72] In 1990, Lucy Dawidowicz—by then politically conservative—delivered a significant attack on its curriculum. In an article in *Commentary* magazine, she criticized the program for attempting to provide a moral education along with teaching a history of the Holocaust and charged, "Facing History was also a vehicle for instructing thirteen-year-olds in civil disobedience and indoctrinating them with propaganda for nuclear disarmament." An article in 1995 by historian Deborah Lipstadt echoed many of these concerns, insisting on the utter uniqueness of the Holocaust and resisting all comparisons and lessons outside of Jewish history. Both Dawidowicz and Lipstadt objected to what they viewed as FHAO's stripping of the Holocaust out of its historical context (which they viewed narrowly as that of antisemitism) and universalizing it as a means to fight oppression and prejudice.[73]

As the scholar Kali Tal has argued, criticisms such as these stem from a fundamental difference in exactly what lessons should be drawn from studying the Holocaust. "For Dawidowicz," Tal writes, "the Holocaust stands as a vindication of traditional (Jewish) religious culture and conservative politics, and places the Jew at the center of the greatest tragedy in the history of the world." In this view, Jewish suffering is unique in the world and any attempts to universalize the Holocaust is, at minimum, a disservice to that history and at worst, an expression of antisemitism. By contrast, she writes, "Rather than emphasizing the particularity of the Jewish victim, Facing History urges its audience to make a direct comparison between antisemitism in the Third Reich and racism in the United States, between Hitler's massive military build-up and our own nuclear arms race, between the apathy of German citizens and the apathy of U.S. citizens in the face of injustice."[74] In spite of criticisms, FHAO has remained committed to its founding mission of using historical lessons to confront present-day prejudice and inculcate moral values in the name of strengthening democratic societies. It currently has 29,000 trained educators who reach 1.9 million students primarily in the United States.[75]

At the university level, the growth of Holocaust studies has been far less contentious, although some have raised concerns over whether its popularity overshadows the study of other historical periods or genocides. University courses on the Holocaust were initially slow to develop. Even by the early 1980s, they remained rare, leading Henry Friedlander to lament that "teaching [the Holocaust] has remained a matter of chance. Unless someone already tenured in the department happens to know the subject and undertakes to teach it, the Holocaust has been offered as a subject only under pressure and without serious intent."[76] Since that time, however, courses on the Holocaust have become ubiquitous. Institutions of higher education tend to enjoy much more freedom when it comes to divvying up their resources, and do not have to contend with the oversight of local school boards and state and national politics. Rather, the growth of courses and academic programs on the Holocaust has often reflected the demands of the academic "marketplace." That is, as interest in such courses has increased, many schools have complied by offering more courses. Given the willingness of many donors to support such programs, they have emerged across all kinds of institutions of higher education—community colleges and four-year institutions, public and private schools, and liberal arts colleges and major research universities alike.

One influential initiative to expand Holocaust education at the university level occurred in 1976, the same year that FHAO began. That summer, Theodore "Zev," Weiss, a Holocaust survivor, and his wife Alice Weiss invited a small group of people to their suburban Chicago home to discuss forming a Holocaust memorial.[77] Zev Weiss's concern over the lack of Holocaust education in schools prompted him to undertake a series of initiatives, such a producing a filmstrip about the Holocaust, and then, following the 1976 meeting, videotaping the testimonies of survivors like himself. Within a few years and with the support of friends and donors, Zev and Alice had formed an organization called the Holocaust Educational Foundation (HEF). Initially concerned with high-school education, the focus of HEF later shifted to higher education, in part because there were fewer administrative and curricular obstacles. By the late 1980s, Zev was spending much of his time contacting the history departments of universities across the country, encouraging them to teach courses on the Holocaust and in several instances, providing money to support faculty training and course preparation. By 1993, the number of such courses, according to the HEF, was at approximately 100, and by the end of that decade, there were more than 400 colleges and universities teaching Holocaust studies. In 2013, HEF became a part of Northwestern University. It holds an annual Summer Institute on the Holocaust and Jewish Civilization that trains faculty and graduate students and organizes a biennial academic conference that draws hundreds of scholars from around the world.

***

The Holocaust has moved from the margins to the very center of American awareness. Reflecting both its enormity and its malleability, its presence is seemingly everywhere. Politicians from across the political spectrum invoke it in speeches to make moral arguments. Each year, new Holocaust films appear on our movie screens. New works of Holocaust scholarship, fiction, and art are produced at a spectacular pace. Most major cities have Holocaust memorials, and very few students graduate from high school without some direct exposure to the Holocaust in their classrooms. Hitler has become a metaphor for the ultimate form of evil, against which all others are compared. The words "Nazi," "kapo," and "führer" are common forms of derision. There are few, if any, other historical events—including those genocidal crimes that occurred within and by the United States—that currently hold such a position within American society. Such a position reflects not only the status of Jews within American society, but also the highly successful efforts by scholars, teachers, artists, and activists to promote its awareness and centrality in our lives.

Conclusion

When originally planning the end of this book, I had assumed that the Holocaust would have an increasingly important place in American society, although it would also likely be affected by shifts within the Jewish community. In particular, I had expected to focus on developments in two areas: new directions within the academic field of Holocaust studies and the possible impact of demographic changes among American Jewry. While I will touch on these areas briefly, the election of Donald Trump to the US presidency has prompted a reconsideration of the racial and social position of American Jews and potentially poses new challenges to the place of the Holocaust within the United States.

The scholarly field of Holocaust studies, now several decades old, continues to expand into new areas of research and education. At universities around the country, as well as in museums and private institutes, support for Holocaust studies remains vibrant and is likely to remain so for some time as new academic programs are established, new positions for faculty appear, and funding for its study increases. At the same time, our understanding of the category of Holocaust victims is shifting—albeit slowly—to include Roma, people whom the Nazis considered disabled, and others, as scholars recognize that while within the Nazi imagination the threat of these groups never paralleled that of Jews, their destruction was no less horrific. The internationalization of Holocaust studies also continues to expand as scholars—many of whom stem from countries of the former Soviet Union—have generated new approaches to studying the murder of Holocaust victims by demonstrating how the mass killing of Jews in Eastern Europe was often dependent on local ethnic rivalries and the cooperation of neighboring populations. As well, the success of Holocaust studies programs has led to the field of comparative genocide studies, as scholars seek to understand the larger role that genocide and ethnic cleansing has played in human history.[1]

The field of gender studies has made particularly strong contributions to how we understand the Holocaust. If in 1986 the scholar Marlene E. Heinemann could write that "the study of the Holocaust literature has focused primarily on men, whose perspectives have been taken as representative of the experience of all Holocaust victims," such a claim would no longer hold true today.[2] Rather, as Myrna Goldenberg convincingly argued in a 2013 essay in the edited volume *Different Horrors, Same Hell*, "Because Jewish women were vulnerable in different ways than men were, gender and sex cannot be dismissed by responsible scholars."[3] This rapidly growing area of analysis is allowing scholars to understand, among other phenomena, the extent to which women and men experienced sexual violence differently, the role of sexual barter among prisoners in ghettos and camps, and women's actions and motivations both as perpetrators of Nazi crimes and as rescuers of Holocaust victims. Finally, Holocaust scholars are increasingly adopting techniques from the field of digital humanities, which is allowing for innovative approaches such as data mining, digital mapping, and new forms of textual visualization.[4]

At the same time as Holocaust scholarship and awareness continues to grow in the United States, the American Jewish community is undergoing profound changes. In 2013, the Pew Research Center released a demographic survey entitled *Portrait of Jewish Americans*. According to the study, which examined the participants' religious attitudes and level of communal affiliation, 94 percent of people considered by the study to be Jewish Americans still proudly identify as Jewish, yet more than one-in-five no longer do so on a religious basis. This shift is most pronounced among younger Jewish Americans, a full third of whom identify as Jewish mainly "on the basis of ancestry, ethnicity or culture."[5] As the study notes, this tendency toward non-religiosity is in keeping with trends within American society as a whole. The rate of intermarriage for nonreligious Jews is particularly high—"Among Jewish respondents who have gotten married since 2000, nearly six-in-ten have a non-Jewish spouse"—yet most children born to at least one Jewish parent identify themselves as Jewish.[6] At the same time as many Jews disaffiliate religiously, new research by the scholar Steven M. Cohen has shown that there is a rapidly growing affiliation with Jewish Orthodoxy among that segment of younger American Jews who identify as religious. He writes, "The Orthodox population (Haredi, centrist, and modern) is exploding. The non-Orthodox are in sharp decline."[7] Over the past three generations, he has shown, the number of Orthodox Jewish children has quadrupled, while the number of non-Orthodox children has shrunk by one-third.

Among the possible consequences of these changes is a shift in American Jewry's attachment to Holocaust memory and the Holocaust's place within American society. If the Holocaust in the United States has grown in importance as American Jews of European ancestry are perceived as white, and if that status was in part a consequence of the turn toward more "American" forms of religious observance, the fact that increasing numbers of youths are either embracing Orthodox Judaism, with its inherent distinctiveness from mainstream American modes of religious conduct, or moving away from religious forms of Jewish identification entirely may result in the Holocaust's place within the United States changing once again. Whether this comes to pass remains to be seen, of course, but given the close correlation between the position of American Jews and the importance of the Holocaust within American society, such demographic changes are bound to influence it.

***

The election of Donald Trump to the presidency has prompted a new set of unexpected questions about the future of the Holocaust's position within American society. Elected to office in November 2016 as part of a wave of right-wing populism and nationalism that has influenced elections in the United Kingdom, Austria, Hungary, the Netherlands, Turkey, the Philippines, and France, Trump's campaign and first year in office have led many American Jews to wonder whether their position in the country is as secure as they had imagined it to be since the end of World War II. Central to Trump's message has been overt animosity toward immigrants and foreigners. He has implemented new travel restrictions against people from predominantly Muslim countries and instituted mass deportations of people from Mexico. Using racist rhetoric to describe these population groups (Muslims as terrorists, and Mexicans as criminals, rapists, and drug smugglers), he has ushered in a new era of racial hostility into an environment that was already severely polarized. According to research by the Southern Poverty Law Center (SPLC), the number of hate groups in the United States has rapidly grown since Trump's campaign. Correspondingly, the level of hate crimes against racial and religious minorities—in particular against Muslims—has escalated. As the SPLC reports, "In the first 10 days after his [Trump's] election, the SPLC documented 867 bias-related incidents, including more than 300 that targeted immigrants or Muslims."[8]

In spite of the position attained by American Jews in the second half of the twentieth century, they have not been exempt from this escalation of hate acts. Since Trump's election, for example, Jewish cemeteries in St. Louis, Philadelphia, and Rochester have been vandalized, with headstones deliberately toppled and damaged. At a "Unite the Right" gathering in Charlottesville, Virginia, in August 2017, torch-bearing marchers carried Nazi and Confederate flags and chanted, "You/Jews will not replace us," while "defending" a statue of Robert E. Lee. Many demonstrators beat protesters, murdering one. A number of observers are connecting this escalation in antisemitic violence with the Trump administration. As reporter Josh Glancy writes in the *Jewish Chronicle*,

"Some of these people may be feeding off Trump's noxious rhetoric about colour and creed, which has emboldened bigots and conspiracists." Glancy also warns, however, that "it may also be subtler than that: history teaches us that in times of stress and social fracture, someone usually decides to give the Jews a kicking."[9] Since Trump's election to office, commentators are pointing to the fact that although one of the president's closest advisers is his Orthodox Jewish son-in-law and that his own daughter has converted to Judaism, his initial chief strategist was Steve Bannon, a figure widely considered to have close ties to antisemitic groups in the United States. He was dismissed from his post following the outcry after the Charlottesville rally and returned to his position as editor-in-chief of a media outlet that has published antisemitic articles.[10] At times, the president's office has appeared overtly hostile to Jewish American concerns about the Holocaust. For example, on International Holocaust Remembrance Day in 2017, the statement from the White House made no specific mention of Jewish deaths in the genocide. When pressed on the matter, the White House defended its statement by noting that others had suffered and died in the Holocaust. While this is factually correct, the absence of any reference to Jewish deaths was a dramatic departure from previous White House statements, and appeared to legitimize the claims of antisemites who downplay or deny Jewish suffering in the Holocaust. In April 2017, White House Press Secretary Sean Spicer, in making a comparison between Syrian President Bashar al-Assad and Adolf Hitler, proclaimed, "You know, you had someone as despicable as Hitler who didn't even sink to using chemical weapons," a statement he later clumsily retracted.[11]

Compounding many Jewish American fears has been the fact that the administration was reluctant to respond to the escalating hate crimes. When pressed for a statement by an Israeli reporter in February 2017, Trump responded with hostility to any insinuation that he was responsible for the uptick in antisemitism and declared himself "the least antisemitic person you've ever seen in your entire life," a statement that many did not find reassuring.[12] When the director of the New York–based Anne Frank Center for Mutual Respect issued a deeply critical statement expressing his concern about the president's refusal to disavow the antisemitism coming out of his administration, Spicer responded that, in fact, the center should have praised the president for "his commitment to civil rights, to voting rights, to equality for all Americans."[13] After a visit to the National Museum of African American History and Culture in Washington, DC, the president finally made reference to the increasing antisemitic threats, "I think it's terrible. I think it's horrible. Whether it's antisemitism or racism or any—anything you wanna think about having to do with the divide. Antisemitism is, likewise, it's just terrible."[14] On April 23, in a video statement commemorating Yom ha-Shoah, the president attempted to set a more respectful tone and paid tribute to the "six million Jews, two-thirds of the Jews in Europe, murdered by the Nazi genocide."[15] Following the violence in Charlottesville, Trump sparked widespread outrage over remarks that placed blame on the white supremacists as well as those who stood to oppose them, claiming, "You had a group on one side that was bad. You had a group on the other side that was also very violent. Nobody wants to say that. I'll say it right now."[16]

As in earlier periods, the currently intensifying antisemitism in the United States is not occurring in a vacuum but within a larger context of racial violence and hatred. Just as Latinos, Muslims and Middle Easterners, African Americans, and undocumented persons in the United States are facing rising violence, so too are Jews. (As in other periods in American history, it should be noted, the violence directed at Jews has not been as extreme or systematic as that faced by many other minority groups.)

This has prompted some Jews to speculate on their status as white Americans. As the journalist Emma Green reports in an article entitled "Are Jews White?," "Trump's election has reopened questions that have long seemed settled in America," in particular the racial status of Jews of European ancestry.[17] Having benefited for the past two generations from the privileges bestowed to white Americans, some Jews are wondering whether their racial status may be once again called into question. As Green writes, "No matter how much prestige Jews may amass, their status is always ambiguous. 'White' is not a skin color, but a category marking power. American Jews do have power, but they are also often viewed with suspicion; and having power is no assurance of protection."[18] The scholar Karen Brodkin, author of *How Jews Became White Folks and What That Says about Race in America*, also addressed this concern in a 2016 essay, "How Jews Became White Folks—and May Become Nonwhite under Trump." Brodkin asks: "Now, Trump's election and the closet of bigotry it has opened raise a question. Have the decades of whiteness we've enjoyed affected American Jews and Jewishness permanently, so that Jews would still be considered white, in the sense of still being included among the racially privileged, those safe from persecution?" She concludes, "We need to challenge all bigotry, not least by building inclusiveness and democracy every chance we get."[19]

The ascendancy of white nationalists and neo-Nazis after Trump's election also raises questions about the future position of the Holocaust in the United States. Since the end of World War II, the various representations of the Holocaust that have appeared in the United States, including the many monuments, memorials, museums, books, films, and pedagogy programs, have largely portrayed Nazism (and the fascist era as a whole) as an enemy that was defeated, and thus as a relic of a past age. The monuments and memorials were in part commemoration, but they also contained a subtext of triumph.

Nazism was vanquished. The Holocaust was past. Each new monument has affirmed these historical narratives. The USHMM on the National Mall was a formal confirmation of this belief and of Jewry's secure position within the American mainstream. Nazism's contemporary supporters in America have very much been on the fringes of society and not perceived as an existential threat to the Jewish people.

It is no longer clear if such triumphalism is warranted. It may be that in the present moment some people will continue to hold a particularistic view of the Holocaust as an event that is limited strictly to the experience of Jewish victims and will place it solely within the history of antisemitism. Such a stance, in my view, would be misguided. As I hope to have demonstrated in this book, the history of antisemitism in the United States is intricately entwined with the country's legacy of racial discrimination and persecution. The present moment is no exception. Instead of perpetuating a narrative of Jewish exceptionalism, we might draw from earlier periods of American history, when Jews linked their fate to that of other oppressed peoples. Just as Jewish and Italian workers organized together for labor unions, as Jewish philanthropists and community leaders contributed to the founding of the NAACP, as Jewish college students participated in voter recruitment drives and desegregation campaigns with African Americans in the South, and religious figures helped foster postwar Jewish-Christian dialogues in the name of mutual understanding, Jewish Americans have the opportunity to forge alliances in the name of combating hatred and intolerance. How we in the United States remember and discuss the Holocaust may shift as the parallels between the experiences of European Jews—as refugees, victims, and survivors—and other victims of mass violence continue to become more apparent. Some of this work is already underway, as groups such as Facing History and Ourselves continue to develop educational materials linking the Holocaust to other acts of racial violence in the United States and the USHMM repeatedly voices its concern over the plight of refugees from the Syrian civil war and ongoing genocidal acts against religious minorities by the Islamic State. By recognizing the similarities between Jews' experience with Nazism and the persecution faced by other oppressed peoples, it may be that nativism and racial hatred can be consigned to the margins of society. To quote Ruth Kluger a final time:

> We would be condemned to be isolated monads if we didn't compare and generalize, for comparisons are the bridges from one unique life to another. In our hearts we all know that some aspects of the Shoah have been repeated elsewhere, today and yesterday, and will return in a new guise tomorrow; and the camps, too, were only imitations (unique imitations, to be sure) of what had occurred the day before yesterday.[20]

Notes

Introduction

1 Ruth Kluger, *Still Alive: A Holocaust Girlhood Remembered* (New York: The Feminist Press, 2003), 148.

2 In some instances, both positions are held simultaneously, such as in the permanent exhibition of the United States Holocaust Memorial Museum, which both critiques the role of the United States in the refugee crisis prompted by Nazism yet begins by highlighting the role of US troops as liberators.

3 In one of the most egregious instances, Rafael Medoff and Bat-Ami Zucker, after independently writing sharply critical reviews of Richard Breitman and Allan J. Lichtman's *FDR and the Jews* (Cambridge, MA: Belknap Press, 2013), together published and distributed widely a pamphlet that charged the authors with violating academic standards of research, over what are, frankly, historical conclusions that differ from theirs. See Rafael Medoff and Bat-Ami Zucker, *Breaking the Rules: Violations of Academic Standards in the Debate over FDR's Response to the Holocaust* (Washington, DC: The David S. Wyman Institute for Holocaust Studies, 2014).

4 See, for example, Arthur D. Morse, *While Six Million Died: A Chronicle of American Apathy* (New York: Random House, 1968); Monty Noam Penkower, *The Jews Were Expendable: Free World Diplomacy and the Holocaust* (Urbana and Chicago: University of Illinois Press, 1983); David S. Wyman, *The Abandonment of the Jews: America and the Holocaust, 1941–1945* (New York: Pantheon Books, 1984); and David S. Wyman, *Paper Walls: America and the Refugee Crisis 1938–1941* (New York: Pantheon Books, 1985).

5 See, for example, William D. Rubinstein, *The Myth of Rescue: Why the Democracies Could Not Have Saved More Jews from the Nazis* (London and New York: Routledge, 1997); and Robert N. Rosen, *Saving the Jews: Franklin D. Roosevelt and the Holocaust* (New York: Thunder's Mouth Press, 2006). For an insightful review of this literature, see Rebecca L. Erbelding, "About Time: The History of the War Refugee Board," PhD dissertation, George Mason University (2015), 4–17. Erbelding characterizes this historiographical debate as one between "moralists" and "contextualists." For examples of the "contextualists" (to adopt Erbelding's categories), see Henry L. Feingold, *The Politics of Rescue: The Roosevelt Administration and the Holocaust, 1938–1945* (New York: Holocaust Library, 1970); Richard Breitman and Alan M. Kraut, *American Refugee Policy and European Jewry, 1933–1945*

(Bloomington: Indiana University Press, 1987); and Breitman and Lichtman, *FDR and the Jews*.

6 See, for example, Peter Novick, *The Holocaust in American Life* (Boston: Houghton Mifflin, 1999); and Norman Finkelstein, *The Holocaust Industry: Reflections on the Exploitation of Jewish Suffering* (London: Verso, 2000). For an equally emphatic defense of American Jewry in the postwar years, see Hasia Diner, *We Remember with Reverence and Love: American Jews and the Myth of Silence after the Holocaust, 1945–1962* (New York: New York University Press, 2010).

7 Lawrence Zuckerman, "FDR's Jewish Problem: How Did a President Beloved by Jews Come to Be Regarded as an Anti-Semite Who Refused to Save Them from the Nazis?," *Nation*, July 17, 2013, 29–32.

8 Ibid., 29.

9 Ibid., 30.

10 Michael André Bernstein, *Foregone Conclusions: Against Apocalyptic History* (Berkeley: University of California Press, 1994), 16.

11 Primo Levi, *The Drowned and the Saved*, trans. Raymond Rosenthal (New York: Vintage International, 1989), 151.

12 Gavriel D. Rosenfeld, "Probing the Limits of Speculation: Counterfactualism and the Holocaust," in *Hi Hitler! How the Nazi Past Is Being Normalized in Contemporary Culture* (Cambridge: Cambridge University Press, 2015), 122–57.

13 W. E. B. DuBois, *The Souls of Black Folk: Essays and Sketches* (Chicago: A. C. McClurg & Co., 1903), vii.

14 See, for example, Karen Brodkin, *How Jews Became White Folks and What That Says about Race in America* (New Brunswick, NJ: Rutgers University Press, 1998); Eric L. Goldstein, *The Price of Whiteness: Jews, Race, and American Identity* (Princeton: Princeton University Press, 2006); and Cheryl Lynn Greenberg, *Troubling the Waters: Black-Jewish Relations in the American Century* (Princeton: Princeton University Press, 2006).

Chapter 1

1 As C. Paul Vincent has put it, "Some observers remove the saga of the St. Louis from its historical context and represent it much as a morality play." See "The Voyage of the St. Louis Revisited," *Holocaust and Genocide Studies* 25, no. 2 (Fall 2011): 273.

2 For example, the annual quota for Great Britain and Northern Ireland was 65,721 and for Romania, 377. For non-European countries, the quota was often fixed at 100 per annum.

3 As of June 30, 1939, the demand for visas under the German quota was 309,782. The Department of State Bulletin, vol. 2 (January–June) (Washington: Office of Media Services, Bureau of Public Affairs, 1940), 215, https://babel.hathitrust.org/cgi/pt?id=uiuo.ark:/13960/t0sr0fr17;view=1up;seq=223 (accessed January 31, 2017).

4 Vincent also makes the case that the Joint's lead representative in Cuba, Lawrence Berenson, mishandled the negotiations.

5 "Cuba Orders Liner and Refugees to Go," *New York Times*, June 2, 1939.

6 Ibid.

7 This charge is rather ubiquitous in popular accounts of the MS *St. Louis*, both in print and online. See, for example, Ted Falcon and David Blatner, *Judaism for Dummies* (Hoboken, NJ: For Dummies, 2012), 203; or see http://holocaustonline.org/significant-events/voyage-of-the-st-louis (accessed February 7, 2017).

8 "Refugee Ship," Editorial, *New York Times*, June 8, 1939.

9 "Refugee Ship Idles Off Florida Coast," *New York Times*, June 5, 1939.

10 Also see Daniela Gleizer, *Unwelcome Exiles: Mexico and the Jewish Refugees from Nazism, 1933–1945* (Leiden: Brill, 2014).

11 "Seeking Refuge in Cuba," *Holocaust Encyclopedia* of the United States Holocaust Memorial Museum, http://www.ushmm.org/wlc/en/article.php?ModuleId=10007330 (accessed September 19, 2014).

12 I thank Dr. Rebecca L. Erbelding for sharing her research on ships arriving to New York in this period. Also see "Immigration to the United States 1933–1941," United States Holocaust Memorial Museum, *Holocaust Encyclopedia*, https://www.ushmm.org/wlc/en/article.php?ModuleId=10008297 (accessed June 2, 2017).

13 On Ford and antisemitism, see Neil Baldwin, *Henry Ford and the Jews: The Mass Production of Hate* (New York: PublicAffairs, 2001); on Coughlin, see Donald Warren, *Radio Priest: Charles Coughlin, the Father of Hate Radio* (New York: Free Press, 1996).

14 See, for example, Gulie Ne'eman Arad, *America, Its Jews, and the Rise of Nazism* (Bloomington and Indianapolis: Indiana University Press, 2000).

15 Christopher McKnight Nicholas, *Promise and Peril: America at the Dawn of a Global Age* (Cambridge, MA: Harvard University Press, 2011).

16 For an overview of the American eugenics movement, see Adam Cohen, *Imbeciles: The Supreme Court, American Eugenics, and the Sterilization of Carrie Buck* (New York: Penguin Press, 2017).

17 Stefan Kühl, *The Nazi Connection: Eugenics, American Racism, and German National Socialism* (Oxford: Oxford University Press, 1994), 51.

18 Ibid., 86–7. As James Q. Whitman has shown, however, Germany's racial laws drew significant inspiration from segregationist, citizenship, and antimiscegenation laws in the United States. See *Hitler's American Model: The United States and the Making of Nazi Race Law* (Princeton: Princeton University Press, 2017).

19 Michael C. Howard, *Transnationalism and Society: An Introduction* (Jefferson, NC: McFarland, 2011), 62.

20 John Higham, *Strangers in the Land: Pattern of American Nativism, 1860–1925* (New Brunswick, NJ: Rutgers University Press, 1955), 312.

21 "Eugenists Dread Tainted Aliens," *New York Times*, September 25, 1921.

22 "Coolidge Proclaims Immigration Quotas," *New York Times*, July 1, 1924.

23 "National Origins Immigrant Plan in Effect," *New York Times*, July 1, 1929.

24 Speech by Ellison DuRant Smith, April 9, 1924, Congressional Record, 68th Congress, 1st Session (Washington, DC: Government Printing Office, 1924), vol. 65, 5961–2.

25 Mark Wischnitzer, *To Dwell in Safety: The Story of Jewish Migration since 1800* (Philadelphia: Jewish Publication Society, 1948), 289.

26 On isolationism and American immigration policy, see Mae Ngai, *Impossible Subjects: Illegal Aliens and the Making of Modern America* (Princeton: Princeton University Press, 2004).

27 Richard Breitman and Allan J. Lichtman, *FDR and the Jews* (Cambridge, MA: Belknap Press, 2013) 36. Also see "White House Statement on Government Policies to Reduce Immigration," March 26, 1931, http://www.presidency.ucsb.edu/ws/?pid=22581 (accessed July 3, 2014).

28 Melissa Jane Taylor, "Bureaucratic Response to Human Tragedy: American Consuls and the Jewish Plight in Vienna, 1938–1941," *Holocaust and Genocide Studies* 21, no. 2 (Fall 2007): 246.

29 Francisco Balderrama and Raymond Rodríguez, *Decade of Betrayal: Mexican Repatriation in the 1930s* (Albuquerque: University of New Mexico Press, 2006).

30 David R. Roediger, *Working toward Whiteness: How America's Immigrants Became White* (New York: Basic Books, 2005), 37. Roediger's use of "inbetween peoples" is drawn in turn from the work of historians John Higham and Robert Orsi.

31 Ibid., 93.

32 Eric L. Goldstein, *The Price of Whiteness: Jews, Race, and American Identity* (Princeton: Princeton University Press, 2006), 145.

33 Henry L. Feingold, *A Time for Searching: Entering the Mainstream, 1920–1945*, vol. 4 of *The Jewish People in America* (Baltimore: Johns Hopkins University Press, 1992).

34 Victoria Saker Woeste, *Henry Ford's War on Jews and the Legal Battle against Hate Speech* (Palo Alto: Stanford University Press, 2013).

35 Henry Ford, Sr., "Angles of Jewish Influence in American Life," *Dearborn Independent*, May 21, 1921. Reprinted in *The International Jew, Aspects of Jewish Power in the United States* (Honolulu, Hawaii: University Press of the Pacific, 2003), 241–2.

36 For a contemporary report on the Silver Shirts, see Jewish Telegraphic Service, "Silver Shirts and Friends of New Germany Plot For, Dream of Fascist Conquest of U.S." April 19, 1934, http://www.jta.org/1934/04/19/archive/silver-shirts-and-friends-of-new-germany-plot-for-dream-of-fascist-conquest-of-u-s#ixzz34GCnqiZ4 (accessed June 10, 2014). For a later account, see Neil R. McMillen, "Pro-Nazi Sentiment in the United States: March, 1933–March, 1934," *The Southern Quarterly* (October 1963): 48–70.

37 Goldstein, 119–37.

38 Editorial Foreword to Lothrop Stoddard, "The Pedigree of Judah," *The Forum*, no. 3 (March 1926): 321.

39 Ibid., 333.

40 Alfred Jay Nock, "The Jewish Problem in America," *The Atlantic*, June and July 1941, http://www.theatlantic.com/magazine/archive/1941/06 (accessed June 10, 2014).

41 As reported by the Jewish Telegraphic Association on February 2, 1933, http://www.jta.org/1933/02/02/archive/statement-of-jewish-congress (accessed February 2, 2014).

42 Arad, *America, Its Jews*, 109.

43 *Holocaust Encyclopedia* of the United States Holocaust Memorial Museum, "Germany: Jewish Population in 1933," https://www.ushmm.org/wlc/en/article.php?ModuleId=10005276 (accessed February 14, 2017).

44 "Roosevelt Asked to Aid Jews," *New York Times*, March 2, 1933.

45 As cited in *The Jewish Chronicle*, February 3, 1942.

46 See Jewish Telegraphic Association articles from January 30, 1933, to February 28, 1933, http://www.jta.org/jta-archive (accessed February 21, 2014).

47 Gennady Estraikh, "The Berlin Bureau of the *Forverts*," in *Yiddish in Weimar Berlin: At the Crossroads of Diaspora Politics and Culture*, ed. Gennady Estraikh and Mikhail Krutikov (Oxford: Legenda Press, 2010), 157–8. For more on the reaction of the American Yiddish press to the rise of Nazism, see Charles Cutter, "The American Yiddish Daily Press Reaction to the Rise of Nazism, 1930–1933," PhD dissertation, The Ohio State University, 1979.

48 "Other Faiths Join In," *New York Times*, March 28, 1933.

49 Ibid.

50 "We Ask Only for the Right, Says Wise," *New York Times*, March 28, 1933.

51 Naomi W. Cohen and Jerome Chanes, "American Jewish Congress," in *Encyclopedia Judaica*, 2nd edn, ed. Fred Skolnik and Michael Berenbaum, vol. 1, 56–7.

52 The biographical Information on Wise is drawn from Carl Hermann Voss, "Wise, Stephen Samuel," *Encyclopedia Judaica*, vol. 21, 100–102.

53 On the Jewish Labor Committee, see Gail Malmgreen, "Labor and the Holocaust: The Jewish Labor Committee and the Anti-Nazi Struggle," in *Labor's Heritage: Quarterly of the George Meany Memorial Archives* 3 no. 4 (October 1991): 20–35.

54 Louis Anthes, "Publicly Deliberative Drama: The 1934 Mock Trial of Adolf Hitler for 'Crimes against Civilization,' " *The American Journal of Legal History* 42, no. 4 (October 1998): 391–410.

55 "Nazis 'Convicted' of World 'Crime' by 20,000 in Rally," *New York Times*, March 8, 1934.

56 World Committee for the Victims of German Fascism, *The Brown Book of the Hitler Terror and the Burning of the Reichstag* (New York: Alfred A. Knopf, 1933).

57 Pierre van Paassen and James Waterman Wise, eds, *Nazism: An Assault on Civilization* (New York: Harrison Smith and Robert Haas, 1934).

58 Karen J. Greenberg, "Missed Chance: Reassessing the Fort Ontario Emergency Refugee Shelter," *The Hudson Valley Regional Review* 9 (1992): 130–1.

59 Michaela Hoenicke Moore, *Know Your Enemy: The American Debate on Nazism, 1933–1945* (Cambridge: Cambridge University Press, 2010), 74. For a fuller discussion, from which this information is drawn, see in particular pp. 41–101. Also see Andrew Nagorski, *Hitlerland: American Eyewitnesses to the Nazi Rise to Power* (New York: Simon and Schuster, 2013).

60 S. Jonathan Wiesen, "On Dachau and Jim Crow: Holocaust Memory in the Postwar African American Press," in *Als der Holocaust noch keinen Namen hatte/Before the Holocaust Had Its Name*, ed. Regina Fritz, Éva Kovács, and Béla Rásky (Vienna: New Academic Press, 2016), 111–31.

61 Hoenicke Moore, *Know Your Enemy*, 70.

62 See the discussion in Uriel Heilman, "What Americans Had to Say about Jewish War Refugees," *Jewish Telegraphic Agency*, December 2, 2015, http://www.jta.org/2015/12/02/news-opinion/united-states/what-americans-had-to-say-about-jewish-war-refugees (accessed February 2, 2016).

63 For references to Roosevelt's scholarly detractors and supporters, see the Introduction.

64 Breitman and Lichtman, *FDR and the Jews*, 317.

65 Ibid., 315.

66 Ibid., 43.

67 Ibid., 69; see the full discussion in chapter 4, "Immigration Wars," 67–83, from which this discussion is in part drawn.

68 Ibid., 90.

69 Saul Friedländer, *Nazi Germany and the Jews: The Years of Persecution 1933–1939* (New York: HarperCollins, 1997), 62.

70 Wischnitzer, *To Dwell in Safety*, 31. The statistics that follow below are also drawn from this essay.

71 Dorothy Thompson, "Refugees: A World Problem," *Foreign Affairs* 16. no. 3 (April 1938): 375.

72 Ibid., 380.

73 Ibid., 382.

74 Melissa Jane Taylor, "Bureaucratic Response to Human Tragedy: American Consuls and the Jewish Plight in Vienna, 1938–1941," *Holocaust and Genocide Studies* 21, no. 2 (Fall 2007): 243–67. Also see "Diplomats in Turmoil: Creating a Middle Ground in Post-Anschluss Austria," *Diplomatic History* 32, no. 5 (November 2008): 811–39.

75 See "Report by Myron C. Taylor on a Meeting of the Intergovernmental Committee on Refugees at Evian, July 20, 1938," in *The Holocaust: Selected Documents in Eighteen Volumes*, Vol. 5 *Jewish Emigration from 1933 to the Evian Conference of 1938*, ed. John Mendelson (New York: Garland Publishing, Inc., 1982), 245–64.

76 Anne O'Hare McCormick, "Europe: The Refugee Question as a Test of Civilization," *New York Times*, July 4, 1938.

77 Clarence K. Streit, "32 Nations Gather to Help Refugees," *New York Times*, July 6, 1938.

78 Stephen Wise, "Memorandum by the WJC to the Delegates of the Évian Conference, July 6, 1938," reprinted in Jürgen Matthäus and Mark Roseman, eds, *Jewish Responses to Persecution, Volume I, 1933–1938* (Lanham, MD: AltaMira Press, 2010), 316.

79 Ibid.

80 See Marion A. Kaplan, *Dominican Haven: The Jewish Refugee Settlement in Sosúa, 1940–1945* (New York: Museum of Jewish Heritage, 2008).

81 "Report by Myron C. Taylor," 260.

82 Unless otherwise noted, information regarding the expulsion of Polish Jews is drawn from Sybil Milton, "The Expulsion of Polish Jews from Germany October 1938 to July 1939: A Documentation," *Leo Baeck Institute Yearbook* 29 (1984): 169–99.

83 Hannah Arendt, *Eichmann in Jerusalem: A Report on the Banality of Evil* (New York: Viking Press, 1963), 228–9.

84 See the description in Richard J. Evans, *The Third Reich in Power* (New York: Penguin Books, 2005), 580–610; also see Alan E. Steinweis, *Kristallnacht 1938* (Cambridge, MA: Belknap, 2009).

85 Herbert A. Strauss, "Jewish Emigration from Germany: Nazi Policy and Jewish Responses (II)," *Leo Baeck Institute Yearbook* 26 (1981): 367.

86 Clarence Pickett, *For More Than Bread* (Boston: Little, Brown and Company, 1953), 133.

87 Ibid., 99.

88 Ibid.

89 Ibid., 135.

90 Rufus M. Jones, "Our Day in the German Gestapo", *The American Friend*, July 10, 1947.

91 William Edward Nawyn, *American Protestantism's Response to Germany's Jews and Refugees: 1933–1941* (Ann Arbor, MI: UMI Research Press, 1981), 122.

92 "A New Use for Scattergood," AFSC archives: CO, RS, PHS, January–June 1939.

93 Nawyn, *American Protestantism's Response*, 132.

94 See "Non-sectarian Body Formed Here, Sponsored by Quakers, to Place Refugee Children in Homes," *Jewish Telegraph Agency*, March 2, 1939, http://www.jta.org/1939/03/02/archive/non-sectarian-body-formed-here-sponsored-by-quakers-to-place-refugee-children-in-homes (accessed September 3, 2014).

95 "America Speaks for the Wagner–Rogers Bill," *News Letter*, American Friends Service Committee, June 12, 1939: 4.

96 Ibid., 2.

97 Press Release, "Leading American Child Welfare Workers Prepare Plan for Care of Refugee Children," AFSC archives: CO, NSC, March 21, 1939.

98 Feingold, *A Time for Searching*, 150. Also see *News Letter—California Division*, August 23, 1939, AFSC archives: CO, NSC, [letterhead].

99 "Many Offers of Free Foster Homes Received," *News Letter*, AFSC archives: CO, NSC, May 8, 1939.

100 Wyman, *Paper Walls*, 77.

101 Pickett, *For More Than Bread*, 151.

102 Ibid., 152.

103 Feingold, *Politics of Rescue*, 150.

Chapter 2

1 Jan Karski, Interview with Claude Lanzmann, winter 1978–79, http://www.ushmm.org/online/film/display/detail.php?file_num=4739 (accessed June 9, 2015). Claude Lanzmann, *Shoah*, disc 5, Supplements, IFC Films: The Criterion Collection 2013.

2 Saul Friedländer, *Nazi Germany and the Jews, 1939–1945: The Years of Extermination* (New York: HarperCollins, 2007), 304. Also see Alan Cowell, "Files Suggest British Knew Early Of Nazi Atrocities Against Jews," *New York Times*, November 19, 1996.

3 Karski, Interview with Claude Lanzmann.

4 As recounted in E. Thomas Wood and Stanislaw M. Jankowski, *Karski: How One Man Tried to Stop the Holocaust* (New York: John Wiley & Sons, Inc., 1994), 199.

5 Karski, Interview with Claude Lanzmann.

6 Ibid.

7 Ibid. Also see the discussion in Wood and Jankowski, *Karski*, 186–9, which is based in part on interviews with the Karski.

8 See, for example, ibid.

9 Karski, Interview with Claude Lanzmann.

10 "Americans Abroad Urged to Return," *New York Times*, August 25, 1939; "474 Americans Return: Some, Back on German Ship, Say They Feared a War," *New York Times*, August 26, 1939; and "American Abroad Rush for Bookings," *New York Times*, August 26, 1939.

11 Lucy S. Dawidowicz, *From That Place and Time: A Memoir, 1938–1947* (New York: W. W. Norton: 1989), 195.

12 Friedländer, *Nazi Germany and the Jews, 1939–1945*, 12–14.

13 Marion A. Kaplan, *Between Dignity and Despair: Jewish Life in Nazi Germany* (Oxford: Oxford University Press, 1998), 150.

14 Richard Breitman and Allan J. Lichtman, *FDR and the Jews* (Cambridge, MA: Belknap Press, 2013), 157.

15 Friedländer, *Nazi Germany and the Jews, 1939–1945*, 83.

16 Ibid., 159–60. Also see "Alaska Weighed as a Refugee Haven," *New York Times*, August 26, 1939.

17 Breitman and Lichtman, *FDR and the Jews*, 162–3.

18 Hanna Diamond, *Fleeing Hitler: France 1940* (Oxford: Oxford University Press, 2007).

19 Henri Sinder, "Countries of Refuge and Settlement C. France," in *The Jewish Refugee*, ed. Arieh Tartakower and Kurt R. Grossman (New York: Institute of Jewish Affairs of the American Jewish Congress and World Jewish Congress, 1944), 133.

20 Diamond, *Fleeing Hitler*, 150.

21 Irène Némirovsky, *Suite Française*, trans. Sandra Smith (New York: Alfred A. Knopf, 2006), 41.

22 Jean Godsall-Myers and Jennifer Marston William, "Anna Seghers," *The Literary Encyclopedia* (October 28, 2005), http://www.litencyc.com/php/speople.php?rec=true&UID=5460 (accessed May 18, 2015).

23 Anna Seghers, *Transit*, trans. Margot Bettauer Dembo (New York: New York Review of Books, 2013), 31.

24 See Mary Jayne Gold's memoir, *Crossroads Marseilles: 1940* (New York: Doubleday, 1980).

25 Varian Fry, *Surrender on Demand* (New York: Random House, 1945), 18.

26 Fry received considerable assistance from the Czechoslovakian consul Vladimir Vochoc, who was stationed in Marseille and provided the ERC with emergency Czechoslovakian passports. See Adam Hájek "Izrael ocení Čecha, který v Marseille devět měsíců vzdoroval Hitlerovi," iDNES.cz, April 7, 2016; http://zpravy.idnes.cz/vladimir-vochoc-spravedlivy-mezi-narody-marseille-konzulat-pr4-/zahranicni.aspx?c=A160406_112234_zahranicni_aha (accessed August 2, 2017).

27 Lisbon itself became a major departure point for many refugees. See Ronald Weber, *The Lisbon Route: Entry and Escape in Nazi Europe* (Lanham, MD: Rowman and Littlefield, 2011). Also see Hans Ulrich Dillmann and Susanne Heim, *Fluchtpunkt Karibik: jüdische Emigranten in der Dominikanischen Republik* (Berlin: Links, 2009); and Marion Kaplan, "Lisbon Is Sold Out! The Daily Lives of Jewish Refugees in Portugal during World War II," Working Paper, The Tikvah Center For Law & Jewish Civilization, http://www.nyutikvah.org/pubs/1213/documents/WP1kaplan.pdf (accessed June 5, 2015).

28 Breitman and Lichtman, *FDR and the Jews*, 169.

29 "Telegram from Freda Kirchwey to David Dubinsky," July 1, 1940, Tamiment Library & Robert F. Wagner Labor Archives, Jewish Labor Committee Collection, Box 39, Folder 1.

30 See Stefan Zweig, *The World of Yesterday*, trans. Anthea Bell (Lincoln: University of Nebraska Press, 2013). Also see George Prochnik, *The Impossible Exile: Stefan Zweig at the End of the World* (New York: Other Press, 2014).

31 Critics of Long, Wise, and Roosevelt include Wyman, *Paper Walls* and *The Abandonment of the Jews*; Rafael Medoff, *The Deafening Silence/American*

Jewish Leaders and the Holocaust (New York: Shapolsky Publishers, 1987) and *FDR and the Holocaust: A Breach of Faith* (Washington, DC: David S. Wyman Institute for Holocaust Studies, 2013); and Arad, *America, Its Jews*.

32 "Nazi, Red Inquiry Widened by Dies," *New York Times*, November 21, 1939.

33 See Breitman and Lichtman, chapter 9, "Tightened Security," in *FDR and the Jews*, 161–83, from where much of this information is drawn.

34 See the discussions of Breckinridge Long in Henry L. Feingold, *The Politics of Rescue: The Roosevelt Administration and the Holocaust, 1938–1945* (New York: Holocaust Library, 1970), 135; Wyman, *Abandonment of the Jews,* 190–1; and Breitman and Kraut, *American Refugee Policy*, 126–45.

35 Breitman and Lichtman, *FDR and the Jews*, 183.

36 " 'Boycott' on Hatred Urged by Coughlin; Priest Says Americans Bar War to Aid German Jews," *New York Times*, January 29, 1939. More infamously, during a Bronx speech in 1937, he gave the Nazi salute and declared, "When we get through with the Jews in America, they'll think the treatment they received in Germany was nothing!"

37 See A. Scott Berg, *Lindbergh* (New York: Putnam, 1998).

38 See Mae Ngai, *Impossible Subjects: Illegal Aliens and the Making of Modern America* (Princeton: Princeton University Press, 2004); Lynne Olson, *Those Angry Days: Roosevelt Lindbergh, and America's Fight over World War II* (New York: Random House, 2013); and Susan Dunn, *1940: FDR, Willkie, Lindbergh, Hitler—the Election amid the Storm* (New Haven: Yale University Press, 2013).

39 Charles A. Lindbergh, "Aviation, Geography and Race," *Reader's Digest*, November 1939, https://web.archive.org/web/20050404092239/http://www.churchoftrueisrael.com/identity/lindberg.html (accessed May 26, 2015).

40 Charles A. Lindbergh, Speech delivered in Des Moines, Iowa, on September 11, 1941, http://www.charleslindbergh.com/americanfirst/speech.asp (accessed on May 26, 2015).

41 Olson, chapter 24, "Setting the Ground for Anti-Semitism" in *Those Angry Days*.

42 Robert L. Fleegler, *Ellis Island Nation: Immigration Policy and American Identity in the Twentieth Century* (Philadelphia: University of Pennsylvania Press, 2013), 64.

43 Mia Sara Bruch, "Religious Pluralism and the Judeo-Christian Tradition," *Frankel Institute Annual*, Jean and Samuel Frankel Center for Judaic Studies, University of Michigan (2012): 21–2.

44 Executive Order No. 9066, February 19, 1942. A reproduction of the original Order can be viewed at http://www.archives.gov/historical-docs/todays-doc/?dod-date=219 (accessed June 1, 2015). The literature on the US imprisonment of persons of Japanese ancestry is substantial. For historical accounts, see, for example, Greg Robinson, *By Order of the President: FDR and the Internment of Japanese Americans* (Cambridge, MA: Harvard

University Press, 2003) and *A Tragedy of Democracy: Japanese Confinement in North America* (New York: Columbia University Press, 2010). For firsthand accounts, see, for example, Jeanne Wakatsuki Houston, *Farewell to Manzanar* (New York: Random House, 1973); and Lawson Fusao Inada, *Only What We Could Carry: The Japanese American Internment Experience* (Berkeley, CA: Heydey Books, 2000).

45 Following the call by activist, scholar, and former concentration camp prisoner Aiko Herzig-Yoshinaga, I deliberately avoid the euphemisms "relocation center," "internment," "detainee," "non-aliens," and "evacuation" for this historical event. See Herzig-Yoshinaga, "Words Can Lie or Clarify: Terminology of the World War II Incarceration of Japanese Americas," https://manzanarcommittee.files.wordpress.com/2010/03/wordscanlieorclarify-ahy.pdf (accessed June 1, 2015).

46 Following the United States' entry into the war, it detained more than 11,500 ethnic Germans, almost all of whom were German citizens and thus "enemy aliens" during wartime. See "German and Italian Detainees," *Densho Encyclopedia*, http://encyclopedia.densho.org/German_and_Italian_detainees/#cite_note-ftnt_ref1-1 (accessed June 28, 2017).

47 See Richard H. Minear, *Dr. Seuss Goes to War: The World War II Editorial Cartoons of Theodor Seuss Geisel* (New York: The New Press, 1999).

48 Minoru Yasi, "Interview," as quoted in Ronald Takaki, *Double Victory: A Multicultural History of America in World War II* (Boston: Little, Brown and Company, 2000), 155.

49 Henry Louis Gates, Jr., "What Was Black America's Double War?," The Root, http://www.pbs.org/wnet/african-americans-many-rivers-to-cross/history/what-was-black-americas-double-war/ (accessed April 20, 2017).

50 Robert L. Allen, *The Port Allen Mutiny* (New York: Warner Books, 1989), from which this information is drawn.

51 Stuart Cosgrove, "The Zoot-Suit and Style Warfare," *History Workshop*, no. 18 (Autumn 1984): 78.

52 For descriptions of the Zoot-Suit Riots, see Mauricio Mazon, *The Zoot-Suit Riots* (Austin: University of Texas, 1984); Eduardo Obregón Pagán, *Murder at the Sleepy Lagoon: Zoot Suits, Race, and Riot in Wartime L.A.* (Chapel Hill: University of North Carolina Press, 2003); and Luis Alvarez, *The Power of the Zoot: Youth Culture and Resistance during World War II* (Berkeley: University of California Press, 2009) from which this information is drawn.

53 *Los Angeles Evening Herald and Express*, June 5, 1943. As quoted in Pagán, *Murder at the Sleepy Lagoon*, 274, fn. 57.

54 For a useful examination of African American–Jewish relations in Detroit and the racial violence of summer 1943, see Eleanor Paperno Wolf, Alvin D. Loving, and Donald C. Marsh, "Negro-Jewish Relationships," in *Wayne University Studies in Inter-Group Conflicts in Detroit*, no. 1 (Detroit: Wayne University Press, 1944).

55 See Goldstein, chapter 8, "World War II and the Transformation of Jewish Racial Identity," in *The Price of Whiteness: Jews, Race, and American Identity* (Princeton: Princeton University Press, 2006).

56 This question is addressed in most of the literature on the United States and the Holocaust. The most thorough examination, now two decades old, remains Richard Breitman, *Official Secrets: What the Nazis Planned, What the British and Americans Knew* (New York: Hill and Wang, 1998).

57 See, for example, the works of Primo Levi and Imre Kertész, both of whom arrived in Auschwitz in the first half of 1944. As they describe it, neither had any conception of what awaited them. Primo Levi, *Survival in Auschwitz* (New York: Summit Books, 1986); Imre Kertész, *Fatelessness* (New York: Vintage, 2007), which is a fictionalized account of his own experience.

58 Walter Laqueur, "The Riegner Cable, and the Knowing Failure of the West to Act During the Shoah," *Tablet*, August 10, 2015, http://www.tabletmag.com/jewish-arts-and-culture/books/192421/riegner-cable-shoah (accessed March 5, 2017).

59 Deborah Lipstadt, *Beyond Belief: The American Press and the Coming of the Holocaust 1933–1945* (New York: The Free Press, 1986).

60 It is incorrect to assert that reports of atrocities against Jews were, as some have asserted, deliberately suppressed by the press. See, for example, Laurel Leff, *Buried by* The Times*: The Holocaust and America's Most Important Newspaper* (Cambridge: Cambridge University Press, 2005). Also see the review by Peter Novick in the *Washington Post*, May 1, 2005, which argues that the *New York Times*, which is the focus of Leff's critical account, behaved in ways similar to most newspapers at the time. As Novick writes, "The great difficulty with blaming the behavior of the *Times* on the particularities of Sulzberger's belief system is that so many others—Jews and gentiles, universalists and particularists, Zionists and anti-Zionists—behaved more or less identically."

61 Doris L. Bergen, *War and Genocide*, 3rd edn (Lanham, MD: Rowman and Littlefield, 2016), 237.

62 Breitman and Lichtman, *FDR and the Jews*, 198; the text of Roosevelt's telegram is reprinted at "Roosevelt Pledges American People Will Hold Nazis Responsible for Atrocities against Jews," *Jewish Telegraphic Agency*, July 22, 1942, http://www.jta.org/1942/07/22/archive/roosevelt-pledges-american-people-will-hold-nazis-responsible-for-atrocities-against-jews (accessed March 2, 2017).

63 https://commons.wikimedia.org/wiki/File:Riegner_Telegram.jpg (accessed March 2, 2017).

64 Elizabeth Bryant, "Rabbi Stephen S. Wise's Actions upon Receipt of the Riegner Telegram: What More Could He Have Done?," *Studia Historyczne* 25, no. 2 (2013): 187–8.

65 Breitman and Lichtman, *FDR and the Jews*, 200–205.

66 "Slain Polish Jews Put at a Million," *New York Times*, November 26, 1942.

67 "President Renews Pledges to Jews," *New York Times*, December 9, 1942.

68 "11 Allies Condemn Nazi War on Jews," *New York Times*, December 18, 1942.

69 For an overview of the Joint's activities in Europe during the Nazi period, see Sara Kadosh, "American Jewish Joint Distribution Committee," in *Encyclopedia Judaica*, 2nd edn, vol. 2. 59–61, from which much of this overview is drawn. Also see Yehuda Bauer, *My Brother's Keeper: A History of the American Jewish Joint Distribution Committee: 1929–1939* (Philadelphia: Jewish Publication Society of America, 1974); *American Jewry and the Holocaust: The American Jewish Joint Distribution Committee 1939–1945* (Detroit: Wayne State University Press, 1981); and Oscar Handlin, *A Continuing Task: The American Jewish Joint Distribution Committee* (New York: Random House, 1964). Also see Weber, *The Lisbon Route*, 183–5.

70 Breitman and Lichtman, *FDR and the Jews*, 198.

71 For example, see Wyman, *Abandonment of the Jews*, 157–77 and Arad, *America, Its Jews*, 205–208.

72 Friedländer, *Nazi Germany and the Jews*, 304.

73 Breitman and Lichtman, *FDR and the Jews*, 310.

74 Judith Tydor Baumel, *The "Bergson Boys and the Origins of Contemporary Zionist Militancy*, trans. Dena Ordan (Syracuse: Syracuse University Press, 2005), from which this information is drawn.

75 Federal Council of the Churches of Christ in America. Department of Research and Education, "The Mass Murder of Jews in Europe," *Information Service* of the Department of Research and Education 22, no. 17 (April 24, 1943).

76 Gertrude Bussey and Margaret Tims, *Pioneers for Peace: Women's International League for Peace and Freedom 1915–1965* (Oxford: Alden Press, 1980); and Catherine Foster, *Women for All Seasons: The Story of the Women's International League for Peace and Freedom* (Athens: University of Georgia Press, 1989).

77 Eleanor M. Barr, "Records of the WILPF, US Section, 1919–1959, Guide to the Scholarly Resources, Microfilm Edition" (Wilmington, DE: Scholarly Resources, Inc., 1988), 6.

78 Mercedes Randall, "The Voice of Thy Brother's Blood" (Washington: WILPF, 1944).

79 Wyman, *Abandonment of the Jews*, 317.

80 William Edward Nawyn, *American Protestantism's Response to Germany's Jews and Refugees: 1933–1941* (Ann Arbor, MI: UMI Research Press, 1981), 62.

81 Randall, "The Voice of Thy Brother's Blood," 19.

82 Ibid., 27–8; emphasis in the original.

83 Mercedes Randall, "Report on the Pamphlet, 'The Voice of Thy Brother's Blood,' " October 12, 1944, Swarthmore College Peace Collection, MR, DG110, Box 2, Correspondence about "Voice ... ." My thanks to Dr. Wendy E. Chmielewski, George R. Cooley Curator of the Swarthmore College Peace Collection, for making these materials available.

84 Virginia C. Gildersleeve, "Letter to MR," May 31, 1944; Kirchwey, "Letter to MR," June 2, 1944; Joseph C. Hyman, "Letter to MR," March 28, 1944; Alexander S. Kohanski, "Letter to MR," July 11, 1945; Glenn J. Talbott, "Letter to MR," June 10, 1944; "The Rescue of Europe's Jews," *New York Herald Tribune*, April 20, 1944, are found in Swarthmore College Peace Collection, MR, DG110. Box 2, Correspondence about "Voice . . ." The only organization to disagree with Randall was Bergson's Emergency Committee to save the Jewish People of Europe, Inc. whose members were displeased at being left out of "Voice."

85 "Refugee Facts," AFSC, CO, RS, PHS, Beginnings; Wyman, *Paper Walls*, 26.

86 Nawyn, *American Protestantism's Response*, 127.

87 Jean Reynolds, Brochure, Scattergood Hostel, American Friends Service Committee archives, CO, RS, PHS, Committee Report, 1939. Also see Robert Berquist, David Rhodes, and Carolyn Smith Treadway, *Scattergood Friends School: 1890–1990* (West Branch, IO: Scattergood Friends School, 1990).

88 Nawyn, *American Protestantism's Response*, 128.

89 Kurt R. Grossmann, "Refugees: Burden or Asset?" *Nation*, December 26, 1942, 708. Grossman himself was a German Jewish refugee who had escaped Germany in 1933 and resettled in Prague. He fled again to France in 1938 and arrived in the United States in 1939, and became an executive assistant to the World Jewish Congress.

90 Breitman and Kraut, *American Refugee Policy*, 139–43.

91 See the advertisement in the *New York Times*, May 4, 1943, 17.

92 See "Pole's Suicide Note Pleads for Jews," *New York Times*, June 4, 1943, 7.

93 See the discussions in Wyman, *The Abandonment of the Jews*, 193–206, and Breitman and Lichtman, *FDR and the Jews*, 228–37, from which this information is drawn.

94 Rebecca L. Erbelding, "About Time: The History of the War Refugee Board," PhD dissertation, George Mason University (2015), 120–1. For a full discussion of the tensions and intrigue between the Departments of State and Treasury, see chapter 2, "The Time to Act Is Long Past Due." This percentage assumes, however, that in the early years of Nazi rule over Germany, there were sufficient numbers of Jews seeking to leave Germany for the United States to fill the quota, an unlikely proposition.

95 Efforts by the Treasury Department included the drafting of a report calling out the State for its obstructionism and was entitled "Report to the Secretary on the Acquiescence of this Government in the Murder of the Jews." It declared that unless the US government took direct action on the refugee issue, it would bear some responsibility for the extermination of Jews held by Germany.

96 The information on the WRB that follows is from Erbelding, "About Time."

97 John Crider, "Roosevelt Warns Germans on Jews," *New York Times*, March 25, 1944 A1, as cited in ibid., 248.

98 See Erbelding, "About Time," 380–7.

99 Historian David S. Wyman was among those to take up this question in the late 1970s. See "Why Auschwitz Was Never Bombed," *Commentary* 65 (May 1, 1978): 37–46.

100 Breitman and Lichtman, *FDR and the Jews*, 281. See the larger discussion on pages 280–8.

101 On the WRB's brief but formative role with the Fort Ontario Emergency Refugee Shelter, see Erbelding, "About Time," 341–51, and 373–6.

102 See Wyman, *Abandonment of the Jews*, pages xiv and 405, fn 129. This number has been subsequently repeated by many historians, such as Breitman and Lichtman, *FDR and the Jews*, 226.

103 See Erbelding, "Appendix A: The Number of People 'Rescued' by the War Refugee Board," in "About Time," 709–15.

104 Sharon Lowenstein, *Token Refuge: The Story of the Jewish Refugee Shelter at Oswego, 1944–1946* (Bloomington: Indiana University Press, 1986), 48. Much of what follows is drawn from Lowenstein's work. Lowenstein's title is a reference to the US Department of the Interior's War Relocation Authority's report, *Token Shipment: The Story of America's War Refugee Shelter* (Washington, DC: US Government Printing Office, 1944).

105 Lowenstein, *Token Refuge*, 75, 111.

106 Interview with Irene Danon, Safe Haven Fiftieth Anniversary Reunion Video Collection at the State University of New York at Oswego, http://www.oswego.edu/library/archives/safe_haven_videos.html (accessed on July 20, 2015).

107 Interview with Eva Kaufman, Safe Haven Fiftieth Anniversary Reunion Video Collection at the State University of New York at Oswego, http://www.oswego.edu/library/archives/safe_haven_videos.html (accessed on July 20, 2015).

108 See Karen J. Greenberg, "Missed Chance: Reassessing the Fort Ontario Emergency Refugee Shelter," *The Hudson Valley Regional Review* 9 (1992): 131–6.

109 Lowenstein, *Token Refuge*, 135–7.

Chapter 3

1 Hannah Arendt, "We Refugees," *Menorah Journal* 31 (1943): 69–77.

2 For a biography of Arendt, see Elisabeth Young-Bruehl, *Hannah Arendt: For Love of the World*, 2nd edn (New Haven: Yale University Press, 2004).

3 See Laura Jockusch, *Collect and Record! Jewish Holocaust Documentation in Early Postwar Europe* (Oxford: Oxford University Press, 2012); and Lisa Moses Leff, *The Archive Thief: The Man Who Salvaged French Jewish History in the Wake of the Holocaust* (Oxford: Oxford University Press, 2015).

4 Arendt, "We Refugees," 69–70.

5 Ibid., 74, 70.

6 Ibid., 77.

7 Ibid., 69.

8 Roscoe C. "Rockie" Blunt, as interviewed in "World War II in HD," History Channel (2009), http://www.history.com/topics/world-war-ii/the-holocaust/videos/concentration-camp-liberation (accessed December 22, 2015). Also see his description in Roscoe C. Blunt, "Liberation," in *Foot Soldier: A Combat Infantryman's War in Europe* (Cambridge, MA: De Capo Press, 2004), chapter 15.

9 Hanna Lévy-Hass, *Diary of Bergen-Belsen, 1944–1945*, trans. Sophie Hand (Chicago: Haymarket Books, 2009), 117–19.

10 Tony Judt, *Postwar: A History of Europe since 1945* (New York: Penguin, 2005), 23; Israel Gutman, ed., *Encyclopedia of the Holocaust*, Vol. I (New York: MacMillan, 1990), 377.

11 The information on the treatment of DPs under US military command is drawn primarily from Leonard Dinnerstein, *America and the Survivors of the Holocaust* (New York: Columbia University Press, 1982).

12 Ibid., 51.

13 See Jan Tomasz Gross and Irena Grudzińska Gross, *Golden Harvest: Events at the Periphery of the Holocaust* (Oxford: Oxford University Press, 2012). Also see Jan T. Gross, *Fear: Anti-Semitism in Poland after Auschwitz* (New York: Random House, 2006).

14 Dinnerstein, *America and the Survivors*, 35.

15 Earl G. Harrison, *The Plight of the Displaced Jews in Europe* (The White House: September 29, 1945), reprinted by United Jewish Appeal for Refugees, Overseas Needs and Palestine.

16 Ibid., 6.

17 Dwight D. Eisenhower, "Letter to President Truman, 8 October 1945," reprinted in *New York Times*, October 17, 1945.

18 "Harrison Strikes Back," *New York Times*, October 18, 1945.

19 As cited in Eric Lichtblau, *The Nazis Next Door: How America became a Safe Haven for Hitler's Men* (Boston: Houghton Mifflin Harcourt, 2014), 5.

20 Harry S. Truman, "Statement and Directive by the President on Immigration to the United States of Certain Displaced Persons and Refugees in Europe," December 22, 1945, https://www.trumanlibrary.org/publicpapers/viewpapers.php?pid=515 (accessed January 15, 2017).

21 For an extended discussion of this famous photo, as well as of the boy depicted in it, see Werner Sollors, *The Temptation of Despair: Tales of the 1940s* (Cambridge, MA: Belknap Press, 2014), 57–82. As Sollors relates, the original photo was altered for publication in *Life* so as to blur the nakedness of the corpses.

22 See Dinnerstein, *America and the Survivors*, 120–1.

23 Maurice R. Davie, *Refugees in America: Report of the Committee for the Study of Recent Immigration from Europe* (New York: Harper and Brother Publishers, 1947).

24 Ibid., 391.

25 See Irving M. Engel, *Americanizing Our Immigration Laws* (New York: American Jewish Committee, 1949), 47.

26 Ibid., 57.

27 Much of the information on Kurt Maier is drawn from Rachel Deblinger's digital exhibition, "Memories/Motifs: Holocaust Survivor Narratives in Postwar America," http://www.memoriesmotifs.com (accessed December 31, 2015). I thank Dr. Deblinger for her willingness to share her deep knowledge of the campaigns in the United States on behalf of DPs.

28 Daniel Lang, "Displaced: A Reporter at Large," *The New Yorker*, September 13, 1947, 100–101.

29 "555 Arrive on Ship as Quota Immigrants," *New York Times*, July 28, 1946.

30 Lang, "Displaced: A Reporter at Large," 100.

31 See the review by Sam Chase, *The Billboard* 61, no. 5 (January 29, 1949): 10.

32 Dinnerstein, chapter 7, "Congress Acts."

33 See, for example, Christopher Simpson, *Blowback: America's Recruitment of Nazis and Its Effects on the Cold War* (New York: Collier Books, 1988); Annie Jacobsen, *Operation Paperclip: The Secret Intelligence Program That Brought Nazi Scientists to America* (New York: Back Bay Books, 2014); and Lichtblau, *The Nazis Next Door*. Also see the report by the US Department of Justice, Office for Special Investigations, *Striving for Accountability in the Aftermath of the Holocaust*, by Judy Feigin (Washington, DC, 2008).

34 Jacobsen, *Operation Paperclip*, xiii.

35 Reprinted in Jesse Zel Lurie, "Nazi Invasion of the U.S.," *The Jewish Veteran* (January 1947): 19.

36 See Dinnerstein, *America and the Survivors*, 217–53.

37 Harry Truman, "Statement by the President upon Signing Bill Amending the Displaced Persons Act. June 16, 1950," The American Presidency Project, http://www.presidency.ucsb.edu/ws/index.php?pid=13531&st=displaced+persons&st1 (accessed March 6, 2017).

38 Dinnerstein, *America and the Survivors*, 251.

39 Ibid., 183, and the table on p. 288.

40 One former DP who refused on principle to accept appropriated Palestinian property was Hannah Lévy, who arrived in the newly established state of Israel in the fall of 1948.

41 Hannah Arendt, *The Origins of Totalitarianism* (New York: Schocken Books, 1951), 293–4, 295–6.

42 Samuel C. Heilman, *Portrait of American Jews: The Last Half of the 20th Century* (Seattle: University of Washington Press, 1995), 8.

43 Karen Brodkin, *How Jews Became White Folks and What That Says about Race in America* (New Brunswick, NJ: Rutgers University Press, 1998), 39–52.

44 Eli Lederhendler, *New York Jews and the Decline of Urban Ethnicity, 1950–1970* (Syracuse, NY: Syracuse University Press, 2001), 148–54. Lederhendler notes importantly that Jewish migration out of New York tended to lag behind that of other white groups. A consequence of this, he suggests, may have been to expose Jews to urban racial tensions sooner and in greater proximity than other non-Hispanic whites (154).

45 Jeffrey S. Gurock, *Jews in Gotham: New York Jews in a Changing City, 1920–2010* (New York: New York University Press, 2012), 203.

46 Brodkin, *How Jews Became White Folks*, 42.

47 Ira Katznelson, *When Affirmative Action Was White: An Untold History of Racial Inequality in Twentieth-Century America* (New York: W. W. Norton & Company, 2005), 114.

48 Also see Ta-Nehisi Coates, "The Case for Reparations," *The Atlantic* (June 2014), http://www.theatlantic.com/features/archive/2014/05/the-case-for-reparations/361631 (accessed January 5, 2016).

49 Hasia R. Diner, "The Myth of Silence: Postwar American Jews Did Not Ignore the Holocaust," *Chronicle of Higher Education*, April 24, 2009.

50 Milton Himmelfarb, "The Jewish Vote (Again)," *Commentary* (June 1973).

51 For a representative example of this literature, see Nathan Glazar, "The Anomalous Liberalism of American Jews," in *The Americanization of the Jews*, ed. Robert M. Seltzer and Norman J. Cohen (New York: New York University Press, 1995), 133–7.

52 Jacob Lestschinsky, *Crisis, Catastrophe and Survival: A Jewish Balance Sheet, 1914–1948* (New York: Institute of Jewish Affairs for the World Jewish Congress, 1948).

53 Ibid., 81.

54 Ibid., 76.

55 Lederhendler, *New York Jews*, 104.

56 Heilman, chapter 1, "Starting Over: Acculturation and Suburbia, the Jews of the 1950s," in *Portrait of American Jews*.

57 David Kaufman, *Shul with a Pool: The "Synagogue-Center" in American Jewish History* (Hanover, NH: University Press of New England, 1999).

58 Philip S. Bernstein, "What the Jews Believe," *Life*, September 11, 1950, 161–79.

59 Morris N. Kertzer, "What Is a Jew?" *Look*, June 1952, 120–8. Referenced in Heilman, *Portrait of American Jews*, 16–17.

60 Neglecting the fact by 1952, American Jews were privately sending millions as a sign of support for the new state. As Dawidowicz reports, between 1939 and 1967, American Jews sent $1.5 billion to Israel. Lucy Dawidowicz, *On Equal Terms: Jews in America 1881–1981* (New York: Holt, Rinehart and Winston, 1982), 129.

61 Arendt, "We Refugees," 69–70.

62 For an example of this argument, see Novick, *The Holocaust in American Life*, 83–4, and chapter 5, "That Is Past, and We Must Deal with the Facts Today," 85–102, in which he argues that much of the silence on the part of Jewish American leaders and organizations (as opposed to American Jews speaking privately) was imposed by the perceived demands of the Cold War. Also see the discussion in Hasia R. Diner, *We Remember with Reverence and Love: American Jews and the Myth of Silence after the Holocaust, 1945–1962* (New York: New York University Press, 2009), 1–17.

63 See Joshua M. Zeitz, *White Ethnic New York: Jews, Catholics, and the Shaping of Postwar Politics* (Chapel Hill: University of North Carolina Press, 2007).

64 On American Jewry's embrace of Israel following the 1967 war, see Arthur Hertzberg, "Israel and American Jewry," *Commentary* (August 1967): 69–73.

65 In addition to Diner, *We Remember with Reverence and Love*, see David Cesarani and Eric J. Sundquist, eds, *After the Holocaust: Challenging the Myth of Silence* (New York: Routledge, 2011); and Rachel Deblinger, "'In a World Still Trembling': American Jewish Philanthropy and the Shaping of Holocaust Survivor Narratives in Postwar America, 1945–1953," PhD dissertation, University of California, Los Angeles, 2014.

66 Jonathan Boyarin, "Yizker-bikher," in *The YIVO Encyclopedia of Jews in Eastern Europe*, Vol. 2, ed. Gershon David Hundert (New Haven: Yale University Press, 2008), 2096. See also Jack Kugelmass and Jonathan Boyarin, trans. and eds, *From a Ruined Garden: The Memorial Books of Polish Jewry* (Bloomington: Indiana University Press, 1998).

67 Max Weinreich, *Hitler's Professors: The Part of Scholarship in Germany's Crimes against the Jewish People* (New York: Yiddish Scientific Institute, 1946).

68 Raphael R. Abramovitch, *Di farshvundene velt/The Vanished World* (New York: Forward Association, 1947).

69 Kluger, *Still Alive*, 149.

70 Art Spiegelman, *Maus: A Survivor's Tale*, Vol. I (New York: Random House, 1986) 12.

71 Dawidowicz, *On Equal Terms*, 127.

72 Rebecca Kobrin, "Beyond the Myths of Mobility and Altruism: Jewish Immigrant Professionals and Jewish Social Welfare Agencies in New York City, 1948–1954," in *A Jewish Feminine Mystique?: Jewish Women in Postwar America*, ed. Hasia Diner, Shira Kohn, and Rachel Kranson (New Brunswick, NJ: Rutgers University Press, 2010), 108.

73 See Beth Cohen, *Case Closed: Holocaust Survivors in Postwar America* (New Brunswick, NJ: Rutgers University Press, 2007), from which much of the information below is derived.

74 Kluger, *Still Alive*, 174.

75 "Jewish Refugees Adjust Themselves Speedily to American Life, Rosenwald Reports," *Jewish Telegraph Agency*, October 30, 1947, http://www.jta.org/1947/10/30/archive/jewish-refugees-adjust-themselves-speedily-to-american-life-rosenwald-reports (accessed January 11, 2016).

76 *New Neighbors: United Service for New Americans*, April 1948–February 1952.

77 Cohen, *Case Closed*, 71.

78 Ibid., 54.

79 See Kobrin, "Beyond the Myths of Mobility and Altruism."

80 Ibid., 113.

81 Adara Goldberg, *Holocaust Survivors in Canada: Exclusion, Inclusion, Transformation, 1947–1955* (Winnipeg: University of Manitoba Press, 2015), 49.

82 For scholarship on the Canadian reception of Holocaust survivors, see Irving Abella and Harold Troper, *None Is Too Many: Canada and the Jews of Europe, 1933–1948* (Toronto: University of Toronto Press, 1983); and Goldberg, *Holocaust Survivors in Canada*.

83 Eva Hoffman, *Lost in Translation: A Life in a New Language* (New York: E. P. Dutton, 1989), 32. Also see Sarah Phillips Casteel, "Eva Hoffman's Double Emigration: Canada as the Site of Exile in *Lost In Translation*," *Biography: An Interdisciplinary Quarterly* 24, no. 1 (Winter 2001): 288–302.

84 Hoffman, *Lost in Translation*, 124–5.

85 Tom Segev, *The Seventh Million: The Israelis and the Holocaust*, trans. Haim Watzman (New York: Hill and Wang, 1993), 119.

86 Ibid., 180.

87 Ibid., 185.

88 Also see Idith Zertal, *Israel's Holocaust and the Politics of Nationhood* (Cambridge: Cambridge University Press, 2005).

Chapter 4

1 Jacob Pat, *Ashes and Fire* (New York: International Universities Press, 1947).

2 S. L. Shneiderman, *Between Fear and Hope*, trans. Norbert Guterman (New York: Arco Publishing Company, 1947), 11.

3 Mary Berg, *The Diary of Mary Berg*, ed. S. L. Shneiderman and Susan Lee (Oxford: Oneworld Publications, 2007). Originally published as Mary Berg, *The Diary of Mary Berg*, trans. S. L. Shneiderman (New York: L. B. Fischer, 1945). Born Miriam Wattenberg, she, like many immigrants at that time, changed her name so that it sounded more American.

4 "Hostages in Vittel: The Rodi Glass Collection," https://www.ushmm.org (accessed October 3, 2016).

5 "Forum for Democracy," *Variety*, April 11, 1945, 26.

6 Berg, *The Diary of Mary Berg*, 168.

7 Amy Rosenberg, "What Happened to Mary Berg," *Tablet*, July 17, 2008, http://www.tabletmag.com/jewish-news-and-politics/981/what-happened-to-mary-berg (accessed October 16, 2016).

8 Ibid.

9 Quoted in ibid.

10 Jennifer Schuessler, "Survivor Who Hated the Spotlight," *New York Times*, November 10, 2014; Mike Argento, "Holocaust Diary Author Lived in York County For Years," *Associated Press*, December 27, 2014.

11 Anne Frank, *The Diary of a Young Girl*, trans. B. M. Mooyaart-Doubleday (New York: The Modern Library, 1952). There are several excellent recent studies on Frank's diary and its reception and impact, including Francine Prose, *Anne Frank: The Book, The Life, The Afterlife* (New York: HarperCollins, 2009); and Barbara Kirshenblatt-Gimblett and Jeffrey Shandler, eds, *Anne Frank Unbound: Media, Imagination, Memory* (Bloomington: Indiana University Press, 2012), both of which inform this discussion.

12 See the "Chronology" in Anne Frank, *The Diary of Anne Frank*, ed. Harold Bloom (New York: Bloom's Literary Criticism, 2010), 164.

13 See the description in Prose, *Anne Frank*, 14–15.

14 Eleanor Roosevelt, "Introduction" to *Anne Frank: The Diary of a Young Girl*, 8.

15 See, for example, the criticism by Cynthia Ozick, "Who Owns Anne Frank?" *New Yorker*, October 6, 1977, 76–87.

16 Prose, *Anne Frank*, 76; italics in the original.

17 Ozick, "Who Owns Anne Frank?" 87.

18 See, for example, the review by Algene Ballif, "On the Horizon: Anne Frank on Broadway," *Commentary*, November 1, 1955.

19 See Edward Wyatt, "The Translation of Wiesel's 'Night' Is New, but Old Questions Are Raised," *New York Times*, January 19, 2006; Geoffrey Stokes and Eliot Fremont-Smith, "Jerzy Kosiński's Tainted Words," *The Village Voice*, June 22, 1982, 1, 41–3; Samuel Moyn, *A Holocaust Controversy: The Treblinka Affair in Postwar France* (Waltham, MA: Brandeis University Press, 2005).

20 Another film of this era that portrays Jews as one of many victims of Nazism is the 1942 comedy *To Be Or Not To Be?*

21 *None Shall Escape*, writ. Lester Cole and Alfred Neumann, dir. André De Toth, perf. Marsha Hunt, Alexander Knox, Henry Travers, Columbia Pictures, 1944. I thank Dr. Eugene R. Sheppard of Brandeis University for this reference.

22 Thomas Doherty, " 'None Shall Escape,' Hollywood's First Holocaust Film, Was All But Unknown for 70 Years. Now It's Been Rediscovered," *Tablet Magazine*, November 1, 2016, http://www.tabletmag.com/jewish-arts-and-culture/216380/none-shall-escape (accessed December 1, 2016).

23 See Jeffrey Shandler, *While America Watches: Televising the Holocaust* (New York: Oxford University Press, 1999), 5–26.

24 The newsreel can be viewed at the website of the United States Holocaust Memorial Museum (www.ushmm.org).

25 On the use of newsreel footage in the service of World War II court proceedings, see Christian Delage, *Caught on Camera: Film in the Courtroom from the Nuremberg Trials to the Trials of the Khmer Rouge*, trans. Ralph Schoolcraft and Mary Byrd Kelly (Philadelphia: University of Pennsylvania Press, 2013).

26 *Death Mills*, writ. and dir. Billy Wilder and Hanuš Burger, United States Department of War, 1946.

27 Another, less successful film in this genre is *Crossfire*, writ. and dir. Edward Dmytryk, perf. Robert Young, Robert Mitchum, and Robert Ryan, RKO Radio Pictures, 1947.

28 Eric J. Sundquist, *Strangers in the Land: Blacks, Jews, Post-Holocaust America* (Cambridge, MA: Harvard University Press, 2009), 67.

29 The film first appeared in Berlin in 1964 and was released in the United States the following year.

30 *The Pawnbroker*, dir. Sidney Lumet, writ. Edward Lewis Wallant, Morton S. Fine, and David Friedkin, perf. Rod Steiger, Allied Artists, 1964.

31 Judith E. Doneson, *The Holocaust in American Film*, 2nd edn (Syracuse: Syracuse University Press, 2002), 112.

32 Shandler, *While America Watches*, 3.

33 "This is Your Life," hosted by Ralph Edwards, directed by Axel Gruenberg, episode airing May 27, 1953. The full episode can viewed on many websites, including http://kmuw.org/post/your-life-hanna-bloch-kohner-story-holocaust-survivor (accessed on November 11, 2016).

34 What they didn't learn about, however, was just as compelling. Many years later, Hanna and Walter's daughter Julie—who formed a charitable organization to promote her parents' desire to further Holocaust remembrance and education—revealed that her mother had a secret abortion while in Auschwitz. Women prisoners who were otherwise fit to work but who were pregnant were routinely murdered. With the help of her brother, who arranged for her to get assistance from a female doctor, Hanna was able to end her pregnancy and avoid being sent to her death. See https://vogcharity.org (accessed November 11, 2016). Hanna and Walter also published their own memoir. See *Hanna and Walter: A Love Story* (New York: Random House, 1984).

35 Shandler, *While America Watches*, 39.

36 Raul Hilberg, *The Politics of Memory: The Journey of a Holocaust Historian* (Chicago: Ivan R. Dee, 1996), 66.

37 For the most comprehensive account of the Ringelblum archive, see Samuel Kassow, *Who Will Write Our History? Emanuel Ringelblum, the Warsaw Ghetto, and the Oyneg Shabes Archive* (Bloomington: Indiana University Press, 2007).

38 This biographical information on Friedman is from Roni Stauber, "Laying the Foundations for Holocaust Research: The Impact of Philip Friedman", *Search and Research" Lectures and Papers* 15 (Jerusalem: Yad Vashem International Institute for Holocaust Research, 2009). Also see Natalia Aleksiun, "Philip Friedman and the Emergence of Holocaust Scholarship: A Reappraisal," *Simon Dubnow Institute Yearbook* 11 (2012): 333–46.

39 Pat, *Ashes and Fire*, 62.

40 Friedman quoted by Pat in ibid., 4.

41 Roni Stauber, *Laying the Foundations for Holocaust Research: The Impact of the Historian Philip Friedman* (Jerusalem: Yad Vashem, 2009), 19.

42 Jacob Robinson and Philip Friedman, *Guide to Jewish History under Nazi Impact* (New York: YIVO Institute for Jewish Research, 1960).

43 Salo Wittmayer Baron, "Introduction," in Philip Friedman, *Roads to Extinction: Essays on the Holocaust*, ed. Ada June Friedman (New York and Philadelphia: Conference on Jewish Social Studies/The Jewish Publication Society of America, 1980), 1.

44 For a collection of his essays in English, see Philip Friedman, *Roads to Extinction*. Also see Laura Jockusch, *Collect and Record! Jewish Holocaust Documentation in Early Postwar Europe* (Oxford: Oxford University Press, 2012).

45 See the discussion in David Engel, *Historians of the Jews and the Holocaust* (Stanford: Stanford University Press, 2010).

46 Lucy Dawidowicz, *The Holocaust and the Historians* (Cambridge, MA: Harvard University Press, 1981), 132.

47 Hilberg, *The Politics of Memory*, 57.

48 Gie Van Den Berghe, "The Incompleteness of a Masterpiece: Raul Hilberg and the Destruction of European Jews," *Belgisch Tijdschrift voor Nieuwste Geschiedenis* XXI, nos 1–2 (1990): 110.

49 Hilberg, *The Politics of Memory*, 59–60.

50 Friedman, and not Baron, it should be noted, served on Hilberg's dissertation committee. See Hilberg, *The Politics of Memory*, 109.

51 On this cohort of scholars, see Doris L. Bergen, "Out of the Limelight or In: Raul Hilberg, Gerhard Weinberg, Henry Friedlander, and the Historical Study of the Holocaust," in *The Second Generation: Émigrés from Nazi Germany as Historians*, ed. Andreas W. Daum, Hartmut Lehmann, and James J. Sheehan (New York: Berghahn, 2016), 229–43.

52 Fritz T. Epstein (*1954*) Washington Research Opportunities in the Period of World War II. *The American Archivist* 17, no. 3 (July 1954): 225–36. On Epstein, see Gerhard L. Weinberg, "Fritz T. Epstein, 1898–1979," *Central European History* 12, no. 4 (December 1979): 399–401.

53 Raul Hilberg, *The Destruction of the European Jews* (Chicago: Quadrangle Books, 1961).

54 Van Den Berghe, "The Incompleteness of a Masterpiece," 110.

55 H. R. Trevor-Roper, Review of *The Destruction of the European Jews*, by Raul Hilberg, *Commentary*, April 1, 1962.

56 Hilberg, *The Destruction of the European Jews*, 22.

57 Ibid., 5.

58 See Michael R. Marrus, *The Holocaust in History* (New York: Penguin, 1987), 48–50.

59 See the comments by Abba Kovner in Yehuda Bauer and Nathan Rotenstreich, eds, *The Holocaust as Historical Experience* (New York: Holmes and Meier, 1981), 250–2.

60 Oscar Handlin, "Jewish Resistance to the Nazis," *Commentary*, November 1, 1962.

61 Lawrence Douglas, *The Right Wrong Man: John Demjanjuk and the Last Great Nazi War Crimes Trial* (Princeton: Princeton University Press, 2016), 6–7.

62 See Charles I. Bevans, ed., *Treaties and Other International Agreements of the United States of America, 1776–1949* (Washington, DC: United States Department of State, 1969), 834.

63 Ian Cobain, "Britain Favoured Execution over Nuremberg Trials for Nazi Leaders," *The Guardian*, October 25, 2012.

64 "Charter of the International Military Tribunal," http://avalon.law.yale.edu/imt/imtconst.asp (accessed November 16, 2016).

65 Robert H. Jackson, "Opening Statement before the International Military Tribunal," https://www.roberthjackson.org (accessed November 16, 2016). On Jackson, see John Q. Barrett, "The Nuremberg Roles of Justice Robert H. Jackson," *Washington University Global Studies Law Review* 6 no. 3 (2007): 511–25.

66 "War-Crimes Court Sees Horror Films," *The New York Times*, November 30, 1945. As quoted in Daniel H. Magilow and Lisa Silverman, *Holocaust Representations in History: An Introduction* (London: Bloomsbury, 2015), 23.

67 Magilow and Silverman, *Holocaust Representations in History*, 25.

68 As quoted in Laura Jockusch, "Justice at Nuremberg? Jewish Responses to Nazi War-Crime Trials in Allied-Occupied Germany," *Jewish Social Studies: History, Culture, Society* n.s. 19, no. 1 (Fall 2012): 108.

69 Michael R. Marrus, "The Nuremberg Trial: Fifty Years After," *The American Scholar* 66, no. 4 (Autumn 1977): 568.

70 *Nuremberg—Les nazis face à leurs crimes*, dir. Christian Delage, La Compagnie des Phares et Balises and ARTE France 2006.

71 Tom Segev, *The Seventh Million: The Israelis and the Holocaust*, trans. Haim Watzman (New York: Hill and Wang, 1993), 334. Segev is quoting Pinhas Rosen, the Israeli minister of justice at the time of the legislation. The information below on the Eichmann trail is derived from Segev's account except where otherwise noted.

72 See William L. Shirer, *The Rise and Fall of the Third Reich* (New York: Simon & Schuster, 1960), 978.

73 "Eichmann in Vengeance Trap," *Washington Post*, May 25, 1960.

74 "Jungle Law," editorial, *Washington Post*, May 27, 1960.

75 "The Eichmann Case as Seen by Ben-Gurion," *New York Times*, December 18, 1960.

76 Shandler, *While America Watches*, 90–1. The quotation is by *New York Times* media critic Jack Gould and is found on p. 91.

77 *Eichmann in Jerusalem* originally appeared in the *New Yorker* editions of February 16, February 23, March 2, March 9, and March 16, 1963.

78 As she writes in the postscript to the 1964 edition, "We are forced to conclude that Eichmann acted fully within the framework of the kind of judgment required of him: he acted in accordance with the rule" (293).

79 Arendt, *Eichmann in Jerusalem*, 117–18.

80 Ibid., 125.

81 Seyla Benhabib, "Who's on Trial, Eichmann or Arendt?" *New York Times*, September 21, 2014.

82 Arendt, "Eichmann in Jerusalem," *New Yorker*, March 2, 1963, 42.

Chapter 5

1 In the interest of full disclosure, over the years, I have had or continue to have professional relationships with several of the institutions discussed in this chapter, including the United States Holocaust Memorial Museum, the Museum of Tolerance, the Holocaust Educational Foundation, and Facing History and Ourselves.

2 See Remarks of President William J. Clinton at the Dedication Ceremonies for the United States Holocaust Memorial Museum, April 22, 1993, https://www.ushmm.org/research/ask-a-research-question/frequently-asked-questions/clinton (accessed December 13, 2016).

3 For two helpful discussions on the implications of this expression, see Yehuda Elkana, "The Need to Forget," *Haaretz*, March 2, 1988; and Doris L. Bergen, "Studying the Holocaust: Is History Commemoration?" in *The Holocaust and Historical Methodology*, ed. Dan Stone (New York: Berghahn Books, 2012), 158–77.

4 Heilman, "Starting Over: Acculturation and Suburbia, the Jews of the 1950s," in *Portrait of American Jews*, chapter 1. The analysis here is also drawn in part from chapter 2, "The Emergence of Two Types of Jews: Choices Made in the 1960s and 1970s."

5 Edward S. Shapiro, *A Time for Healing: American Jewry since World War II* (Baltimore: The Johns Hopkins University Press, 1992), 223.

6 It is important to note, as Cheryl Greenberg has shown, that few Southern Jews favored desegregation and saw little comparison between the anti-Semitism faced by Jews and racism faced by African Americans. See *Troubling the Waters*, 209.

7 Ibid., 206–207.

8 Shapiro, *A Time for Healing*, 216. Also see Peter Novick's discussion of this in "Would They Hide My Children?," in *The Holocaust in American Life*, chapter 9, 170–203.

9 Yehuda Bauer, *The Jewish Emergence from Powerlessness* (Toronto: University of Toronto Press, 1979), 26.

10 As related in Leonard Dinnerstein, "What Should American Jews Have Done to Rescue Their European Brethren?" *Simon Wiesenthal Center Annual* 3 (1986), http://motlc.wiesenthal.com/site/pp.asp?c=gvKVLcMVIuG&b=395049 (accessed December 8, 2016, from which this account is drawn).

11 Seymour Maxwell Finger, *American Jewry during the Holocaust* (New York: Holmes & Meier, 1984), 36–7.

12 Haskel Lookstein, *Were We Our Brothers' Keepers? The Public Response of American Jews to the Holocaust 1938–1944* (New York: Hartmore House, 1985).

13 Ibid., 216.

14 For a contemporary response to critics of American Jewish leadership during the Nazi period, see Henry L. Feingold's essays from the 1980s, as collected in *Bearing Witness: How America and Its Jews Responded to the Holocaust* (Syracuse: Syracuse University Press, 1995).

15 Feingold, "Did American Jewry Do Enough during the Holocaust?," in ibid., 10, 2.

16 "American Jewish Groups Faulted on a Report on Holocaust Victims," *New York Times*, March 21, 1984.

17 Richard J. Jensen, *Reagan at Bergen-Belsen and Bitburg* (College Station: Texas A&M University Press, 2007), 62.

18 Ibid., 64.

19 The information regarding the Demjanjuk trial is drawn primarily from Lawrence Douglas, *The Right Wrong Man: John Demjanjuk and the Last Great Nazi War Crimes Trial.*

20 See Nicolas Werth, "Mass Deportations, Ethnic Cleansing, and Genocidal Politics in the Later Russian Empire and the USSR," in *The Oxford Handbook of Genocide Studies*, ed. Donald Bloxham and A. Dirk Moses (Oxford: Oxford University Press, 2010), 386–406.

21 Douglas, *The Right Wrong Man*, 33.

22 In Israel, as Yehudit Dori-Deston has shown, one consequence of the Demjanjuk case was that survivor testimony, once held as the "gold standard" for evidence, was no longer viewed as reliable in such cases. " 'When One Door Closes, Another Opens': Demjanjuk's Trials in Israel (1986–93) and in Germany (2009–11)," paper presented at the XIV Lessons and Legacies Conference, November 3, 2016, Claremont, CA.

23 Felix Eliezer Shinnar and Michael Bazyler, "Reparations, German," in *Encyclopedia Judaica*, 2nd edn, vol. 17, ed. Fred Skolnik (Detroit: Thomson Gale, 2007), 220–1. Later, the German government also paid compensation to former slave laborers.

24 Norman Finkelstein, *The Holocaust Industry: Reflections on the Exploitation of Jewish Suffering* (London: Verso, 2000), 86–8.

25 Peter Novick refers to this campaign as "exploitation [of the Holocaust] by politicians," in *The Holocaust in American Life*, 230. Norman Finkelstein dubbed it a "double shakedown" and an "outright extortion racket" in *The Holocaust Industry*, 79, 89. Angelo M. Codevilla called it "moral blackmail" in his *Between the Alps and a Hard Place: Switzerland in World War II and Moral Blackmail Today* (Washington, DC: Regnery Publishing, Inc., 2000).

26 "Switzerland Winds Up Holocaust Fund," December 18, 2002, Swissinfo.ch, http://www.swissinfo.ch/eng/switzerland-winds-up-holocaust-fund/7146 (accessed January 5, 2017). "Swiss Bank Holocaust Fund Paid Out $1.24 Billion for Survivors & Relatives, Magazine Reports," *Huffington Post*, July 15, 2013, http://www.huffingtonpost.com/2013/07/15/swiss-bank-holocaust-fund_n_3597359.html (accessed January 5, 2017).

27 In English, *Night*, translated from the French by Stella Rodway (New York: Hill and Wang, 1960). A new translation by Marion Wiesel (published by Farrar, Straus & Giroux) appeared in 2006. *Night* has also faced challenges by scholars for its veracity and some have speculated whether the work should be classified as autobiographical-fiction for Wiesel's invention of some of its characters. See Ruth Franklin, "A Thousand Darknesses," *The New Republic*, March 20 and 27, 2006.

28 Gertrude Samuels, "When Evil Closed In," *New York Times*, November 13, 1960.

29 *I Never Saw Another Butterfly: Children's Drawings and Poems from Theresienstadt Concentration Camp, 1942–1944* (New York: McGraw-Hill Book Co., 1959); Simon Wiesenthal, *The Sunflower* (New York: Schocken Books, 1976).

30 *Marathon Man*, dir. John Schlesinger, writ. William Goldman, perf. Dustin Hoffman, Lawrence Olivier, Roy Scheider, Paramount, 1976.

31 *Holocaust: The Story of the Family Weiss*, writ. Gerald Green, dir. Marvin J. Chomsky, National Broadcasting Company (NBC), 1978. Also see the extended discussion in Jeffrey Shandler, "The Big Event," in *While America Watches: Televising the Holocaust* (New York: Oxford University Press, 1999), chapter 6, 155–78.

32 "NCB-TV Says 'Holocaust' Drew 120 Million," *New York Times*, April 21, 1978.

33 Frank Rich, "Reliving the Nazi Nightmare," *Time*, April 17, 1978.

34 John J. O'Connor, "TV Weekend," *New York Times*, April 14, 1978.

35 Diane Henry, " 'Holocaust' On TV Stirs Poles' Anger," *New York Times*, September 23, 1978.

36 Elie Wiesel, "Trivializing the Holocaust: Semi-Fact and Semi-Fiction," *New York Times*, April 16, 1978.

37 Gerald Green, "TV View," *New York Times*, April 23, 1978.

38 Elie Wiese, "Wiesel Answers Green," *New York Times*, April 30, 1978.

39 Shandler, "The Big Event," 159–67. Also see the discussion of the miniseries in Paul Warne Mathewson, "Mandatory Holocaust Education Legislation in the State of Illinois: A Historical Study," PhD dissertation, University of Illinois at Urbana-Champaign, 2015, 21–37.

40 *Sophie's Choice*, writ. William Styron, dir. Alan J. Pakula, perf. Meryl Streep, Kevin Kline, Peter MacNicol, ITC, 1982; *Shoah*, writ. and dir. Claude Lanzmann, BBC, Historia, Les Films Aleph, 1985.

41 *Schindler's List*, writ. Steven Zaillian, dir. Steven Spielberg, perf. Liam Neeson, Ralph Fiennes, and Ben Kingsley, Universal, 1993.

42 For scholarly critiques of *Schindler's List*, see Yosefa Loshitzky, ed., *Spielberg's Holocaust: Critical Perspectives on Schindler's List* (Bloomington: Indiana University Press, 1997), 119–39; Tim Cole, *Selling the Holocaust: From Auschwitz to Schindler, How History Is Bought, Packaged, and Sold* (New York: Routledge, 2000); and Daniel H. Magilow and Lisa Silverman, "United States Holocaust Memorial Museum: How Do Countries Outside Germany Commemorate the Holocaust?" in *Holocaust Representations in History*, chapter 12, 123–31. Also see the author, Auschwitz survivor, and Nobel Laureate Imre Kertész's essay "Who Owns Auschwitz," *The Yale Journal of Criticism* 14, no. 1 (Spring 2001): 267–72, which takes Spielberg to task for a number of aspects of the film, including his attempt to make a "realistic" film about an event of which he can have no firsthand knowledge, and for making a film "that seek[s] to establish the Holocaust once and for all as something foreign to human nature; that seek to drive the Holocaust out of the realm of human experience" (270).

43 See the discussions in Edward T. Linenthal, *Preserving Memory: The Struggle to Create America's Holocaust Museum* (New York: Viking, 1995); Novick, *The Holocaust in American Life*; and Cole, *Selling the Holocaust*.

44 "Criminal Complaint (U.S v. James Wenneker von Brunn)."

45 Florence Hartmann and Ed Vulliamy, "How Britain and the US Decided to Abandon Srebrenica to Its Fate," *The Guardian*, July 4, 2015.

46 Linenthal, *Preserving Memory*, 263.

47 See "Selected List of Holocaust Memorial Sites," in *In Fitting Memory: The Art and Politics of Holocaust Memorials*, Sybil Milton and Ira Nowinski (Detroit: Wayne State University Press, 1991), 317–35.

48 "Cornerstone Set Here for Memorial to 6,000,000 Jews Killed by Nazis," *New York Times*, October 20, 1947.

49 James E. Young, *Texture of Memory: Holocaust Memorials and Meaning* (New Haven, CT: Yale University Press, 2000), 287–94.

50 Sabrina, "Warsaw Ghetto Memorial," Riverside Park Conservancy, https://riversideparknyc.org/places/warsaw-ghetto-memorial (accessed December 16, 2016).

51 Young, *Texture of Memory*, 304.

52 For a recent impression on Hier, see Curt Schleier, "How Did Marvin Hier Become the Rabbi Who Blesses Movies?," *Forward*, May 11, 2016.

53 According to Novick (*The Holocaust in American Life*, 216), Hier paid Wiesenthal a "subsidy" for use of his name on the new building.

54 See Bradley Burston, "Visit Jerusalem's New Museum of Tolerance: Feel Your Blood Boil," *Haaretz*, June 7, 2012.

55 See, for example, the blog entry from the LAMOTH's president, "No, We're Not The Museum on Pico," in which he seeks to distinguish his museum from the Museum of Tolerance, "At our Museum, no two visitors will get the same experience; at MOT, they all do. When people get through our Museum, they tell us they need to come back to learn more. That's not something you'll hear over on Pico." http://losangelesmuseumoftheholocaust.blogspot.com/2013/03/no-were-not-museum-on-pico.html (accessed December 16, 2016).

56 See "Project to Identify and Document Holocaust Memorials & Museums in the Americas," http://www.avotaynuonline.com/2016/01/holocaust-memorial-project (accessed December 23, 2016).

57 Arthur Hertzberg, "A Lifelong Quarrel with God," *New York Times*, May 6, 1990.

58 Nora Levin, *The Holocaust: The Destruction of European Jewry, 1933–1945* (New York: T.Y. Crowell Co., 1968).

59 Karl A. Schleunes, *The Twisted Road to Auschwitz: Nazi Policy toward German Jews, 1933–1939* (Urbana: University of Illinois Press, 1970).

60 The most notable of these early studies of Holocaust historiography is Michael R. Marrus, *The Holocaust in History* (New York: Penguin, 1987).

61 Robert Alter, "Deformations of the Holocaust," *Commentary* (February 1981): 49.

62 In 2006, the rate was more than 300 per year, a number that has only grown. See Gregory Weeks, "Understanding the Holocaust: The Past and Future of Holocaust Studies," *Contemporary European History* 1, no. 1 (February 2006): 117–29.

63 More about the project can be found at https://sfi.usc.edu.

64 See the work, for example, by Edwin Black, *IBM and the Holocaust: The Strategic Alliance between Nazi Germany and America's Most Powerful Corporation* (New York: Crown Publishers, 2001); Reinhold Billstein, *Working for the Enemy: Ford, General Motors, and Forced Labor in Germany during the Second World War* (New York: Berghahn Books, 2004); and Jane Mayer, *Dark Money: The Hidden History of the Billionaires behind the Rise of the Radical Right* (New York: Doubleday, 2016).

65 See Deborah Lipstadt, *Denying the Holocaust: The Growing Assault on Truth and Memory* (New York: Free Press, 1993); Richard J. Evans, *Lying about Hitler: History, Holocaust, and the David Irving Trial* (New York: Basic Books, 2001); *Denial* dir. Mick Jackson, writ. David Hare, perf. Rachel Weisz, Tom Wilkinson, Timothy Spall, BBC Films, 2016.

66 See Doris L. Bergen, *War and Genocide*, 1–11; and Saul Friedländer, "An Integrated History of the Holocaust, Possibilities and Challenges," in *Years of Persecution, Years of Extermination: Saul Friedländer and the Future of Holocaust Studies*, ed. Christian Wiese and Paul Betts (London: Bloomsbury, 2010), 21–9.

67 Henry Friedlander, "On the Holocaust: A Critique of the Treatment of the Holocaust in History Textbooks Accompanied by an Annotated Bibliography" (New York: Anti-Defamation League of B'nai B'rith, 1972, 1973). Note his early use of the term "Holocaust" to name this event.

68 Also see the discussion of Friedlander's subsequent writing on the subject by Fred M. Hechinger, "About Education," *New York Times*, May 15, 1979.

69 Thomas D. Fallace, *The Emergence of Holocaust Education in American Schools* (New York: Palgrave Macmillan, 2008), 5.

70 Mathewson, "Mandatory Holocaust Education Legislation," 3.

71 This history of FHAO is drawn primarily from Fallace, *The Emergence of Holocaust Education*, 61–6. Also see Karen L. Riley et al., "Facing History and Ourselves: Noble Purpose, Unending Controversy," in *Teaching and Studying Social Issues: Major Programs and Approaches*, Samuel Totten (Charlotte, NC: Information Age, 2010), 119–38. Also see Dennis J. Barr and Betty Bardige, "Facing History and Ourselves," in *Handbook of Prosocial Education*, Vol. 2, ed. Philip M. Brown, Michael W. Corrigan, and Ann Higgins-D'Alessandro (Lanham, MD: Rowman and Littlefield, 2012), 665–80.

72 See Stephen Labaton, "Gingrich Dismisses New Historian as Holocaust View Raises Furor," *New York Times*, January 10, 1995.

73 Lucy S. Dawidowicz, "How They Teach the Holocaust," *Commentary* December 1, 1990. Deborah Lipstadt, "Not Facing History," *New Republic*, March 6, 1995.

74 Kali Tal, *Worlds of Hurt: Reading the Literatures of Trauma* (Cambridge: Cambridge University Press, 2006), 26.

75 https://www.facinghistory.org.

76 Quoted in Stephen R. Haynes, "Holocaust Education at American Colleges and Universities: A Report on the Current Situation," *Holocaust and Genocide Studies* 12 no. 2 (Fall 1998): 282.

77 Anita Weiner, *Expanding Historical Consciousness: The Development of the Holocaust Educational Foundation* (Skokie, IL: Holocaust Educational Foundation, 2002). The work is an institutional history and tribute to the HEF, written by a former director.

Conclusion

1 For recent studies on non-Jewish victims of the Holocaust, see Center for Advanced Holocaust Studies, *Roma and Sinti: Under-Studied Victims of Nazism: Symposium Proceedings* (Washington, DC: United States Holocaust Memorial Museum, 2002); and Susanne C. Knittel, *The Historical Uncanny: Disability, Ethnicity, and the Politics of Holocaust Memory* (New York: Fordham University Press, 2014). For examples of scholarship on non-German perpetrators in Eastern Europe, see Jan T. Gross, *Neighbors: The Destruction of the Jewish Community in Jedwabne, Poland* (Princeton: Princeton University Press, 2001); and Jan Grabowski, *Hunt for the Jews. Betrayal and Murder in German-Occupied Poland* (Bloomington: Indiana University Press, 2013). On comparative genocide, see Donald Bloxham and A. Dirk Moses, eds, *The Oxford Handbook of Genocide Studies*.

2 Marlene E. Heinemann, *Gender and Destiny: Women Writers and the Holocaust* (New York: Greenwood Press, 1986), 2.

3 Myrna Goldenberg and Amy H. Shapiro, eds, *Different Horrors, Same Hell: Gender and the Holocaust* (Seattle: University of Washington Press, 2013), 100. For a discussion of the impact and contribution of women's studies and gender studies on Holocaust research, see especially the essays in the volume's first part, "History of Feminist Theory and Gender Analysis of the Holocaust."

4 As an example, see Anne Kelly Knowles, Tim Cole, and Alberto Giordano, *Geographies of the Holocaust* (Bloomington: Indiana University Press, 2014).

5 Pew Research Center, *A Portrait of Jewish Americans: Overview* (Washington, DC: Pew Research Center, 2013), 7.

6 Ibid., 10.

7 Steven M. Cohen, "Dramatic Orthodox Growth Is Transforming the American Jewish Community," *Forward*, December 19, 2016, http://forward.com/opinion/357517/dramatic-orthodox-growth-is-transforming-the-american-jewish-community (accessed March 14, 2017).

8 Southern Poverty Law Center, "Hate Groups Increase for Second Consecutive Year as Trump Electrifies Radical Right," February 15, 2017, https://www.splcenter.org/news/2017/02/15/hate-groups-increase-second-consecutive-year-trump-electrifies-radical-right (accessed March 16, 2017).

9 Josh Glancy, "Creeping Fear Is Here," *Jewish Chronicle*, March 9, 2017, https://www.thejc.com/comment/comment/glancy-creeping-fear-is-here-1.433967 (accessed March 16, 2017).

10 Michael D. Shear, Maggie Haberman, and Michael S. Schmidt, "Critics See Stephen Bannon, Trump's Pick for Strategist, as Voice of Racism," *New York Times*, November 14, 2016, https://www.nytimes.com/2016/11/15/us/politics/donald-trump-presidency.html?_r=0 (accessed April 18, 2017).

11 Nicholas Fandos and Mark Landler, "Sean Spicer Raises Outcry with Talk of Hitler, Assad and Poison Gas," *New York Times*, April 11, 2017, https://www.nytimes.com/2017/04/11/us/politics/sean-spicer-hitler-gas-holocaust-center.html (accessed April 12, 2017); Michael M. Grynbaum, " 'I Screwed Up': Sean Spicer Apologizes for Holocaust Comments," *New York Times*, April 12, 2017, https://www.nytimes.com/2017/04/12/business/media/sean-spicer-apology-holocaust-comments.html (accessed April 12, 2017).

12 Jonathan Easley, "Trump Clashes with Jewish Reporter over Anti-Semitism Question," *Hill*, February 16, 2017, http://thehill.com/homenews/administration/319954-trump-clashes-with-jewish-reporter-over-antisemitism-question (accessed March 16, 2017).

13 See the original statement by Steven Goldstein, executive director of the Anne Frank Center for Mutual Respect, https://twitter.com/AnneFrankCenter/status/834072801736814592 (posted to Twitter on February 21, 2017, at 8:10 am, accessed March 16, 2017). See Sean Spicer's response in Rachael Revesz, "Sean Spicer: 'I wish the Anne Frank Center Had Praised Donald Trump for Fighting Anti-Semitism,' " *The Independent*, February 21, 2017, http://www.independent.co.uk/news/world/americas/sean-spicer-anne-frank-centre-donald-trump-antisemitism-press-conference-a7592401.html (accessed March 16, 2017).

14 See Trump's comments in Craig Melvin and Erik Ortiz, "Trump at African-American History Museum Denounces Anti-Semitism and Racism: 'It Has to Stop,' " NBC News, February 21, 2017, http://www.nbcnews.com/politics/donald-trump/trump-african-american-history-museum-denounces-antisemitism-racism-it-n723521 (accessed March 16, 2017).

15 See Trump's comments in Abby Phillip, "After Earlier Omission, Trump Mourns Murder of 6 Million Jews in Video Message to World Jewish Congress," *Washington Post*, April 23, 2017, https://www.washingtonpost.com/news/post-politics/wp/2017/04/23/after-earlier-omission-trump-mourns-murder-of-six-million-jews-in-video-message-to-world-jewish-congress/?utm_term=.923911ff3468 (accessed April 24, 2017).

16 Michael D. Shear and Maggie Haberman, "Trump Defends Initial Remarks on Charlottesville; Again Blames 'Both Sides,' " *New York Times*, August 15, 2017, https://www.nytimes.com/2017/08/15/us/politics/trump-press-conference-charlottesville.html?mcubz=3 (accessed September 15, 2017).

17 Emma Green, "Are Jews White?," *Atlantic*, December 5, 2016.

18 Ibid.

19 Karen Brodkin, "How Jews Became White Folks—and May Become Nonwhite under Trump," *Forward*, December 6, 2016.

20 Kluger, 64.

Selected bibliography

Please note: The books in this bibliography are listed according to the chapter in which they first appear.

Introduction

Bernstein, Michael André. *Foregone Conclusions: Against Apocalyptic History.* Berkeley: University of California Press, 1994.
Breitman, Richard and Alan M. Kraut. *American Refugee Policy and European Jewry, 1933–1945.* Bloomington: Indiana University Press, 1987.
Breitman, Richard and Allan J. Lichtman. *FDR and the Jews.* Cambridge, MA: Belknap Press, 2013.
Brodkin, Karen. *How Jews Became White Folks and What That Says about Race in America.* New Brunswick, NJ: Rutgers University Press, 1998.
Diner, Hasia. *We Remember with Reverence and Love: American Jews and the Myth of Silence after the Holocaust, 1945–1962.* New York: New York University Press, 2010.
Erbelding, Rebecca L. *Rescue Board: The Untold Story of America's Efforts to Save the Jews of Europe.* New York: Doubleday, 2018.
Feingold, Henry L. *The Politics of Rescue: The Roosevelt Administration and the Holocaust, 1938–1945.* New York: Holocaust Library, 1970.
Finkelstein, Norman. *The Holocaust Industry: Reflections on the Exploitation of Jewish Suffering.* London: Verso, 2000.
Goldstein, Eric L. *The Price of Whiteness: Jews, Race, and American Identity.* Princeton: Princeton University Press, 2006.
Greenberg, Cheryl Lynn. *Troubling the Waters: Black-Jewish Relations in the American Century.* Princeton: Princeton University Press, 2006.
Kluger, Ruth. *Still Alive: A Holocaust Girlhood Remembered.* New York: The Feminist Press, 2003.
Levi, Primo. *The Drowned and the Saved.* Trans. Raymond Rosenthal. New York: Vintage International, 1989.
Morse, Arthur D. *While Six Million Died: A Chronicle of American Apathy.* New York: Random House, 1968.
Novick, Peter. *The Holocaust in American Life.* Boston: Houghton Mifflin, 1999.
Penkower, Monty Noam. *The Jews Were Expendable: Free World Diplomacy and the Holocaust.* Urbana and Chicago: University of Illinois Press, 1983.
Rosen, Robert N. *Saving the Jews: Franklin D. Roosevelt and the Holocaust.* New York: Thunder's Mouth Press, 2006.

Rosenfeld, Gavriel D. *Hi Hitler! How the Nazi Past Is Being Normalized in Contemporary Culture*. Cambridge: Cambridge University Press, 2015.
Rubinstein, William D. *The Myth of Rescue: Why the Democracies Could Not Have Saved More Jews from the Nazis*. London and New York: Routledge, 1997.
Wyman, David S. *The Abandonment of the Jews: America and the Holocaust, 1941–1945*. New York: Pantheon Books, 1984.
Wyman, David S. *Paper Walls: America and the Refugee Crisis 1938–1941*. New York: Pantheon Books, 1985.
Zuckerman, Lawrence. "FDR's Jewish Problem: How Did a President Beloved by Jews Come to be Regarded as an Anti-Semite Who Refused to Save Them from the Nazis?" *The Nation* (July 17, 2013): 29–32.

Chapter 1

Arad, Gulie Ne'eman. *America, Its Jews, and the Rise of Nazism*. Bloomington and Indianapolis: Indiana University Press, 2000.
Arendt, Hannah. *Eichmann in Jerusalem: A Report on the Banality of Evil*. New York: Viking Press, 1963.
Evans, Richard J. *The Third Reich in Power*. New York: Penguin Books, 2005.
Friedländer, Saul. *Nazi Germany and the Jews: The Years of Persecution 1933–1939*. New York: HarperCollins, 1997.
Higham, John. *Strangers in the Land: Pattern of American Nativism, 1860–1925*. New Brunswick, NJ: Rutgers University Press, 1955.
Hoenicke Moore, Michaela. *Know Your Enemy: The American Debate on Nazism, 1933–1945*. Cambridge: Cambridge University Press, 2010.
Kühl, Stefan. *The Nazi Connection: Eugenics, American Racism, and German National Socialism*. Oxford: Oxford University Press, 1994.
Milton, Sybil. "The Expulsion of Polish Jews from Germany October 1938 to July 1939: A Documentation." *Leo Baeck Institute Yearbook* 29 (1984): 169–99.
Roediger, David R. *Working toward Whiteness: How America's Immigrants Became White*. New York: Basic Books, 2005.
Taylor, Melissa Jane. "Bureaucratic Response to Human Tragedy: American Consuls and the Jewish Plight in Vienna, 1938–1941." *Holocaust and Genocide Studies* 21, no. 2 (Fall 2007): 243–67.
Thompson, Dorothy. "Refugees: A World Problem." *Foreign Affairs* 16, no. 3 (April 1938): 375–87.
Vincent, C. Paul. "The Voyage of the St. Louis Revisited." *Holocaust and Genocide Studies* 25, no. 2 (Fall 2011): 252–89.
Whitman, James Q. *Hitler's American Model: The United States and the Making of Nazi Race Law*. Princeton: Princeton University Press, 2017.
Wiesen, S. Jonathan. "On Dachau and Jim Crow: Holocaust Memory in the Postwar African American Press." In Regina Fritz, Éva Kovács, and Béla Rásky, eds, *Als der Holocaust noch keinen Namen hatte/Before the Holocaust Had Its Name*. Vienna: New Academic Press, 2016, 111–31.
Woeste, Victoria Saker. *Henry Ford's War on Jews and the Legal Battle against Hate Speech*. Palo Alto: Stanford University Press, 2013.

Chapter 2

Allen, Robert L. *The Port Allen Mutiny*. New York: Warner Books, 1989.
Alvarez, Luis. *The Power of the Zoot: Youth Culture and Resistance during World War II*. Berkeley: University of California Press, 2009.
Bacon, Margaret Hope. *The Quiet Rebels: The Story of the Quakers in America*. Philadelphia: New Society Publishers, 1985.
Bauer, Yehuda. *American Jewry and the Holocaust: The American Jewish Joint Distribution Committee 1939–1945*. Detroit: Wayne State University Press, 1981.
Bauer, Yehuda. *My Brother's Keeper: A History of the American Jewish Joint Distribution Committee: 1929–1939*. Philadelphia: Jewish Publication Society of America, 1974.
Baumel, Judith Tydor. *The "Bergson Boys" and the Origins of Contemporary Zionist Militancy*. Trans. Dena Ordan. Syracuse: Syracuse University Press, 2005.
Bergen, Doris L. *War and Genocide*, 3rd edn. Lanham, MD: Rowman and Littlefield, 2016.
Breitman, Richard. *Official Secrets: What the Nazis Planned, What the British and Americans Knew*. New York: Hill and Wang, 1998.
Bryant, Elizabeth. "Rabbi Stephen S. Wise's Actions upon Receipt of the Riegner Telegram: What More Could He Have Done?" *Studia Historyczne* 25, no. 2 (2013): 185–202.
Dawidowicz, Lucy S. *From That Place and Time: A Memoir, 1938–1947*. New York: W. W. Norton, 1989.
Diamond, Hanna. *Fleeing Hitler: France 1940*. Oxford: Oxford University Press, 2007.
Dunn, Susan. *1940: FDR, Willkie, Lindbergh, Hitler—the Election amid the Storm*. New Haven: Yale University Press, 2013.
Fleegler, Robert L. *Ellis Island Nation: Immigration Policy and American Identity in the Twentieth Century*. Philadelphia: University of Pennsylvania Press, 2013.
Friedländer, Saul. *Nazi Germany and the Jews, 1939–1945: The Years of Extermination*. New York: HarperCollins, 2007.
Fry, Varian. *Surrender on Demand*. New York: Random House, 1945.
Gold, Mary Jayne. *Crossroads Marseilles: 1940*. New York: Doubleday, 1980.
Kaplan, Marion A. *Between Dignity and Despair: Jewish Life in Nazi Germany*. Oxford: Oxford University Press, 1998.
Lipstadt, Deborah. *Beyond Belief: The American Press and the Coming of the Holocaust 1933–1945*. New York: The Free Press, 1986.
Lowenstein, Sharon. *Token Refuge: The Story of the Jewish Refugee Shelter at Oswego, 1944–1946*. Bloomington: Indiana University Press, 1986.
Mazon, Mauricio. *The Zoot-Suit Riots*. Austin: University of Texas, 1984.
Némirovsky, Irène. *Suite Française*. Trans. Sandra Smith. New York: Alfred A. Knopf, 2006.
Olson, Lynne. *Those Angry Days: Roosevelt Lindbergh, and America's Fight over World War II*. New York: Random House, 2013.
Pagán, Eduardo Obregón. *Murder at the Sleepy Lagoon: Zoot Suits, Race, and Riot in Wartime L.A.* Chapel Hill: University of North Carolina Press, 2003.

Seghers, Anna. *Transit*. Trans. Margot Bettauer Dembo. New York: New York Review of Books, 2013.

Shoah. Directed by Claude Lanzmann. Disc 5, Supplements, IFC Films: The Criterion Collection, 2013.

Takaki, Ronald. *Double Victory: A Multicultural History of America in World War II*. Boston: Little, Brown and Company, 2000.

Weber, Ronald. *The Lisbon Route: Entry and Escape in Nazi Europe*. Lanham, MD: Rowman and Littlefield, 2011.

Wood, E. Thomas and Stanislaw M. Jankowski. *Karski: How One Man Tried to Stop the Holocaust*. New York: John Wiley & Sons, Inc., 1994.

Zweig, Stefan. *The World of Yesterday*. Trans. Anthea Bell. Lincoln: University of Nebraska Press, 2013.

Chapter 3

Arendt, Hannah. *The Origins of Totalitarianism*. New York: Schocken Books, 1951.

Arendt, Hannah. "We Refugees." *Menorah Journal* 31 (1943): 69–77.

Bernstein, Philip S. "What the Jews Believe." *Life*, September 11, 1950: 161–79.

Coates, Ta-Nehisi. "The Case for Reparations." *The Atlantic*, June 2014.

Cohen, Beth. *Case Closed: Holocaust Survivors in Postwar America*. New Brunswick, NJ: Rutgers University Press, 2007.

Davie, Maurice R. *Refugees in America: Report of the Committee for the Study of Recent Immigration from Europe*. New York: Harper and Brother Publishers, 1947.

Dawidowicz, Lucy. *On Equal Terms: Jews in America 1881–1981*. New York: Holt, Rinehart and Winston, 1982.

Deblinger, Rachel. "Memories/Motifs: Holocaust Survivor Narratives in Postwar America." http://www.memoriesmotifs.com.

Dinnerstein, Leonard. *America and the Survivors of the Holocaust*. New York: Columbia University Press, 1982.

Engel, Irving M. *Americanizing Our Immigration Laws*. New York: American Jewish Committee, 1949.

Glazar, Nathan. "The Anomalous Liberalism of American Jews." In Robert M. Seltzer and Norman J. Cohen, eds, *The Americanization of the Jews*. New York: New York University Press, 1995, 133–43.

Gross, Jan Tomasz. *Fear: Anti-Semitism in Poland after Auschwitz*. New York: Random House, 2006.

Gross, Jan Tomasz and Irena Grudzińska Gross. *Golden Harvest: Events at the Periphery of the Holocaust*. Oxford: Oxford University Press, 2012.

Harrison, Earl G. *The Plight of the Displaced Jews in Europe*. Washington, DC: The White House: September 29, 1945. Reprinted by United Jewish Appeal for Refugees, Overseas Needs and Palestine.

Heilman, Samuel C. *Portrait of American Jews: The Last Half of the 20th Century*. Seattle: University of Washington Press, 1995.

Jacobsen, Annie. *Operation Paperclip: The Secret Intelligence Program That Brought Nazi Scientists to America*. New York: Back Bay Books, 2014.

Judt, Tony. *Postwar: A History of Europe since 1945*. New York: Penguin, 2005.
Katznelson, Ira. *When Affirmative Action Was White: An Untold History of Racial Inequality in Twentieth-Century America*. New York: W. W. Norton & Company, 2005.
Kaufman, David. *Shul with a Pool: The "Synagogue-Center" in American Jewish History*. Hanover, NH: University Press of New England, 1999.
Kertzer, Morris N. "What Is a Jew?" *Look*, June 1952: 120–8.
Lang, Daniel. "Displaced: A Reporter at Large." *The New Yorker*, September 13, 1947: 100–11.
Lederhendler, Eli. *New York Jews and the Decline of Urban Ethnicity, 1950–1970*. Syracuse, NY: Syracuse University Press, 2001.
Lestschinsky, Jacob. *Crisis, Catastrophe and Survival: A Jewish Balance Sheet, 1914–1948*. New York: Institute of Jewish Affairs for the World Jewish Congress, 1948.
Lévy-Hass, Hanna. *Diary of Bergen-Belsen, 1944–1945*. Trans. Sophie Hand. Chicago: Haymarket Books, 2009.
Lichtblau, Eric. *The Nazis Next Door: How America Became a Safe Haven for Hitler's Men*. Boston: Houghton Mifflin Harcourt, 2014.
Segev, Tom. *The Seventh Million: The Israelis and the Holocaust*. Trans. Haim Watzman. New York: Hill and Wang, 1993.
Simpson, Christopher. *Blowback: America's Recruitment of Nazis and Its Effects on the Cold War*. New York: Collier Books, 1988.
Young-Bruehl, Elisabeth. *Hannah Arendt: For Love of the World*. 2nd edn. New Haven: Yale University Press, 2004.
Zertal, Idith. *Israel's Holocaust and the Politics of Nationhood*. Cambridge: Cambridge University Press, 2005.

Chapter 4

Aleksiun, Natalia. "Philip Friedman and the Emergence of Holocaust Scholarship: A Reappraisal." *Simon Dubnow Institute Yearbook* 11 (2012): 333–46.
Bauer, Yehuda and Nathan Rotenstreich, eds. *The Holocaust as Historical Experience*. New York: Holmes and Meier, 1981.
Berg, Mary. *The Diary of Mary Berg*. Trans. S. L Shneiderman. New York: L. B: Fischer, 1945.
Bergen, Doris L. "Out of the Limelight or In: Raul Hilberg, Gerhard Weinberg, Henry Friedlander, and the Historical Study of the Holocaust." In Andreas W. Daum, Hartmut Lehmann, and James J. Sheehan, eds, *The Second Generation: Émigrés from Nazi Germany as Historians*. New York: Berghahn, 2016, 229–43.
Dawidowicz, Lucy. *The Holocaust and the Historians*. Cambridge, MA: Harvard University Press, 1981.
Doneson, Judith E. *The Holocaust in American Film*. 2nd edn. Syracuse: Syracuse University Press, 2002.
Douglas, Lawrence. *The Right Wrong Man: John Demjanjuk and the Last Great Nazi War Crimes Trial*. Princeton: Princeton University Press, 2016.

Engel, David. *Historians of the Jews and the Holocaust.* Stanford: Stanford University Press, 2010.
Frank, Anne. *The Diary of a Young Girl.* Trans. B. M. Mooyaart-Doubleday. New York: The Modern Library, 1952.
Friedman, Philip. *Roads to Extinction: Essays on the Holocaust.* Ed. Ada June Friedman. New York and Philadelphia: Conference on Jewish Social Studies/ The Jewish Publication Society of America, 1980.
Hilberg, Raul. *The Destruction of the European Jews.* Chicago: Quadrangle Books, 1961.
Hilberg, Raul. *The Politics of Memory: The Journey of a Holocaust Historian.* Chicago: Ivan R. Dee, 1996.
Jockusch, Laura. *Collect and Record! Jewish Holocaust Documentation in Early Postwar Europe.* Oxford: Oxford University Press, 2012.
Kassow, Samuel. *Who Will Write Our History? Emanuel Ringelblum, the Warsaw Ghetto, and the Oyneg Shabes Archive.* Bloomington: Indiana University Press, 2007.
Kirshenblatt-Gimblett Barbara, and Jeffrey Shandler, eds, *Anne Frank Unbound: Media, Imagination, Memory.* Bloomington: Indiana University Press, 2012.
Magilow, Daniel H. and Lisa Silverman. *Holocaust Representations in History: An Introduction.* London: Bloomsbury, 2015.
Marrus, Michael R. *The Holocaust in History.* New York: Penguin, 1987.
Ozick, Cynthia. "Who Owns Anne Frank?" *New Yorker*, October 6, 1977: 76–87.
Pat, Jacob. *Ashes and Fire.* New York: International Universities Press, 1947.
Prose, Francine. *Anne Frank: The Book, the Life, the Afterlife.* New York: HarperCollins, 2009.
Robinson, Jacob and Philip Friedman. *Guide to Jewish History under Nazi Impact.* New York: YIVO Institute for Jewish Research, 1960.
Shandler, Jeffrey. *While America Watches: Televising the Holocaust.* New York: Oxford University Press, 1999.
Shneiderman, S. L. *Between Fear and Hope.* Trans. Norbert Guterman. New York: Arco Publishing Company, 1947.
Stauber, Roni. *Laying the Foundations for Holocaust Research: The Impact of the Historian Philip Friedman.* Jerusalem: Yad Vashem, 2009.
Van Den Berghe, Gie. "The Incompleteness of a Masterpiece: Raul Hilberg and the Destruction of European Jews." *Belgisch Tijdschrift voor Nieuwste Geschiedenis* XXI, nos 1–2 (1990): 110–24.

Chapter 5

Bauer, Yehuda. *The Jewish Emergence from Powerlessness.* Toronto: University of Toronto Press, 1979.
Bergen, Doris L. "Studying the Holocaust: Is History Commemoration?" In Dan Stone, ed., *The Holocaust and Historical Methodology.* New York: Berghahn Books, 2012.
Cole, Tim. *Selling the Holocaust: From Auschwitz to Schindler, How History Is Bought, Packaged, and Sold.* New York: Routledge, 2000.

Dawidowicz, Lucy. *The War against the Jews, 1933–1945*. New York: Holt, Rinehart and Winston, 1975.
Evans, Richard J. *Lying about Hitler: History, Holocaust, and the David Irving Trial*. New York: Basic Books, 2001.
Fallace, Thomas D. *The Emergence of Holocaust Education in American Schools*. New York: Palgrave Macmillan, 2008.
Feingold, Henry L. *Bearing Witness: How America and Its Jews Responded to the Holocaust*. Syracuse: Syracuse University Press, 1995.
Hausner, Gideon. *Justice in Jerusalem*. New York: Schocken Books, 1968.
Hertzberg, Arthur. "A Lifelong Quarrel With God." *New York Times*, May 6, 1990.
Levin, Nora. *The Holocaust: The Destruction of European Jewry, 1933–1945*. New York: T.Y. Crowell Co., 1968.
Lipstadt, Deborah. *Denying the Holocaust: The Growing Assault on Truth and Memory*. New York: Free Press, 1993.
Lookstein, Haskel. *Were We Our Brothers' Keepers? The Public Response of American Jews to the Holocaust 1938–1944*. New York: Hartmore House, 1985.
Robinson, Jacob. *And the Crooked Shall Be Made Straight: The Eichmann Trial, the Jewish Catastrophe, and Hannah Arendt's Narrative*. New York: Macmillan, 1965.
Schleunes, Karl A. *The Twisted Road to Auschwitz: Nazi Policy toward German Jews, 1933–1939*. Urbana: University of Illinois Press, 1970.
Shapiro, Edward S. *A Time for Healing: American Jewry since World War II*. Baltimore: The Johns Hopkins University Press, 1992.
Trunk, Isaiah. *Judenrat: The Jewish Councils in Eastern Europe under Nazi Occupation*. New York: Macmillan, 1972.
Weiner, Anita. *Expanding Historical Consciousness: The Development of the Holocaust Educational Foundation*. Skokie, IL: Holocaust Educational Foundation, 2002.
Wiesel, Elie. *Night*. Trans. from the French by Stella Rodway. New York: Hill and Wang, 1960.
Young, James E. *Texture of Memory: Holocaust Memorials and Meaning*. New Haven, CT: Yale University Press, 2000, 287–94.

Conclusion

Brodkin, Karen. "How Jews Became White Folks—and May Become Nonwhite under Trump." *Forward*, December 6, 2016.
Center for Advanced Holocaust Studies. *Roma and Sinti Under-Studied Victims of Nazism: Symposium Proceedings*. Washington, DC: United States Holocaust Memorial Museum, 2002.
Cohen, Steven M. "Dramatic Orthodox Growth Is Transforming the American Jewish Community." *Forward*, December 19, 2016.
Glancy, Josh. "Creeping Fear Is Here." *Jewish Chronicle*, March 9, 2017.
Goldenberg, Myrna and Amy H. Shapiro, eds. *Different Horrors, Same Hell: Gender and the Holocaust*. Seattle: University of Washington Press, 2013.

Green, Emma. "Are Jews White?" *The Atlantic*, December 5, 2016.

Heinemann, Marlene E. *Gender and Destiny: Women Writers and the Holocaust*. New York: Greenwood Press, 1986.

Knittel, Susanne C. *The Historical Uncanny: Disability, Ethnicity, and the Politics of Holocaust Memory*. New York: Fordham University Press, 2014.

Knowles, Anne Kelly, Tim Cole, and Alberto Giordano. *Geographies of the Holocaust*. Bloomington: Indiana University Press, 2014.

Pew Research Center. "A Portrait of Jewish Americans: Overview." Washington, DC: Pew Research Center, 2013.

Index

Page numbers in *italics* denote figures.